WORLD WAR I
COMPANION

Edited by

MATTHIAS STROHN

First published in Great Britain in 2013 by Osprey Publishing,
Osprey Publishing, PO Box 883, Oxford, OX1 9PL, UK
Osprey Publishing, PO Box 3985, New York, NY 10185-3985, USA

E-mail: info@ospreypublishing.com

Osprey Publishing is part of the Osprey Group
© 2013 Osprey Publishing Ltd.

A CIP catalogue record for this book is available from the British Library

Gary Sheffield, Michael Neiberg, Thorsten Loch, Bruce Gudmundsson, James Corum, Michael Epkenhans, François Cochet, Matthias Strohn, Lothar Höbelt, Stephen Walsh, Andrew Macdonald, David Murphy, Andrew Wiest and Peter Lieb have asserted their right under the Copyright, Designs and Patents Act, 1988, to be identified as the Authors of this Work.

ISBN: 978 1 78200 188 1

e-book ISBN: 978 1 4728 0710 6

PDF ISBN: 978 1 4728 0709 0

Index by Angela Hall

Cartography by Bounford.com

Typeset in Adobe Garamond Pro

Originated by PDQ Digital Media Ltd, Bungay, Suffolk, NR35 1BY, UK

Printed in China through Worldprint

13 14 15 16 17 10 9 8 7 6 5 4 3 2 1

Front and Back cover: Men of the 8th Battalion, East Yorkshire Regiment going up to the line near Frezenberg during the Third Battle of Ypres, 1917. (Q 2978, Imperial War Museum)

Osprey Publishing is supporting the Woodland Trust, the UK's leading woodland conservation charity, by funding the dedication of trees.

www.ospreypublishing.com

Acknowledgements

A book such as this cannot be written without the help and support of numerous people and this is the place to thank them.

First and foremost, I would like to thank the contributors to this book. It is often said that looking after academics is worse than herding cats, but this was most definitely not the case in this project. All the contributors worked with a high level of professionalism which made my work as the editor an enjoyable task.

My role as the editor was made even easier by the outstanding support provided by Marcus Cowper and his team at Osprey. I know that without this support the road to publication of this book would have been far bumpier than it turned out to be.

I would also like to thank the Royal Military Academy Sandhurst, in particular the Director of Studies Sean McKnight, my colleagues in the War Studies Department and Andrew Orgill and his team from the library.

Even though his role in the project was only a small one I would like to thank Professor Sir Hew Strachan from Oxford University for his continuous support. Without him, I would not be where I am today.

Last, and by no means least, I would like to thank my family, and in particular my wife Rocio, for their help and understanding. Rocio had to share my attention with old generals and chapter drafts for far too long. Without her infinite patience and love it would have been much harder to complete this book.

This book is dedicated to the soldiers from all nations who fought and suffered in World War I, believing that they were fighting for a just course.

CONTENTS

CONTRIBUTORS

Professor Gary Sheffield is Professor of War Studies at the University of Wolverhampton. He has published widely on military history, especially World War I. His books include *The Chief: Douglas Haig and the British Army* (2011); the bestselling *Forgotten Victory: The First World War – Myths and Realities* (2001); and *Leadership in the Trenches* (2000). He previously held Chairs at the University of Birmingham and King's College London. A Fellow of the Royal Historical Society, he is currently editing, with John Bourne, the World War I letters and diaries of General Sir Henry Rawlinson, and researching a book on the experiences of the British and Commonwealth soldiers in World War II. He frequently broadcasts on television and radio, and writes for a variety of newspapers, journals and magazines.

Professor Michael Neiberg is Professor of History in the Department of National Security and Strategy at the United States Army War College in Carlisle, Pennsylvania. He is the author or editor of numerous books and articles about World War I, most recently *Dance of the Furies: Europe and the Outbreak of War in 1914* (Harvard University Press, 2011). He is also the author of the World War I article in the forthcoming Cambridge History of Warfare series. He is a founding member of the International Society for First World War Studies and a trustee of the Society for Military History. His latest book is *The Blood of Free Men: The Liberation of Paris, 1944* (Basic Books, 2012).

Major Dr Thorsten Loch, MA, works at the German Armed Forces Office for Military History and Social Sciences in Potsdam, Germany. He studied history and social sciences at the German armed forces university in Hamburg and has held several postings related to military history (e.g. as lecturer in military history at the German officer training academy) and as an infantry company commander. His publications include *Das Gesicht der Bundeswehr.*

Kommunikationsstrategien in der Freiwilligenwerbung der Bundeswehr. 1956 bis 1989 (Munich, 2008), *Wie Friedrich der Große" wurde. Eine kleine Geschichte des Siebenjährigen Krieges 1756 bis 1763* (Freiburg, 2012), *Wie die Siegessäule nach Berlin kam. Eine kleine Geschichte der Reichseinigungskriege 1864 bis 1871* (Freiburg, 2011), and *Das Wachbataillon beim Bundesministerium der Verteidigung (1957–2007). Geschichte – Auftrag – Tradition* (Hamburg, 2007)

Major Bruce Gudmundsson, USMC (Retired) is a military historian who studies tactical innovation, professional education, and organizational culture. He has written six books on these subjects, as well as a large number of short books, doctrinal manuals, case studies, concept papers, magazine articles, translations, and tactical decision games. A graduate of Oxford University (D.Phil), Yale College (BA) and the Marine Corps Recruit Depot, Parris Island (PFC), Dr. Gudmundsson has taught at the Marine Corps School of Advanced Warfighting, Oxford University, and the Royal Military Academy at Sandhurst.

Dr James S. Corum is the Dean of the Baltic Defence College since 2009. From 1991 to 2004, he was a professor at the US Air Force School of Advanced Air and Space Studies at Maxwell Air Force Base, Alabama. In 2005 he was a visiting fellow at All Souls College, Oxford, where he held a Leverhulme Fellowship, and then an associate professor at the US Army Command and General Staff College, Fort Leavenworth, Kansas. Dr Corum is the author of several books on military history, including *The Roots of Blitzkrieg: Hans von Seeckt and German Military Reform* (1992); *The Luftwaffe: Creating the Operational Air War, 1918–1940* (1997); *The Luftwaffe's Way of War: German Air Doctrine, 1911–1945*, with Richard Muller (1998); *Airpower in Small Wars: Fighting Insurgents and Terrorists*, with Wray Johnson (2003); and *Fighting the War on Terror: A Counterinsurgency Strategy* (2007). His eighth book on Cold War History is *Rearming Germany* (Leiden, Brill Press, 2011). He is the editor in chief of the translation (from German) of the *Encyclopedia of the First World War* (2 volumes) (Leiden, Brill, 2012). He has also authored more than 60 major book chapters and journal articles on a variety of subjects related to air power and military history, and was one of the primary authors of *Field Manual 3-24*, the US Army and US Marine Corps doctrine on counterinsurgency. Dr Corum served in Iraq in 2004 as a lieutenant-colonel in the US Army Reserve. He holds a master's degree from Brown University, a Master of Letters from Oxford University, and a PhD from Queen's University, Canada.

Professor Dr Michael Epkenhans is currently the director of Historical Research at the German Armed Forces Office for Military History and Social Sciences in Potsdam. Between 1996 and 2009 he was the director of the Otto-von-Bismarck-Foundation in Friedrichsruh. He has published widely on the German history of the 19th and 20th centuries as well as on naval history. His publications include *Preußen. Aufstieg und Fall einer Großmacht* (Stuttgart, 2011), *The Danish Straits and German Naval Power, 1905–1918* (Potsdam, 2010), and *Grand Admiral Alfred von Tirpitz. Architect of the German Battle Fleet* (Washington, DC, 2008).

Professor Dr François Cochet is Professor of Contemporary History at Lorraine University, Metz. Before taking up his position in Metz in 2002 he was he was a professor at the University of Limoges. Francois Cochet is a Chevalier de l'ordre des Palmes académiques and Chevalier de l'ordre des Arts et des Lettres. He is the author of a number of books on the subject of World War I, with a particular emphasis on the experience of combat and prisoners of war. His publications include *Les soldats inconnus de la Grande Guerre* (Saint-Cloud, 2012), *Former les soldats au feu, premier volume de la collection l'Expérience combattante, 19e–21e siècles* (Paris, 2011), *Ferdinand Foch (1851–1929), «Apprenez à penser»* (Saint-Cloud, 2010), and *La Première Guerre mondiale: Dates, thèmes, noms* (Paris, 2001)

Dr Matthias Strohn was educated at the Universities of Münster (Germany) and Oxford. He has lectured at Oxford University, the German Staff College (Führungsakademie der Bundeswehr) and the Joint Services Command and Staff College at Shrivenham. Since 2006 he has been a Senior Lecturer in the Department of War Studies at the Royal Military Academy Sandhurst, and in 2011 he was also made a Senior Research Fellow at the University of Buckingham. He holds a commission in the German army and is currently a member of the military attaché reserve. In this role he acts as the historical advisor to the German embassy in London on matters related to the World War I centenary commemorations. His publications include *The Great Adventure Ends: New Zealand and France on the Western Front* (Christchurch, 2013), and *The German Army and the Defence of the Reich: Military Doctrine and the Conduct of the Defensive Battle 1918–1939* (Cambridge, 2010).

Professor Dr Lothar Höbelt was born in Vienna in 1956, graduated with honours from the University of Vienna 1982, Assistant Visiting Professor University of Chicago 1992, Associate Professor of Modern History at

University of Vienna since 1997, Lecturer at Military Academy Wiener Neustadt since 2001. The main focus of his research lies on the history of Austria(-Hungary) in the 19th and 20th centuries. His publications include *Franz Joseph I. Der Kaiser und sein Reich. Eine politische Geschichte* (Vienna, 2009), and *Die Habsburger. Aufstieg und Glanz einer europäischen Dynastie* (Stuttgart, 2009).

Dr Stephen Walsh is a Senior Lecturer in the Department of War Studies at the Royal Military Academy, Sandhurst. He has a BA in History and an MA in War Studies. Dr Walsh's doctoral thesis analysed Marshal Konstantin Rokossovskiy and the Red Army's style of leadership and command on the Eastern Front during World War II. He is the author of *Stalingrad, The Infernal Cauldron 1942–43* (2001) and co-author of *The Eastern Front* (2001).

Dr Andrew Macdonald is a New Zealand military historian who specializes in tactical effectiveness among Commonwealth formations during World War I. He has published two books about this subject, the first about the Somme, 1916, and the second about the closing phases of Third Ypres, 1917. He has a particular interest in matters concerning the Western Front 1916–18, Gallipoli, 1915, the Greek campaign of 1941, and the media at war. Prior to becoming a military historian, Macdonald was a correspondent for the global news agency Reuters. He is married and lives in London.

Dr David Murphy is a lecturer with the Centre for Military History & Strategic Studies at the Department of History, NUI Maynooth. Since 2006, he has also taught defence studies programmes at the Irish Military College. He has previously taught at University College Dublin and Trinity College, Dublin. In recent years he has given guest lectures at various military institutions, including the Dutch staff college and cadet academy, the US Army Command and General Staff College, Fort Leavenworth, and the US Military Academy, West Point. David Murphy has carried out extensive research on the service of Irish soldiers in British and European armies. His current research is focused on World War I and he is completing a book on the failed Nivelle Offensive of 1917, which will be published in 2015. His other publications include *T. E. Lawrence* (Oxford, 2011), *The Arab Revolt, 1916–18* (Oxford, 2008), *The Irish Brigades, 1685–2006* (Dublin, 2007) and *Ireland and the Crimean War* (Dublin, 2002).

Professor Andrew Wiest is Professor of History at the University of Southern Mississippi and is also the founding director of the Center for the Study of War and Society. After attending the University of Southern Mississippi for his undergraduate and masters degrees, Dr Wiest went on to receive his Ph.D. from the University of Illinois, Chicago in 1990. Specializing in the study of World War I and Vietnam, he has served as a Visiting Senior Lecturer at the Royal Military Academy, Sandhurst and as a Visiting Professor in the Department of Warfighting Strategy in the United States Air Force Air War College. Since 1992 Dr Wiest has been active in international education, developing the award-winning Vietnam Study Abroad Program. A widely published author, Wiest's titles include *Vietnam's Forgotten Army: Heroism and Betrayal in the ARVN* (2009), which won the Society for Military History's Distinguished Book Award; *America and the Vietnam War* (2010); *Rolling Thunder in a Gentle Land* (2006); *Passchendaele and the Royal Navy* (1995); and *The Boys of '67* (2012). Additionally Dr Wiest has appeared in and consulted on several historical documentaries for the History Channel, Granada Television, PBS, the BBC, and for Lucasfilm. Wiest lives in Hattiesburg with his wife Jill and their three children Abigail, Luke and Wyatt.

Dr Peter Lieb is a Senior Lecturer at the Royal Military Academy Sandhurst, Department of War Studies, and Research Fellow at the European Studies Research Institute, University of Salford. Prior to this he was a research fellow at the Institut für Zeitgeschichte in Munich, and the German Historical Institute in Paris. He holds a PhD and an MA from the University of Munich. His research interests are the German Army in World War I and World War II, and insurgencies and counterinsurgency in the 20th century. His publications include 'Suppressing Insurgencies in Comparison: The Germans in the Ukraine, 1918, and the British in Mesopotamia, 1920', *Small Wars & Insurgencies*, Volume 23, 2012, *Die Ukraine zwischen Selbstbestimmung und Fremdherrschaft 1917–1922* (Graz, 2011), and *Konventioneller Krieg oder NS-Weltanschauungskrieg? Kriegführung und Partisanenbekämpfung in Frankreich 1943/44* (Munich, 2007).

FOREWORD

Professor Gary Sheffield

As I write these words, the date is 1 July 2013. The 97th anniversary of the 'First Day on the Somme' has not gone unnoticed, for 1 July 1916 has, for Britons, become the single most infamous date of the entire war. By the end of that terrible day, 57,000 British Empire soldiers had become casualties, with over 19,000 being killed. The hoped-for breakthrough simply failed to materialize. This day, above all others, has come to epitomize all that is wrong with World War I: incompetent generalship leading to horrendous losses for negligible gains of ground. All this futile sacrifice took place in a war that is widely believed to lack purpose.

Yet this very common view of the First Day of the Somme conceals much. Few if any reputable historians hold that World War I was futile. On the contrary, great issues were at stake, and throughout the people of Britain and the Empire demonstrated an amazingly high level of support for the war effort. The fact that the much maligned Commander-in-Chief of the British Expeditionary Force, General (later Field Marshal) Sir Douglas Haig, fought on the Somme at the behest of the French before he believed his army was ready is also generally unknown, as is the fact that the 'Battle of the Somme' did not last for one day, like Hastings or Waterloo, but for four-and-a-half months.

While lay people generally regard the Somme as an unmitigated British defeat, in fact given the considerable success on the southern part of the battlefield on 1 July 1916 (and the complete success of the French on the BEF's right flank) the failure to reinforce success led to defeat being snatched from the jaws of victory. Certainly the German high command did not regard the four-month Somme campaign as a clear victory. I believe an objective assessment of the

Somme campaign reveals it as an attritional strategic success for the Allies that provided an invaluable platform for the eventual Allied victory. Professor William Philpott has goes further, proclaiming the Somme as an outright Allied victory. 'Victory' is a term I avoid, since I believe the term is unhelpful in this context, but our arguments are essentially similar. Certainly, Haig did not acquire the nickname 'the Butcher of the Somme' as many people seem to think; I am unaware of any contemporary evidence for this soubriquet. I have written elsewhere that I suspect that the large numbers of teachers who take their charges to the Beaumont Hamel Battlefield park, which commemorates the disastrous attack of the Newfoundland Regiment on 1 July 1916 a) tell their pupils about Haig's incompetence and callousness and b) would be amazed to know that Haig, a hero across the Empire in the 1920s, himself unveiled the 'Caribou' memorial.

While it is right and proper to commemorate the sacrifice of the men of the First Day of the Somme, excessive concentration on this disaster does a disservice to the cause of understanding World War I in at least two ways in addition to those described above. First, the great Allied victories of 1918 are airbrushed from public memory. Second, such a relentlessly Anglocentric approach ignores the wider international context: there was more to the Great War than one day's fighting by the British Army, no matter how traumatic it might have been. Thankfully, this book will help to address the latter problem, by presenting a range of greatly differing perspectives in a highly accessible format.

On the eve of the centenary of World War I, it is clear that the conflict remains highly controversial in both academic and lay circles. The prominent view among historians is that Germany and Austria-Hungary were primarily responsible for the outbreak of the war. Berlin gave Vienna a 'blank cheque', an unconditional offer of support for actions taken in response to the assassination of Archduke Franz Ferdinand in Sarajevo in June 1914. Austria decided to crush its upstart Balkan rival Serbia, heedless of the risk of provoking Russia and thus bringing about a general war; in this book, Lothar Höbelt gives a good concise summary of the Austrian role in launching the war. Many historians believe that Germany took advantage of the crisis engendered by the Sarajevo murder to achieve foreign policy objectives, even at the risk of war; some believe Berlin actually planned and executed a war of aggression. Recently attempts have been made both to blame Russia for the war, and return to the earlier idea of a war that no great power really wanted. Neither has succeeded in supplanting the dominant theories.

World War I was a global conflict, but while this fact is at the centre of 'high end' books such as Hew Strachan's *To Arms* (2001), the first volume of a projected trilogy on the war, and David Stevenson's *1914–18: The History of the First World War* (2004), it is simply not reflected in the vast majority of publications on the war. The titanic struggle between Russia and the Central Powers has been particularly poorly served in this respect. Although Austria-Hungary played a critical role in the outbreak of the war, in terms of military history it has been all but invisible to an Anglophone audience. Russia has fared a little better, but not much, and even Germany's Eastern Front campaigns have received short shrift. Norman Stone's *The Eastern Front 1914–17*, published as far back as 1975, continues to hold the field although as Stone himself admits it should have been superseded by now. Nevertheless, recent work has begun to address the gap. Dennis Showalter's *Tannenberg* (1991) has been joined by other excellent studies of Eastern Front campaigns, such as Graydon Tunstall, *Blood on the Snow: The Carpathian Winter War of 1915* (2010) Richard DiNardo, *Breakthough: The Gorlice-Tarnow Campaign, 1915* (2010) and Timothy C. Dowling, *The Brusilov Offensive* (2008). It is particularly pleasing to see that the Eastern Front is given good coverage in this book. Höbelt's study of, as he puts it, 'the rollercoaster' of Austro-Hungarian 'experience' during the war is a particularly impressive chapter which, among many other things brings out the pitfalls as well as the advantages of being the junior partner to the Germans. Stephen Walsh's chapter, although more narrowly focused, is a very useful synthetic piece on the Russian army, while Peter Lieb's superb study of the German Army in the Ukraine brings into sharp focus a campaign that will be almost wholly unknown even to readers with a good general knowledge of the war.

World War I was not one conflict but many. While the Allied war against the Ottoman Empire had many points of contact with the war with Germany, it was pursued for rather different reasons. The conflict with Germany was primarily concerned with preventing a bid for hegemony in Europe, while the Russians, British and French fought the Turks in large part out of motives of imperial expansion. While much of Ottoman Turkey's war is almost completely unknown, two aspects have been perennial favourites of writers: the campaigns at the Dardanelles/Gallipoli, and in Palestine. Until very recently, the Turkish perspective of the former has been largely absent, although Edward J. Erickson's pioneering work has done much to rectify this. The Palestine campaign remains famous largely because of the enigmatic, charisma-laden figure of T. E. Lawrence ('of Arabia'). Lawrence was responsible for much myth-making about the Arab Revolt, and David Murphy's nuanced chapter in this book will surprise those who base their knowledge on *Revolt in the Desert* and the many popular works that use it. Rather than seeing it in romantic terms, Murphy emphasizes such unfamiliar factors as air power and Ottoman counter-insurgency methods, arguing that 'the Arab Revolt of 1916–18 established many of the methods in the modern desert warfare playbook'.

However important it is establish the global context, the Western Front remains at the heart of World War I. Here too, Anglophone readers have been, until recently, ill-served. Not until the late 20th and early 21st centuries did major works on the French army begin to appear in English in the numbers that the importance of this force warrants. Works by historians such as Michael Neiberg (who has an excellent chapter on Allied and Central Powers high command in this book), Robert Doughty, William Philpott and Elizabeth Greenhalgh have filled the gap, and to this must now be added the name of François Cochet, whose chapter on the French army appears in this book.

In contrast to the French, there has been a little more work in English on the German army, but some of it dating from the Cold War era was rather uncritical: seeing Germany as a paradigm of military efficiency was always rather strange, given that in the 20th century it fought two major wars and lost both of them. More recently, scholars such as Robert Foley, Holger Afflerbach, David T. Zabecki, Jonathan Boff and Jack Sheldon have given more nuanced perspectives on the German army and its commanders. The chapters by Thorsten Loch and Matthias Strohn in this book are worthy additions to the literature in English on the German army of 1914–18, and help the reader see 'the other side of the hill'.

As a glance at the military history shelves of American book stores indicates that, in contrast to the Civil War and World War II, World War I does not attract much interest in the United States. Earlier studies of the American Expeditionary Forces were often nationalistic in tone, and gave very positive assessments of the operational performance of the US Army. They have been replaced by more scholarship that takes a much more sober and downbeat view that highlights the problems faced by raw American formations in 1918. General John J. Pershing, the AEF's staff work and doctrine have not emerged unscathed from this reassessment. Andrew Wiest's chapter in this book follows scholars such as Timothy Nenninger, Robert Ferrell and Mark Grotelueschen in this respect.

Some of the fiercest historiographical battles have been fought over the performance of the British army, with issues of command and the existence or otherwise of a 'learning curve' to the fore. After Bruce Gudmundson's useful assessment of the organization of the army, Andrew Macdonald's chapter affirms the reality of the learning curve – better described as 'learning process' – debate by concentrating on the New Zealand Division. This was regarded by both contemporaries and historians as a highly effective formation, but the reputation of the Division is bound up with the myth that 'colonials' were better soldiers than men from the British Isles. He debunks the 'colonial supermen' idea, concluding although the NZ Division indeed had an impressive record of innovation, adaptation and battlefield performance, this needs to be placed into the context of a number of 'British and Dominion formations that were together treading the often difficult path towards tactical maturation that culminated in the attainment of a British army-wide critical mass of expertise and ultimately the victory of 1918'.

Together with James Corum's and Michael Epkenhans's fine chapters, on air power and the war at sea respectively, the pieces in this book form an excellent introduction to the military history of World War I that will also prove valuable to specialists in the subject. While it does not – cannot – cover every single aspect, the book shows how much more there was to the war than just the First Day of the Somme. The centenary years of 2014 to 2018 offer an unparalleled opportunity for education about a conflict that has more than its fair share of myths. It is my hope that this book, written by an international team of experts, will enhance the educational process. All those who fought in World War I are now dead. We owe it to them to try to understand the terrible conflict that consumed so many and marked the post-war lives of survivors.

Gary Sheffield
Professor of War Studies
University of Wolverhampton
1 July 2013

CHAPTER 1

COMMANDING THROUGH ARMAGEDDON

Allied Senior Leadership in World War I

Professor Michael S. Neiberg

The road to the Marne

In 1909, five years after historic rivals France and Great Britain buried their hatchets and signed the diplomatic agreement known as the *Entente Cordiale*, the French Army sent a high-level delegation to the British Staff College at Camberley. It was led by the cerebral commander of the French *École Supérieur de Guerre*, Général Ferdinand Foch. Hosting him was his British counterpart and friend General Sir Henry Wilson. Although the two governments had made it clear that the *Entente Cordiale* was not a military alliance in any sense of the term, the two men quasi-officially discussed possible joint responses to a European war. Presciently, Wilson is supposed to have introduced Foch to a colleague by saying 'This fellow is going to command the Allied armies when the big war comes on.'[1]

It took about a decade, but Wilson's prophecy came true in March 1918, when the Allied governments named Foch supreme commander. The road from Wilson's introduction at Camberley to the historic 1918 decision in a city hall in the provincial town of Doullens was a rocky and bloody one. At base, the main issue revolved around how much sovereignty states and commanding generals were willing to cede to a supranational command. During most of the war, the Allies realized that the absence of such a body hindered the execution of a single, unified strategy. Still, they had good reasons for resisting a true coalition command structure for four long and murderous years.

Although Wilson's comment about 'the big war' suggests that planners expected a war, few saw it coming when it did break out in the summer of 1914. Even Foch, then serving as the commander of the elite 20e Corps d'armée in eastern France, reacted to the assassination of Archduke Franz Ferdinand in Sarajevo in June 1914 by going to his country house in Brittany for a few weeks of vacation as planned. Russian General Alexei Brusilov did not even see the need to cut short his vacation in, of all places, Germany. Only when the Austro-Hungarian government issued its lightning bolt of an ultimatum to Serbia on 23 July did most Europeans begin to worry about the imminence of war.

The rapid transformation of a third-rate diplomatic quarrel in the Balkans into a possible world war did not give the British and French much time to coordinate their movements. The British, moreover, were going through turmoil associated with the government's March 1914 decision to give Ireland Home Rule. Officers at the Curragh barracks in Ireland made it clear to the British government that they did not support Parliament's policy. Threats by these and other British officers not to obey orders to disarm Protestant paramilitaries in Ireland had led to command shakeups and numerous resignations from officers who wished to dissociate themselves from what they saw as mutinous behaviour.[2]

One of those who had resigned on principle in the wake of the Curragh incident was Sir John French, a womanizing cavalryman who was frequently in debt to his fellow officers. Despite the lack of faith that most generals in the British Army had in him, the politicians were reassured by his resignation that he would obey their orders and thus they gave him command of the British Expeditionary Force (BEF), a well-trained force of 100,000 men designed for rapid deployment to the continent.

Sir John did not have the kind of warm friendships with French generals that Wilson enjoyed. He did not speak the language of his allies nor did he fully trust them. He initially wanted the BEF deployed to Antwerp, where it would be independent of the French; have the direct support of the Royal Navy; and where its position would be consistent with Britain's stated reason for entering the war, the defence of neutral Belgium. The politicians overruled him and ordered him to go to France, with Secretary of State for War Lord Kitchener telling Sir John that he would need to subordinate British strategy to Allied strategy. In practical terms, Kitchener was telling France that Britain could only win the war by hewing to the strategic direction of its senior partner. As Kitchener later told Winston Churchill, 'Unfortunately, we have to make war as we must, not as we should like to.'[3]

Sir John did not agree, establishing a strategic relationship with the French that was characterized by improvisation and ad hoc measures. British leaders struggled to find a way to maintain full control over their own forces while the French tried to force the British to hew to their own strategic vision. Sir John undoubtedly saw the value of the Allies having one unified strategy, but he argued vociferously that only he had the legal and constitutional authority to command British forces and, furthermore, that no foreigner could issue orders to him or his men. Sir John, moreover, had had a very bad introduction to his French allies. When his BEF finally achieved liaison with 5e Armée to its right in late August, its chief of staff greeted the British with the comment, 'At last you are here… If we are beaten we will owe it all to you.'[4] Sir John's loathing of his allies intensified when 5e Armée retreated without informing him, dangerously exposing one of his flanks.

The August defeats of the Allied armies, caused in part by the lack of a unified strategy, forced their retreat towards Paris. The retreat further demonstrated the limits of Allied strategy. Sir John wanted to reposition the BEF behind Paris to allow its soldiers to rest and recover; he had also considered moving it as far as Le Havre from where the Royal Navy could take it home if necessary. French Chief of Staff Général Joseph Joffre – who often acted as if the BEF belonged to him – disagreed, arguing for the BEF to move forward in coordination with the French armies ranged east of the capital.

Joffre was a massive man who had been too busy directing French responses to the German invasion of his homeland to worry much about his allies or their strategic needs. In late August, as the battle for Paris was beginning to take shape, however, Joffre reacted with decisiveness. He replaced the commander of 5e Armée that Sir John blamed for retreating without informing him. In his place came Général Louis Franchet d'Espèrey, a more aggressive and more diplomatic general that Sir John came to respect. Changing French commanders, however, did not guarantee that the British would move into a gap in the line between 5e and 6e Armées, as Joffre thought vitally necessary.

Joffre reluctantly concluded that he had no authority to order the British to move as he wished. In the absence of such authority, he relied on personal persuasion. He made an appearance at Sir John's headquarters on 5 September, just as the battle that was likely to determine the outcome of the war was beginning. Joffre implored Sir John, grabbing his hand and telling him that 'the lives of all French people, the soil of France, the future of Europe' depended on what the BEF did next. Growing more emotional, Joffre continued, 'I cannot believe that the British Army will refuse to do its share in this supreme crisis… History would severely judge your absence.' Leaning over to stare into Sir John's eyes, Joffre then pounded his fists on the table and said, 'The honor of England is at stake!'[5]

The exchange was typical of this first stage of allied command relationships. Neither man had any formal authority to determine the actions of the other. Thus did Joffre have to rely on emotion and persuasion to influence his British counterpart. In this case, it worked. Sir John grew red with emotion and tears welled in his eyes. He tried to recall enough of his schoolboy French to respond in Joffre's own language but the words failed him. Instead he turned to the best French speaker on his staff, none other than Henry Wilson, and said, 'Damn it. I can't explain. Tell him we will do all we possibly can.'[6] Joffre then turned and left the room without arranging any of the details. French's word, he said, was all he needed.

Persuasion was sufficient this time to help the Allies win a great victory on the Marne. It was not, however, a model for the future because such emotional appeals could not substitute for genuine coalition strategy. Another model, if used only briefly, did appear at the end of 1914 when Joffre assigned Foch to command the Northern Army Group, a hastily thrown together assemblage of French, British, and Belgian units that tried to hold the line of the Yser River and the Ypres canal in the small slice of Belgium not yet in German hands. Foch was, in fact, junior in rank to both the British commander, Field Marshal French, and the Belgian commander, King Albert. Nevertheless, his energy and his determination allowed the Allies to hold the line through the autumn and winter.

Fighting separate wars

After poor weather and mutual exhaustion had set in on both sides, the British and French established their own parts of the Western Front, thus ending this brief experiment in conducting coalition operations. Throughout 1915 the British and French ran virtually separate wars, both from one another and from their other main allies, Italy and Russia. Partly, the experience of 1915 was a response to the problems of 1914. Although the Allies had succeeded in fending off German offensives, enough friction had developed to make a unified command – such as that temporarily exercised by Foch on the Yser/Ypres line – impractical. Joffre still tried to influence British strategy, especially its timing, but he had little success.

As a result, Allied efforts were poorly timed and poorly coordinated. British and French offensives did not mutually support one another in either time or space; nor did offensives on the Italian or Eastern Front sufficiently distract German attention. If part of warfare was to divide one's enemies, then the Germans need only sit back. The Allies were doing the dividing for them, as Foch had already divined. As a result, the Germans were able to use what military strategists call interior lines of communication. Such lines enabled the Germans to move men and *matériel* from the Western Front to the Eastern Front in a way that was both logistically and politically impossible for the Allies.

Germany also had the advantage of near-total strategic dominance over its main ally, Austria-Hungary. The two coalition systems offered stark contrasts in methods and results. Increasingly dependent on Germany for men and supplies, the Austro-Hungarians were in no position to challenge their senior partner over matters of strategy. Thus while the Central Powers were conducting one war, the Allies were in effect running four: one French, one British, one Italian, and one Russian. On the Western Front, the consequence was that the Germans could move men along their interior lines of communication to meet emergencies as they arose or to concentrate resources for attacks.

It also meant that the Germans could take risks. In the spring of 1915, the Germans attacked the northern meeting point of French and British lines, using poison gas for the first time at the Second Battle of Ypres. The attack created a huge hole in Allied lines, but the Germans were in no position to exploit it, in large part because exploitation was not their goal. Instead, they wanted to fix Allied attention in the west while they used their interior lines to move men undetected to the east. Then, in May, 1915, they struck between the towns of Gorlice and Tarnów in Galicia, inflicting a massive defeat on the Russians. In just a few weeks, the Russians lost an estimated 410,000 men and had retreated more than 100 miles. By the end of summer, the Germans had Warsaw and almost all of Poland in their possession.

One of the lessons of the catastrophe at Gorlice-Tarnów, and of 1915 more generally, was the need for better inter-Allied strategic coordination. Without it, the Germans would be free once again to shift resources between theatres of war. The failure of the mostly British adventure at Gallipoli and the joint failure at Salonika in Greece also underscored the need to focus on the Western Front.[7] But doing so would require more coordination and more joint strategy than the Allies had employed in the frustrating year of 1915.

The Allies gave it a try at the end of the year, in a meeting at Joffre's headquarters at the massive Château de Chantilly, north-east of Paris. The French, British, Russians, Italians, and Serbians all sent senior representatives to the meeting. The Russians, not surprisingly, were anxious to find a way to prevent a repeat of their disaster at Gorlice-Tarnów. All of the representatives understood the root cause of that defeat: by failing to properly coordinate their offensives, the Allied armies failed to make maximum advantage of their resources. Nevertheless, if they agreed on the central problem they disagreed on the proper remedy. None of the representatives at the meeting was willing to consider naming a single strategic commander for the Allied armies. Instead they agreed that all of the Allied armies would launch offensives if one of them was threatened as Russia had been at Gorlice-Tarnów.

This promise was unlikely to solve the problem, unconnected as it was to any specific strategic situation. Major offensives, moreover, do not materialize at a moment's notice. As such, the promise mollified the increasingly fearful Russians without giving them any real help. The French, moreover, insisted that the Salonika front in Greece continue, despite the objections of the Russians and the British that it was a waste of resources. Chantilly therefore exposed the basic strategic disagreements between the Allies; as such, it is unlikely that they could have reached any accord on major strategic questions that would have sufficiently satisfied them.

The frustrations of 1916

Chantilly did, however, produce a joint Franco–British agreement to launch a major offensive in mid-summer, 1916, near the Somme River. Neither side was willing to agree to a joint commander, even for so large an operation. Consequently, the plan called for the French to command their forces, 40 divisions strong, to the south of the river, while the less experienced British attacked with eight divisions to the north. Ferdinand Foch, the French commander of the operation, might have been an excellent choice to assume overall command, but the new British commander, Sir Douglas Haig, was opposed to allowing a foreign general to command British divisions. The British government supported him, meaning that the central command problems of 1915 remained.[8]

Consequently, because the enormous German offensive in and around Verdun, launched in February, 1916, targeted the French only, the crisis that ensued was primarily a French crisis that required British help rather than a coalition crisis that called for fundamental changes to the system.[9] The French Army went through a massive transformation during 1916 as it rotated units in and out of a ten-month battle of unprecedented ferocity. Instead of becoming the coalition's largest joint attempt to date to win a major campaign on the

Western Front, the offensive on the Somme now became, in French eyes, a means to distract German attention from Verdun. The emergency at Verdun, moreover, meant that the French could not contribute anywhere close to the 40 divisions it had promised. Joffre openly worried that without British help the French Army might be out of reserves in three months. The Somme would thus have to become a primarily British offensive with the French in a supporting role.

But British strategic aims were not the same as French aims. While the French were imploring their allies to attack as soon as possible, the British were trying to delay the Somme offensive in order to give them time to train and amass their new volunteer armies. Joffre urged a reconsideration of that policy, begging the British to reconceive the Somme offensive as an operation to relieve the desperate French Army. Such strategic goals failed to motivate the British, who, naturally, had aims of their own for the offensive. British leaders, moreover, either could not, or would not, understand just how badly the French were suffering at Verdun, with General William 'Wully' Robertson ungraciously remarking in late March that Joffre had 'no idea of ever taking the offensive if he can get other people to take it for him'.[10]

That comment was unduly harsh. The French Army was then undergoing a trial the likes of which the British had never seen. Scholars still argue over how much the crisis at Verdun affected British strategic thinking on the Somme, but two points are clear. First, there was to be no supreme commander of the operation. British commander Douglas Haig became the de facto commander-in-chief not because the arrangement made the most military sense, but simply from the old military maxim of preponderance of force. Because most of the divisions on the Somme were British, Haig became the commander. Thus most of the key strategic decisions were British.

Second, the Allied system had not noticeably advanced since 1914. Joffre still tried to persuade Haig to push forward the date of the offensive not by ordering him to do so, but by making a personal appeal. In a meeting in mid-May, Haig favored a delay until mid-August; Joffre convinced him to attack in early July only by telling him that if he waited until August the French Army might be out of reserves and the French government might even fall. With the question of timing resolved, the inexperienced British Army began to organize the details, while the French prepared to support their allies as well as they could.[11]

Whatever its role in wearing down the German Army, the Somme failed to break German lines or create the conditions necessary for French victory at Verdun.[12] The enormous British casualties in the campaign struck many British political leaders as wasteful. In October, Britain's new Secretary of State for War, David Lloyd George, even came to the Somme to ask Foch why French forces had advanced further at lower costs than British troops did. Foch refused to take the bait, aware as he was that Lloyd George was looking for ammunition in his quest to remove Haig from command.

Had he given Lloyd George an answer, however, Foch might have pointed out several important factors, including the higher level of training and experience in the French Army as well as the relatively weaker German positions opposite French lines. He might also have noted that without a single, unified command the French and British continued, two years into the war, to operate essentially separate wars unified only by their proximity in space and time. Instead of one commander, the Somme had two. Instead of a single strategic and operational vision for the battle, Haig and Foch found themselves disagreeing and debating, thus preventing the development of what Foch called a 'suitable rhythm' for exploiting successes. For Foch, who had commanded the only successful (if temporary) unified command of the war, the experience was immensely frustrating. Foch wrote to his wife complaining of this command arrangement, saying that it forced him to find a patience within himself that he did not know he possessed.[13]

The Somme revealed two important barriers to the formation of a unified command. First, British generals remained adamantly opposed. Their objections may appear unwarranted with the benefit of hindsight, but they had logical arguments on their side. Few of them were unreservedly impressed with their French colleagues' strategic vision. Typical of a smaller power in a coalition, they were sensitive about being used to achieve the strategic aims of the larger power. Unless and until they believed that Allied strategy could represent their strategic needs on a roughly equal basis, they saw no benefit in a joint command; indeed, they saw a great deal of potential harm.

They also argued that British officers (and only British officers) had a legal, constitutional right to command British troops. Although sometimes couched as an issue of honour, this argument had the additional benefit of putting the onus for a unified command on British politicians who would need to take responsibility for any decision to place British troops under French command.

This last point flowed logically into the second main barrier to a unified command: the unwillingness of British politicians to take a larger role in the formation of allied strategy. British Prime Minister Herbert Asquith (in office until December 1916) had had virtually no experience of foreign affairs or military strategy. The British foreign secretary, Edward Grey, was far more expert on Asia than he was on Europe and he, too, had little understanding of military strategy. Britain's main military strategist had been the Secretary of State for War, the imperial hero Lord Kitchener, but he had an awkward and uneasy relationship with British politicians; Asquith had once quipped that Kitchener was not a great man, but a great poster, referring to the myriad recruitment posters across Britain with a stern Kitchener telling young men to enlist.[14] In any event, Kitchener's death at sea in June 1916 permanently silenced the voice of Britain's most experienced strategist.

The elevation of David Lloyd George to Prime Minister in December 1916 represented a sea change in British strategy. Lloyd George hated Haig, frequently referring to him as a 'dunce'.[15] Yet Haig was well connected to the royal family and there was no obvious general in line to replace him. Thus Lloyd George knew that if he wanted to reduce Haig's power and influence he would need to find a way to do so without removing him from command. Lloyd George was also more willing to see the war in far-reaching global terms, a strategic vision that had the side benefit of undercutting Haig, whose authority did not extend beyond the Western Front.

The failure of 1917

Lloyd George began to scheme with the new French commander, Général Robert Nivelle, who replaced Joffre at the end of 1916. Unlike Joffre, Nivelle was comfortable around politicians and projected an air of easy confidence. He also spoke excellent English and understood British culture because of his English mother. Although most Allied generals, British and French alike, thought Nivelle was too glib and confident for his own good, to the politicians he stood as a welcome contrast to the dour Haig and the tired Joffre.

Lloyd George sought to put Haig under Nivelle's authority, both to undercut Haig and to take advantage of Nivelle's confidence. He sprung a trap on his own commander at a conference at Calais in February, 1917. Ostensibly called to discuss mundane, but important, matters related to railways, Lloyd George spent the first day avoiding Haig but talking to French Premier Aristide Briand. When the conferees gathered for the first plenary session, Lloyd George patiently listened to a discourse on strategy from Nivelle. At the end, Lloyd George asked Nivelle to sum up his key points of disagreement with Haig. A stunned Nivelle did not quite know how to reply, so Haig replied in his best French (thus forcing Lloyd George to follow through an interpreter), explaining some of the key technicalities. The British Prime Minister then asked for the French to write up a description of the strategic problems as they understood them.[16]

So far, there seemed little to alarm Haig, but after dinner, he learned that Lloyd George had been floating a plan to reduce the power of the British commander-in-chief, meaning that Haig would thereafter be responsible for administration and discipline, but not strategy. An enraged Haig and his colleague General Sir William Robertson went to Lloyd George's room to confront him. Lloyd George told them that he planned to go even further, placing Haig directly under the orders of Nivelle. He was thus proposing a joint command that subordinated British interests to those of France.

Haig, predictably, was furious, calling the scheme 'madness' and openly raising the possibility that British soldiers would not fight under French command. Haig recalled the tensions between the British and French in 1914 and 1915 as reasons to avoid the very idea Lloyd George was then proposing. The two generals, soon joined by one more, met in Robertson's room and agreed to face a court martial rather than accept Lloyd George's plan. Haig wrote in his diary that he went to bed that night 'thoroughly disgusted with our Government and our Politicians'.[17]

Lloyd George's scheme was more than simply underhand; it threatened to tear the Allied coalition apart. Several senior French generals, including Nivelle and the legendary soldier-general Hubert Lyautey (then serving as France's minister of war), rushed to Haig and Robertson to assure them that they had had nothing to do with Lloyd George's plot. As Foch had done on the Somme, they displayed loyalty to a fellow general, showing the complications involved in such a tense series of relationships as well as the barriers to forming a functioning coalition.

In the face of such strenuous opposition from his own generals, Lloyd George quickly agreed to compromise. Within just a few hours, the Prime Minister and his generals signed a document putting the direct command of British troops under Haig, although the strategic direction of the battle Nivelle planned for spring, 1917 remained with the French. In practice, the agreement meant that for an approximately two-week period the French would tell the British where to attack, but the methods and execution of that attack were to remain in Haig's hands.

The offensive Nivelle designed predictably turned into a disaster. It became known either as the Chemin des Dames Offensive to mark the ridge it targeted or, more appropriately, the Nivelle Offensive. Nivelle made number of critical mistakes in his preparations, most importantly in not maintaining proper operational security. As a result, the Germans, perched high atop a commanding ridge, were in an excellent position to see what Nivelle was planning. They were also able to build strong defensives and move many of their units to a position that was safe from French attack but perfectly poised for a counter-attack.

Many French officers had been highly critical of Nivelle's preparations. Lyautey went as far as to resign as war minister and return to Algeria in order to avoid the responsibility for an offensive he believed was doomed to fail. The French government nevertheless let the attack go forward. It proved to be a complete disaster that led not only to battlefield defeat but to a series of mutinies inside the French Army and the rise to command of the cautious and taciturn Philippe Pétain.[18]

From a coalition perspective, the offensive only confirmed in the minds of British generals the folly of tying British strategy to French strategy. The failure on the Chemin des Dames stood in stark contrast to the Anglo-Canadian success at roughly the same time at Vimy Ridge. Haig predicted that the French would complain of a lack of British support, thus showing 'the womanly side of their nature, wounded vanity, jealousy and disappointment at their failure and our success'.[19]

As Haig had predicted, the French soon demanded that the British resume their offensive near Arras and Vimy Ridge in order to draw off German troops from the battered French on the Chemin des Dames. Although they hated the idea, and resented the unwillingness of the French to be honest with them about their losses on the Chemin des Dames, the British complied. What became known as the Second Battle of Arras (23 April to 17 May 1917) was a source of great bitterness to British generals, who now had even more reason to resist all suggestions of a joint command.

The Allies ran separate wars through the rest of 1917 on the Western Front, but events elsewhere kept the idea of a unified command alive. In October, Foch and British general Sir Hubert Plumer rushed troops and artillery to Italy to help the Italians recover after their devastating defeat at the battle of Caporetto. Foch's time in Italy convinced him more than ever that the entire Allied war effort needed a single commander who could fuse together the efforts of all of the belligerents. He also advocated for the formation of a general reserve, a large body of troops from all of the Allied nations that could respond to threats anywhere.

The Americans, who entered the war in April, presented another problem. American manpower, money, and arms held out the promise of providing the Allies with a decisive edge, but American stubbornness threatened to throw those advantages away. President Wilson aimed to keep American forces as separate as possible from those of the Allies. He even refused to sign the Treaty of London that formally created the alliance and called the Americans an 'associated power' of that alliance. The American commander, John Pershing, left for France with a letter signed by the President forbidding him from allowing American soldiers to serve under European command.

Wilson hoped that his policy would maintain his country's strategic and operational independence, thereby allowing him to pursue his post-war goals. But to the Europeans, his stance carried with it the risk of wasting American resources. No American commander had any experience of leading large formations of men under conditions remotely similar to those of the Western Front. Far better, the British and French argued, to place those Americans under European generals while they learned the art of modern warfare. Pershing and Wilson, however, refused almost all of their efforts, only agreeing to place one division (and that, notably, was an African-American division) under European command.

In place of a joint command came strategic direction by committee. In November, the Allies formed the Supreme War Council (SWC) which was dominated by politicians. Although the politicians, who had the legal responsibility for grand strategy, had a perfect right to assume the direction of the SWC, in practice it tended to pit the 'brass hats' against the 'frocks'. Neither Britain's Lloyd George nor France's new premier, Georges Clemenceau, had any great love of generals; it was Clemenceau who coined the phrase, 'War is too important a business to be left to the generals.'[20] Being a political body, the SWC was far better suited to discuss and debate than it was to decide. Foch soon concluded that the SWC, although ostensibly a step in the direction of a unified command, might have been worse than the disorganized system it replaced.

From disaster to victory

The Allies entered 1918 without a unified command structure. Foch blamed the failure to create one for the widespread success of the German spring offensives. Without a single commander and a large general reserve there was no way to move reinforcements quickly to areas before they became crises. Recent scholarship argues that the Germans missed a great opportunity to exploit this weakness in the Allied command by failing to target the juncture of the French and British armies near Amiens. Had they done so, they might have forced the British to fall back towards their lines of communication on the English Channel and the French towards their own line of communication near Paris. The Germans would then have had two open flanks to turn.[21] Because they failed to see the strategic opportunity that a lack of an Allied unified command presented, the Germans gave the Allies the crucial gift of time. Germany's spring offensives, which began on 21 March 1918, were therefore successful at the tactical level, but not at the strategic level. They gained enormous swaths of territory but they did not capture operationally vital places like Amiens. They did, however, strike fear into the hearts of politicians and force the French government to abandon Paris.

The offensives also became the impetus for creating – at long last – a unified Allied command structure. Just five days after the German offensives began, the main participants of the SWC met in the small town of Doullens, close enough to hear the fighting on the approaching Western Front. The success of the Germans had forced the British to accept the idea of a unified command in return for badly needed French troops to close up critical gaps in the line. In return, the French agreed that national commanders would have the right to appeal any decisions to their national governments, although in practice they rarely did so.

The man in charge of the new command structure was none other than Foch, thus finally fulfilling Wilson's prophecy at Camberley. Foch's authority, as agreed to at Doullens, gave him power over the strategic direction of the Allied armies only. In practice, he could move Allied armies and he could tell them when and where to fight, but he could not give them operational orders. His real power came from his force of personality, his uncanny ability to read German intentions, and his control over reserves.

This system had flaws, but it worked well enough to turn the tide of the war by mid-summer. Foch organized and directed (although he did not personally lead) true joint and coalition battles with the men of several Allied nations fighting alongside each other. Even the Americans participated, agreeing to abide by Foch's overall direction. In September, they agreed to fight in the Meuse-Argonne sector rather than in the direction of Metz as they preferred because the former operation conformed more closely to Foch's overall vision than did the latter.

The unified command system that Foch led played a decisive role in ending the war in 1918. Foch's carefully coordinated hammer blows across the Western Front gave Allied offensives a punching power that was greater than the sum of its parts. For the first time in the war, the Germans were facing not a detached series of uncoordinated offensives, but a carefully managed plan that used the power of national troops to execute a single strategic vision. Whether such a system would have ended the war more quickly had it been in place in 1914, 1915, or 1916 is irrelevant. The political and military conditions did not yet exist. Only the threat of an imminent defeat was sufficient to force Allied political and military leaders to take a step that all resisted, no matter how obvious its benefits.

Foch, as supreme commander, led the delegation that accepted the German surrender in the forest of Compiègne on 11 November 1918. Even then, however, he had to balance the divergent interests of the French, the British, the Americans, and the coalition he had forged. He also had to balance the goals of the soldiers and those of the politicians. He did so by sheer force of will, but once he delivered the armistice to Georges Clemenceau, the war moved from its military phase to its political phase, and in that phase, there was to be no coalition, only the wide divergence of national interests. The experience of 1919 showed that if making war by coalition was hard, making peace by coalition was almost impossible.

CHAPTER 2

GERMAN OPERATIONAL THINKING IN WORLD WAR I

Major Dr Thorsten Loch

The development of operational thinking in the German armed forces has held a fascination for historians throughout the 20th century and beyond.[1] The reason for this is that the German understanding of the term and its application in war has been seen as the explanation for the German military successes in the German wars of unification and, in particular, in the two world wars. However, quite often the fact is overlooked that, despite the mythical or actual superiority of the German armies at the operational level of war, the Germans were defeated in the two major conflicts of the 20th century. The lesson is clear: operational art can only produce decisive results if it is supported by successful strategy.

'Operation' in the German sense of the word means the interdependency of manoeuvre, geography, and available forces with the aim of achieving the element of surprise and local supremacy in order to create a situation that leads to a decisive battle. The origins of German operational thinking go back as far as Frederick II and especially Napoleon I.[2] As a consequence of the French Revolution and the associated social changes within France, Napoleon was able to recruit or draft enough soldiers for the mass army – an army that was too big to be effectively controlled, commanded, and supplied if kept together as one contingent. As a consequence, Napoleon started dividing a large army into several smaller elements, which would then manoeuvre independently for a common purpose.

One of the most important lessons (or perceived lessons) of this period was that the newly united Germany – surrounded by actual or potential enemies – would not be able to sustain a prolonged war of attrition.[3]

The conclusion drawn from this was apparently a simple one: any war had to be of short duration in order to have the prospect of political success.[4] Owing to the location of Germany in the centre of Europe the general staff's thinking was therefore determined by the assumption that it was vital to defeat in a swift campaign at least one of the potential enemies surrounding the fatherland. Only a swift success would ensure that Germany would not be drawn into the disastrous downward spiral of a war of exhaustion. So time became the third vital element, alongside the determining factors of geography and manpower. To solve this fundamental political dilemma, which Bismarck in 1877 called the '*cauchemar des coalitions*',[5] the general staff came to rely on the paradigm of the strategic offensive, which was preferred to the strategic defence. An offensive promised – despite a higher overall risk – a swift decision, but also required manoeuvring and thus movement in the open, as it is the precondition for 'operation' in the German sense. Mobilization and an initial deployment planned with military precision would allow the one decisive advantage of lead time; the other would arise from the initiative to be taken and the 'imperative to act' which rests with the attacker. Moreover, an attack – rather than a drawn-out war of attrition – offered a greater chance of success if the adversary could be enveloped and thus destroyed.[6] This would lead to the one swift, decisive battle that would solve the political dilemma, which had its roots in historical examples such as Cannae, Leuthen, Königgrätz, and Sedan.[7] Other than the geographical factor, which at the operational level cannot be conceived without considering time and manpower, society and technology were also vital factors and both had been transformed throughout the 19th century, as had been shown in the US Civil War and the German wars of unification. With the increasing sophistication of nation states, wars were becoming more an affair for citizens and less for dynasties. Citizens aspired for political participation and this found one of its expressions in the growth of compulsory military service.[8] This universal conscription saw the development of the mass armies that were to form the basis for the future 'popular war'.

At the same time weapons development experienced a dynamic hitherto unknown, with the introduction of bolt-action breech-loading weapons both for the infantry and artillery. These weapons ushered in the age of industrialized warfare. What is often overlooked is that this development benefited the defender, not the attacker, which posed a unique problem for the Germans as it meant that an offensive seeking a decisive battle would be even more difficult to conduct than before. The introduction of automatic weapons and the ensuing strengthening of the defence were bound to cause a crisis of the attack.[9] The German military, and in a similar way the French, tried to compensate for this by an increased emphasis on morale and combat efficiency. In the face of these changes Helmuth Graf von Moltke the Elder (1801–91), the victor of Königgrätz and Sedan, warned in his last speech before the Reichstag in 1890:

> Gentlemen, if the war that has been hanging over us like the sword of Damocles for the past ten years – if this war breaks out, neither its duration nor its end can be foreseen. It is the greater powers of Europe which, prepared as never before, are ready to fight each other; not one of them can be defeated in one or two campaigns to such a degree that it would have to declare itself beaten, that it would have to make peace under harsh conditions, that it would never rise again, and that only after one year is out, to renew the fight. Gentlemen, it may be a seven-year war, it may be a thirty-year war – and woe betide he who sets Europe on fire, he who lights the fuse to the powder keg.[10]

Envelopment battle: certainty or risk?

It was Moltke the Elder who shaped operational thinking before 1890. After 1890 his successor as Chief of the General Staff of the Army, Alfred Graf von Schlieffen (1833–1913) was as influential as Moltke had been. Neither of them left a complete outline or doctrine for operational thinking.[11]

Yet those elements of their thinking that can be reconstructed were increasingly concerned with the assumed two-front war against France and Russia.[12] This predicted war against two land powers would be condemned to failure if fought defensively and would only have a chance of success if fought offensively. The key to this continued to be the decisive battle,[13] brought about through an offensive designed to destroy the adversary psychologically and morally. The envelopment was based on manoeuvring, with Cannae and Leuthen serving as historical blueprints. The site of the decisive battle, which should be imagined not as one great battle but as a sequence of several small-scale engagements, was to be located in a border region, an indication that operational thinking in its conception, particularly with a view to logistic endurance of a mass army, was limited. The Germans' predicted numerical inferiority was intended to be compensated for by the higher quality of the German soldiers and their military leadership.

Since 1879 German planners had been prepared for a likely two-front war. Their solution for that scenario had been an 'offensive defence in the East and West with the centre of gravity in the East'.[14] As of 1892 Schlieffen re-assessed Russia's and France's options and came to the conclusion that, due to changing circumstances in Russia, no decision could be brought about there and that France, on account of its improved transport infrastructure, would be capable of launching an offensive of its own at a very early stage. Hence, France was the more dangerous of the two adversaries. From then on, the centre of gravity of German operational planning – as far as this is indicated in the initial deployment plans – was in the West. Schlieffen had formulated the final version of his ideas in his memorandum 'Krieg gegen Frankreich', the oft-quoted 'Schlieffen Plan', which he committed to his successor Helmuth von Moltke the Younger (1848–1916) in 1906.[15] This memorandum does not, as is often claimed, contain the plans for a two-front war 'but rather the plan for a possible campaign against France'.[16] The memorandum was not based on any current operational plan but on the initial deployment and mobilization plan for the years 1906–07. It presented a possible operational scenario and was at the same time the repository of much of Schlieffen's operational thinking.[17] What was intended was not a simultaneous two-front war, but rather that, using the advantages of interior lines of communication, both sides should be engaged separately and successively with the centre of gravity being in the West. In other words, France as the first adversary had to be destroyed within a short time, while in the East delaying defence operations should be conducted, if at all. Although the initial deployment plans for the East were frequently updated, Austria and the German Empire did not fully exploit the potential in their strategic cooperation with a view to a coalition war against Russia.

The initial deployment against France was based on the assumption that any frontal attack from the area of south-west Germany would be halted at the French belt of obstacles and fortifications. Therefore the decision was made was to pass through Luxembourg, Belgium, and the Netherlands – in violation of their neutrality – in order to achieve a northern envelopment at an early stage. According to Schlieffen's memorandum, weak German forces coming from Alsace-Lorraine would frontally contain the adversary, while the bulk of the German Army would launch an enveloping attack on the right wing. The ratio of the right to the left wing was to be 7:1, with the centre of rotation/pivot point in the area of Metz-Diedenhofen. The core elements of Schlieffen's operational thinking were offensive warfare, the usage of interior lines of communication, the dissolving of the two-front problem into two single-front wars, a centre of gravity in the West, swift battles of destruction through envelopment, and the formation of a strong right wing.[18]

The Schlieffen Plan and French Plan XVII

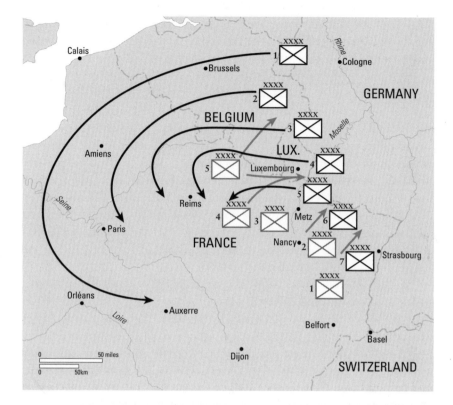

Schlieffen's successor, Moltke the Younger, agreed with the former's basic considerations; however, based on his own assessments Moltke drew a different conclusion where a war with France was concerned. His disposition of forces assumed an early French offensive into the German Empire; therefore he reinforced the left instead of the right wing with recently established forces. In the summer of 1914 seven out of eight armies were deployed on the Western border, with one army protecting East Prussia against any Russian attacks. At the same time, he renounced a passage through the Netherlands on political grounds; therefore, unlike Schlieffen, he had no alternative but to define the fortress of Liége as an intermediate target. One consequence thereof was that he put the German operations under an even higher time pressure, which offered less scope for attempting to find a political solution to any possible conflict. These crucial changes mean that it was the 'Moltke Plan'[19] rather than the Schlieffen Plan with which the German Empire went to war in August 1914.

The aim of winning the multi-front war, initially against France, with inferior resources and within a realistic time span failed within a few weeks.[20] The 'Miracle of the Marne'[21] ended the German advance, and a lack of resources, combined with leadership failures, caused the previously successful German attack to grind to a halt. The French moved forces from the Lorraine area to the Marne after they had identified the German centre of gravity. There, on 5 September, 24.5 German and 41 Allied divisions faced each other. The German advance slowed; the attempt at envelopment changed into a frontal encounter during which the potential threat of being enveloped caused the German forces to withdraw northwards. The ability to manoeuvre, existentially important for any offensive, had not yet been lost. What followed was the 'race to the sea', in which both sides tried to envelop the adversary on the northern flank in order to restart manoeuvre warfare in the depth of area. The culmination of this race was the First Battle of Ypres, with fighting around Ypres and Langemarck. Eventually the front, stretching from the polders of Flanders down to the Jura of Switzerland, became static and the war of attrition and the trenches, feared by all sides, was about to begin.

The lack of fresh forces before the battle of the Marne had yet another reason – events on the German Eastern Front, the forgotten front.[22] While the decision was to be brought about in the West, the soldiers of 8. Armee were tasked with holding East Prussia and taking the offensive wherever possible. Due to the unexpectedly early attack of two Russian armies and a crisis in the command of 8. Armee, Moltke was forced to move forces from the West to the East by rail to avert the imminent loss of East Prussia. Those forces were lacking on the Marne, but were not yet available for the battle of Tannenberg.[23] While the operational idea was heading towards one of its peaks in military history in one place, it ground to a halt in another place due to an inability to manoeuvre. The German offensive in the West had failed.

The search for a breakthrough battle

The armies of millions and the impact of inconceivably ferocious defence fire had ground to a halt any manoeuvring in the West. Soldiers were no longer on the march; instead they dug in. The war of exhaustion had begun. From a German perspective, any hope of swiftly ending the war had gone. There was the danger of another seven-year war, the outcome of which was uncertain. In order to uphold the prospect of a successful outcome of the war, attempts were made in the course of it to 'regain the tactical and operational manoeuvrability in offensive operations'.[24]

Initially, the centre of gravity continued to be in the West. Envelopment was no longer an easy option here. This would have required a breaking up of the static front. German operational thinking was neither rigid nor exclusively intent on envelopment. Alternative approaches such as the frontal attack with break-in and breakthrough had been discussed as early as before the war. A frontal attack had been considered an effective means, provided a gap could be discovered in the battle disposition of the adversary. The purpose of envelopment and breakthrough was the same – to cut off the enemy from his rearward lines of communication and to then destroy him in a decisive battle. Since autumn 1914 there had no longer been sufficient space for an operational envelopment; therefore the only remaining option was to attempt a frontal attack in the hope that a tactically and locally limited break-in could be expanded to an operational breakthrough. If an operational breakthrough could be achieved in one section of the front and a sufficient number of reserves could be moved up, the front line could be ruptured and rolled up in one or the other direction in a flanking operation. For fear of being cut off, soldiers in the trenches would have to move back, and the field would be open for envelopment operations.

Whereas before 1914 military leaders would normally have permitted a breakthrough attack only where gaps had been identified – the deterrent impact of defensive fire was generally known – the unique situation on the Western Front compelled commanders on all sides to order frontal attacks on gapless positions, despite the knowledge that the enemy's defensive fire would be murderous. Against this background the use of poisonous gas should be seen in the context of the continually more professionalized use of artillery on either side.[25] The purpose of the two types of long-range weapon – gas and artillery – was to reduce the adversary's defensive fire and to weaken his artillery to such an extent that the assaulting infantry could launch a successful break-in, which could possibly be expanded into a breakthrough. While the British and French launched frontal attacks in the Champagne and Artois between February and September 1915 and suffered high losses, the Germans tried to do this in Flanders in 1915. While over the years the Allies again and again sought salvation in frontal attacks, the Germans never got beyond attempting such attacks.

Erich von Falkenhayn[26] (1861–1922), who succeeded Moltke as Chief of the Supreme Army Command (*Oberste Heeresleitung*, OHL) in 1914, was compelled to shift his centre of gravity eastwards in order to stabilize the south-eastern front and Germany's ally Austria-Hungary, and to that end an offensive was launched in the area of Gorlice-Tarnów in May 1915. Here in the East was the theatre where the very operations were conducted, which, prior to 1914, one had hoped to conduct in the West. This showed the dilemma of the two-front war and the distribution of resources in a war of exhaustion. While in the eastern and south-eastern theatres of war the operational idea of the OHL unfolded, albeit not without having caused controversy locally, the much-feared war of attrition raged in the West and caused horrendous casualties on all sides. Yet a decisive battle in the East failed to materialize, not least because the Russian forces frequently succeeded in averting the intended envelopment by withdrawing into the depth of the area, even at Gorlice-Tarnów.[27] Here another limit of German operational thinking became apparent: the degree of manoeuvrability in the German Army was not sufficient to allow the idea of envelopment conceived in theory to be translated into practice. The problem of manoeuvrability continued to be directly linked to the logistic endurance of forces, which in pre-war plans hardly extended far beyond any borders. Conceptual flaws in German operational thinking were thus revealed as early as 1915. The concept of fully mobile warfare was ahead of its time, yet it failed more or less on account of technical-logistical limits which had not been duly considered in the search for the 'big operational success'.

In 1916, Falkenhayn moved the centre of gravity back to the West, although he knew that no decisive victory could be expected here. If it was not possible to bring about a breakthrough, the manpower superiority of Allies had be reduced to a minimum, and this was to be achieved by enticing the Allied commanders into accepting extremely high numbers of casualties. For this purpose Falkenhayn chose an objective that he assumed the French would strive to hold at any cost: the fortress town of Verdun. This town was not only an important cornerstone in the French defence plan, but also a political symbol. The French, so the Germans assumed, would most certainly deploy their reserves on a large scale to defend the town. Verdun in a way was intended to become the second French front, which would force them – like the Germans in the East – to withdraw forces from other sections of the front. The overall intention was that Verdun – while using German forces in a calculated manner – would achieve an equalization of force numbers and thus a stabilization of the entire Western Front. Yet Verdun turned into a 'blood pump' for all sides, not least because the leadership of 5. Armee had formulated as the tactical and operational objective to take Verdun and seize terrain instead of destroying the enemy and thus forces. In the end, the Germans got entangled in fights and used a great number of reserves in the course of them.

Operation *Gericht*, the plan for the battle of Verdun, was not based on classic operational concepts as it lacked the element of movement in a large scale. As well as Verdun, 1916 saw the battle of the Somme, also a synonym for phenomenal loss of life. In the West, operational art – the art of war – was being replaced by output of armaments factories. The British naval blockade exacerbated this aspect of the war, as economic issues rather than battlefield ones increasingly dominated the likely outcome of the war. World War I was developing more and more into a war of attrition and exhaustion, much like the Seven Years War. This type of war has no room for the concept of a decisive battle, and is inimical to the operational art.

A virtue out of necessity: exhaustion caused by mobile defence

Falkenhayn eventually failed because of Verdun. His successor as the third Chef der Heeresleitung (Chief of the Supreme Army Command) was Paul von Hindenburg (1847–1934), previously the Supreme Commander East, with his Erster Generalquartiermeister (First Quartermaster General) Erich Ludendorff (1865–1937).

In view of the force ratio in theatre and the Allied offensive on the Western Front, which was expected to happen in 1917, the Third Supreme Army Command established a new defence concept: flexible defence. The priority was no longer to rigidly hold a line with associated losses, but to use the depth of area.[28] At the same time the front line east of the Somme was shortened to the new 'Siegfriedstellung', known in English as the 'Hindenburg Line'. Both measures were the product of a strategic idea that was defensive in nature and aimed at consolidation. In the West, the operational effect of this idea was the establishment of the new defence concept. This concept provided the basis for manoeuvring – something that had not been possible on a large scale since 1914. This new form of manoeuvring was revived only at the tactical level on the Western Front, as even in 1916, the operational idea could be realized only on the Eastern Front. It was Falkenhayn, now in command of 9. Armee, who conducted successful manoeuvre operations against Romania in 1916.[29]

The reorganized defence on the Western Front had its baptism of fire in April 1917 near Arras.[30] After initial difficulties the new tactical concept took full effect and caused a high number of British casualties. The British offensive at Arras was only the precursor of the major French offensive between Reims and Soissons under Robert Nivelle, and due to the new German defensive systems the offensive failed with extremely high casualty figures.

The British fared no better in Flanders. While their attack on the Messines Ridge could be considered as one of the most successful Allied offensives, the ensuing engagements during the Third Battle of Ypres ended again in a bloody disaster, the price for just a few miles of terrain gained in a gruesome attritional battle. The German defence also succeeded in repelling the offensive at Cambrai, which began soon afterwards, and in rectifying the break-in by conducting counter-attacks. Soldiers on all sides bled to death, regardless of how much or how little terrain had been gained.

Allied artillery fire fell on sparsely manned front lines, while the defence in depth enabled the Germans to launch quick counter-attacks. The local superiority achieved through offensive action enabled the Germans again and again to envelop and destroy the Allies at a small scale. These offensives *en miniature* concomitantly interacted with the local defence in an extremely confined area, and the defence exploited the combined firepower of direct and indirect fire in order to engage the assaulting enemy from the front and the flanks. The flexible defence combined the advantages of defensive operations with those of offensive operations within a confined area which was divided into a forward zone, a major combat zone, and a rear zone. Flexible defence required highly trained soldiers and leaders, and not least soldiers' trust in their leaders' initiative – the willingness of the superior command level to delegate decisions which resulted in mission-type command and control and the individualization of war.[31] Necessity had created an environment that led to the revival of the operational idea, albeit in a tactically confined area. Together with the introduction of a new method of attack, the so-called stormtroop tactics, the German command demonstrated its overall ability to innovate.[32] However, Falkenhayn's overall assessment of the Western Front remained valid: the conditions for a decisive battle remained absent. The stabilization of the German position in 1917 was only achieved by the high Allied losses caused by the new German system of defence in depth coupled with the shortened front line caused by the withdrawal to the Hindenburg Line.

While defensive battles were the focus on the Western Front, the Eastern Front and the Isonzo Front saw mobile operations in the classical sense. The taking of a few isles in the Bay of Riga through an amphibious operation,[33] the countering of the Kerensky Offensive in summer 1917, and the combined offensive in northern Italy with a breakthrough of more than 80 miles showed what strategic and tactical flexibility the war in the East and West demanded of soldiers and commanders.

Last hope Operation *Michael* : break-in but no breakthrough

The year 1917 had proved to be one of change. The Western Front had become unstable as a result of the British and French offensives, but it still held. In the South the situation had stabilized to the benefit of Austria and to the detriment of Italy. In the East, the revolution had led to the conclusion of a peace agreement with Russia, and all of this prompted the OHL to revise their options for 1918. It was now time for a major offensive on the Western Front; the time for the 'Grand Battle in France'[34] had come. That consideration was based on many ideas, amongst them the necessity of seeking a decision in the West before the mobilized and deploying US forces would become effective and before the forces of the Kaiserreich and its allies would completely fail.

A frontal attack with all reserves available was planned in order to achieve a breakthrough and envelop the British or the French troops and break the enemy's will to fight. That plan was not met with unconditional consent even by the top military. Nevertheless, the preparations and plans were comprehensive. By late March, more than 70 divisions were made available for the attack, codenamed Operation *Michael*, which was launched on 21 March between Arras and La Fère. It ultimately failed to achieve its goal of a breakthrough, 'although the success of that outbreak from trench warfare was without precedence'.[35] Paradoxically enough, Operation *Michael* did fulfil its purpose, even though not in the desired outcome: the German forces were physically and mentally exhausted, and the war was shortened.[36]

The integration of the plans for Operation *Michael* into German operational thinking is in line with the concept of a frontal breakthrough battle, which was developed as early as 1914. As a rule, this concept was given second priority behind envelopment and only implemented in exceptional cases, when a gap was found in the enemy line. The solution to that tactical-operational problem was one of Ludendorff's major concerns. His plans oscillated between the strategic and the tactical levels, with operational considerations initially receding into the background.[37]

Although the deployment was prepared down to the smallest detail, the German attack remained strangely inaccurate. The spearheads of the attack were to turn to those points where resistance was weakest. Points of resistance – the capture of which would need too much time, materiel, and personnel – were to be bypassed or evaded. The attack was to flow like water in order to infiltrate enemy positions and terrain.[38] The aim was to find the weakest point in the trench system, penetrate the front there, and, if possible, achieve an operational breakthrough in order to create the conditions for the intended field battle. That was strange insofar as the OHL tried to find solutions to tactical issues in the planning phase. On the other hand, that indeterminate course of planning illustrated one of the pillars of German military operational art which had been adhered to since the times of Moltke the Elder – conceptual flexibility to the largest degree possible. That was in line with the basic assumption that any planning would be obsolete once the battle had started and that the leadership would adhere to a 'system of expedients'. This partially explains why Schlieffen in his planning of 1906 did not deal with battles beyond a specific timeline. Obviously thinking along the same lines, Ludendorff time and again gave priority to tactical considerations when he was planning the German Spring Offensive. One of the conclusions drawn from this tactical approach was the consistent implementation of mission command and even forward command by higher commands. It was only personal reconnaissance that enabled the higher commander to assess as to whether a penetration would likely be successful and whether the employment of reserves in this place would have to be ordered. This forward command principle followed by higher military leadership would be essential more than ever to future mechanized operations.

The actual attack was moving on like a snake. The original target of the attack, the British troops deployed in the north, was extended to the south only two days later. The troops that had been deployed at the left flank to protect it against the French forces were planned to advance further to the south-west in order to separate the British from the French troops. There was no longer a clear point of main effort. A short time later, Ludendorff further extended the offensive to the south and at the same time ordered additional attacks against the British troops in Flanders.[39] After the war, Ludendorff was criticized for that erratic and irresolute style of command, with some people missing his 'operational intentions'.[40] That criticism – despite all contemporary implications – is justified insofar as Ludendorff first wanted to wait for the tactical success of that penetration and only then start the operation and thus manoeuvre warfare.[41] So he took a 'bottom up' approach to war, in much the same way as Moltke the Elder did, which means from the tactical to the strategic level.[42] Ludendorff's actions can therefore be interpreted as rational.

Nevertheless, Operation *Michael* remained an offensive of tactical, rather than operational, nature, which was driven by strategic considerations. The main reason for its failure was the lack of mobility of the German units. Artillery, ammunition, and all other logistic assets needed for an industrialized mass army were unable to follow the advancing infantry owing to the lack of suitable transport assets – neither horses nor trucks. The supporting arms were not flexible enough to follow the spearheads, which repeatedly changed the direction of their attacks. Establishing a clear point of main effort and sustaining the attack from the deep was impossible. Due to breaches of operational principles the tactical approach therefore failed to result in a possible strategic success.[43]

Operational solutions to strategic problems

In the late 18th century, operational thinking evolved from the necessity of commanding ever-growing military forces over long distances from several headquarters. Subsequently, it evolved in the Prussian-German area 'as a military solution to waging a two- or multi-front war in the border regions close to Germany and Central Europe'.[44] Operational thinking thus was a conceptual approach to cutting the Gordian knot of the strategic disadvantages of a central position in Europe and the lack of resources by using military operational procedures.

Operational thinking focused on the factors of space, time, and resources as the decisive criteria. The relevant parameters were mobility, speed, and initiative, as well as superior operational art and the high-quality training of troops. Focusing on the supposed constants of space, time, and resources, however, the general staff overlooked the revolutionary power resulting from the changes in society and technology. The evolution of mass armies in the industrialized people's war called for a logistical and transport organization sufficient for meeting the operational requirements with regard to offence and manoeuvrability. This organization did not exist, as was illustrated by the battles at the Marne in 1914, Gorlice-Tarnów in 1915 and the German Spring Offensive in 1918.

If we refer to that narrow context and place emphasis on the limitations on operational thinking at that time we can conclude that the general staff was rigid and inflexible. But if we extend our view and acknowledge that the German military leadership acted within a complex construct and adapted to continuously changing situations we see that the German High Command was able to engage in a wide range of different operations. The battle of Tannenberg in 1914, the Romania campaign in 1916, the amphibious landings on the Baltic islands and in Finland in 1917, and, in particular, the flexibly led defensive battles on the Western Front are clear examples of this. The flexibility was achieved to a large degree by a certain air of liberalism and a culture of constructive critique which dominated the thinking of the general staff.

That intellectual liberty possibly is – despite all hierarchies – the overarching and connecting element of German operational thinking in the era of the world wars.[45]

The lessons learned between 1914 and 1918 shaped German operational thinking over the following decades. The factors of space, time, and resources remained the focus of interest and the overall concept of operational thinking was not questioned; rather, it was even emphasized by the central question: 'How can the offensive, which is the fundamental condition for German operational thinking, regain mobility?'[46] The answer was given by the increasing mechanization of the war machine, which demonstrated its capability in the first campaigns of World War II.

Although operational art was perfected at all levels after 1918, its unchallenged fundamental idea was still the same: to be a military operational solution to a fundamentally political problem. Operational art reached its perfection during World War II, but the course of the war shows that even excellent operational art cannot outweigh the lack of a politico-strategic strategy, or a flawed strategy.

Finally, the war of annihilation against the Soviet Union revealed the weaknesses and, once more, the limits of German operational thinking. The objective of that war, which was to undermine the enemy's superior potential by staging a 'Blitzkrieg', was thwarted as a result of exhaustion in the expanses of Russia. Like World War I, World War II did not see any decisive battles; rather, it remained a war of exhaustion, in which the leaders of the Wehrmacht became entangled and increasingly lost the initiative.

CHAPTER 3

THE EXPANSION OF THE BRITISH ARMY DURING WORLD WAR I

Dr Bruce Gudmundsson

In the course of World War I the British Army grew by a factor of five.[1] At first glance, this great expansion seems to have been the product a long series of ad hoc measures. Upon closer inspection, however, a different pattern emerges. Just below the surface of a great exercise in improvisation, one can see the interaction of two very different approaches to the problem of mass mobilization. One of these approaches belonged to Horatio Herbert Kitchener, the walrus-moustached professional soldier who was, among many other things, the poster child for the British war effort. The other was the brainchild of Richard Burdon Haldane, a lifelong civilian, who, notwithstanding mannerisms that led some contemporaries to compare him to a penguin, might safely be described as the architect of the military forces available to the United Kingdom at the outbreak of the war.

The pre-war organization of the British Army

In August of 1914, the United Kingdom possessed two distinct military forces. The first of this was the Regular Army, a force of long-term volunteers that provided garrisons to the port cities of the British Empire, the British contingent of the Indian Army, and, with the help of a large number of reservists, a home-based Expeditionary Force. The second was the Territorial Force, a body of part-time soldiers that was primarily concerned with the defence of the British Isles against sea-borne invasion. In the course of shaping the component units and formations of both forces, the responsible authorities had taken great pains to ensure a high degree of interoperability. Thus, war planners were able to contemplate situations where the infantry divisions and mounted brigades of the Territorial Force served side-by-side with the infantry divisions and cavalry brigades of the Regular Army. At the same time, the administration of each force was an entirely separate affair. Indeed, the work of recruiting, clothing, and training the members of the Regular Army was carried out by agencies that were not only separate from those that provided the same services to members of the Territorial Force, but organized along very different lines.

For most of its history, the Regular Army had been a highly decentralized organization in which most administrative functions were performed by individual units or corps.[2] However, in the decades leading up to 1914, the Regular Army had begun to centralize some of these functions. In the case of clothing, the displacement of brightly coloured 'regimentals' by general service khaki completed a long-term trend towards the centralized procurement of nearly all of the items worn by enlisted men. In the case of recruiting, the work was divided between individual corps, many of which had traditional recruiting areas, and the recruiting stations established in the larger cities.[3] In the case of entry-level training, the task of teaching the rudiments of the soldier's trade was the responsibility of individual corps. Thus, while recruits for the infantry, cavalry, and Royal Garrison Artillery were trained in home-based operational units, those for the Royal Field Artillery and Royal Engineers spent their first few months 'with the colours' in specialized training organizations.[4]

Where the administration of the Regular Army was divided between individual corps and common agencies, that of the Territorial Force was given entirely to the 93 County Associations, each of which was a board of local notables that was responsible for the recruiting, clothing, and training of all of the Territorial units originating in a particular county, borough, city, or riding. In addition to this, each County Association was charged many other functions that, in the Regular Army, were performed by central offices of one sort or another. These included the acquisition and maintenance of rifle ranges, drill halls, storage facilities, and manoeuvre grounds provision, as well as the provision of horses used in peacetime training.[5] In short, there was much truth in the contemporary characterization of a County Association as a 'miniature War Office'.[6]

The County Associations, like the Territorial Force itself, were the creation of Richard Burdon Haldane. Indeed, the design and implementation of the system of County Associations may fairly be called one of the two great achievements of Haldane's 79 months as Secretary of State for War. The second of these was not, as is commonly supposed, the establishment of the Expeditionary Force. That, after all, was largely a matter of organizing existing units into divisions. Rather, the second great project on Haldane's agenda was the creation of the Special Reserve. This latter institution, the design and fostering of which required nearly as much effort as the care and feeding of the Territorial Force, ensured that the Expeditionary Force would be much more than a collection of understrength combatant units. More specifically, the Special Reserve provided the means to fill the many vacancies in the units of the peacetime Regular Army that were stationed in the United Kingdom. The Special Reserve also made possible the provision of a robust logistics infrastructure, the base and lines-of-communication organizations that enabled the Expeditionary Force to begin active operations a few days after landing on a foreign shore.

The Special Reserve was composed of men with no prior military service who made themselves liable for service with the Regular Army in the event of mobilization. While the exact conditions of service varied from one corps to another, most Special Reservists underwent several months of full-time training at the beginning of their enlistments. As this entry-level training was often identical to that received by recruits who had enlisted for several years of full-time duty, there was considerable overlap between the facilities where Special Reservists were trained and those that catered to the men destined to spend several years 'with the colours'. The Royal Field Artillery, for example, had 'reserve batteries' for the training of Special Reservists and 'depots' for the training of men who had engaged for three or more years of full-time duty. The six years between the establishment of the Special Reserve and the outbreak of war in 1914, however, saw many proposals for the eventual merger of the two sorts of training units and the building of barracks to accommodate the resulting organizations.[7]

From the point of view of mobilization, the great virtue of the Special Reserve was the fact that it was custom tailored to the needs of the Regular Army. Those corps, such as the Brigade of Guards and the Household Cavalry, that had a sufficient number of Regular Reservists (men who had already spent a term of service 'with the colours') to meet the needs of mobilization, had no Special Reservists at all.[8] Likewise, those corps, such as the Cavalry of the Line and the Royal Garrison Artillery, that only required Special Reservists in order to mobilize a small number of specialized units, maintained but a small number of Special Reservists.[9] However, those corps that had many vacancies to fill before their units were ready to take the field, particularly the Army Service Corps and the various regiments of the Infantry of the Line, were richly supplied with Special Reservists.[10]

Distribution of men within each arm,[11] 1 October 1913

Arm	With the colours	Reserve Regular	Reserve Special
Infantry of the Line	49%	34%	17%
Royal Field Artillery[12]	54%	37%	9%
Brigade of Guards	45%	55%	-
Cavalry of the Line	61%	35%	4%
Household Cavalry	84%	16%	-
Army Service Corps	69%	15%	16%
Royal Garrison Artillery	70%	26%	4%
Royal Engineers	56%	34%	10%

The mobilization of the British Army

On 5 August 1914, the Regular Army began to mobilize. Thanks to a combination of meticulous preparation and the trained manpower provided by the Special Reserve, this process was an extraordinarily smooth one. Within a week, the lion's share of this gargantuan exercise in administration and logistics had been completed, and many elements of the Expeditionary Force were already embarked on the ships that would take them to the Continent. Soon thereafter, the great task was complete, and the Special Reserve took up its principle wartime duty of training the men (and, in some corps, the horses) needed to keep the Expeditionary Force up to strength.

The mobilization of the Regular Army coincided with the 'embodiment' of the Territorial Force, a measure that called for all members of that body to report to their drill halls for continuous active service. In many respects, 'embodiment', which involved the drawing of the stores, the preparation of equipment, and the requisition of horses, bore a close resemblance to mobilization. In one key respect, however, the two processes were different. Where the mobilization of the Regular Army provided the United Kingdom with a force that was immediately ready to take the field, the embodiment of the Territorial Force provided a body that was ready to begin a course of serious military training.

Neither the rules governing the mobilization of the Regular Army nor those that dealt with the embodiment of the Territorial Force made any explicit provision for expansion in time of war. Thus, the first measures taken to reinforce the original Expeditionary Force involved the redeployment of elements of the Regular Army located overseas. On 6 August 1914, an interagency 'council of war' resolved to recall all units of the Regular Army then serving in South Africa. Three days later, the senior leadership of the War Office decided to repatriate some of the Regular Army units then serving in Gibraltar, Malta and Egypt.[13] These transfers provided a sufficient number of infantry battalions, but only half of the field artillery batteries and engineer companies needed to create a seventh infantry division for the Expeditionary Force. Even when some of the missing units were provided from among the small number of Regular Army units that had not been part of the original Expeditionary Force, the resulting formation was both short of field gun batteries and entirely bereft of divisional cavalry, field howitzers, and heavy field guns.[14]

The cause of the many lacunae in the order of battle of 7th Division was the lopsided nature of the peacetime Regular Army. That is, rather than having a permanent place in a British formation (whether infantry division or cavalry brigade), a substantial proportion of the units of the British Army were assigned either directly to overseas garrisons or to one of the formations of the Indian Army. This, in turn, created a situation in which the Regular Army had enough infantry battalions for 13 infantry divisions, enough field gun batteries for 12 infantry divisions, and sufficient howitzer batteries and engineer companies for seven infantry divisions, but only as many heavy batteries and divisional cavalry squadrons as were needed by the six infantry divisions of the original Expeditionary Force.

Distribution of units in the Regular Army, 5 August 1914

Type of unit	Assigned to formations	Assigned elsewhere	Total available
Infantry Battalion[15]	72	85	157
Field Gun Battery	54	60	114
Howitzer Battery	18	3	21
Heavy Battery[16]	6	-	6
Cavalry Squadron (Divisional)[17]	6	-	6
Engineer Field Company[18]	12	3	15

In sharp contrast to the Regular Army, the Territorial Force had been designed, from the ground up, as a balanced force. With a few notable exceptions (most of which were connected with coast defence), each unit of the Territorial Force was part of an all-arms formation. (Half of these formations were infantry divisions formed on the same basic pattern as the infantry divisions of the Expeditionary Force. The other half were mounted brigades that had been modelled on the cavalry brigades of the Expeditionary Force.) Thus, field artillery batteries were in proportion to infantry battalions, horse artillery batteries were in proportion to cavalry regiments, and the various service units (ammunition columns, transport companies, mobile medical units, and bridging trains) were in proportion to all.[19]

The well-balanced structure of the Territorial Force made it much easier to expand than the Regular Army. In particular, this organizational advantage greatly facilitated the widespread use of a technique that was used on the Continent, a form of military mitosis that the French and Belgian armies called 'doubling' (*dédoublement*).[20] This process began with the division of an existing unit into two parts, each of which received an equal proportion of officers, non-commissioned officers, specialists, and experienced soldiers. Once this had been accomplished, each unit would be provided with a sufficient number of recruits to bring it up to establishment.

The great advantage of 'doubling' was the transmission of various forms of social capital from the old unit to the new organization. These included regimental tradition, the 'vertical' cohesion that bound peers within the unit to each other, and the 'horizontal' cohesion that connected superiors to subordinates. Moreover, the structure of the Territorial Force was such that it was not only possible to 'double' units but also to 'double' complete formations. Thus, in addition to preserving the internal cohesion of units, 'doubling' made possible the preservation of many of the social and professional connections that bound units and staffs to each other.

While the technique of 'doubling' does not seem to have played any significant role in the debates leading up to the creation of the Territorial and Reserve Forces Act of 1907, the possibility of using the Territorial Force as the chief means of expanding the British Army in time of war did. Towards the end of his first year at the War Office, Haldane had made a number of public pronouncements on the subject of the use of the (as yet unnamed) Territorial Force as the basis of a much larger 'nation-in-arms' of as many as 900,000 men. According to this idea, a long war would find a large number of recruits flocking to the Territorial Force, thereby enabling it to expand well beyond its original size of 300,000 or so.[21] This growth, in turn, would make it possible for many, if not most, of the formations of the Territorial Force to be used to reinforce the Expeditionary Force.[22] However, this idea was poorly received in many quarters, and, what was even worse, caused a great deal of confusion about the scale of Haldane's proposal.[23] It is thus not surprising that the idea is conspicuously absent from the text of the Territorial and Reserve Forces Act, the memoranda Haldane wrote in support of that bill, and, for that matter, all of the public speeches that Haldane made after the autumn of 1906.[24]

Once the Territorial and Reserve Forces Act had passed, Haldane devoted much of his remaining time at the War Office to the execution of his scheme and, in particular, to the daunting task of inducing large numbers of his countrymen to support the new organization. In the course of doing this, he managed to convince some of the County Associations to make modest preparations for a possible expansion of the Territorial Force in the course of a general war. Nonetheless, Haldane proved unable to pass the sort of legislation that would have been needed to implement his vision for a locally rooted 'nation-in-arms'.[25] As a result, the use of the County Associations to form large numbers of new units in the months after the embodiment of the Territorial Force remained an inherent capability rather than a formal plan, an option available to a future Secretary of State for War rather than an integral part of the well-established plan for general mobilization.[26]

The greatest obstacle to the implementation of Haldane's concept of a locally based 'nation-in-arms' was the rule that neither the officers nor the men of the Territorial Force could be sent beyond the borders of the United Kingdom without their explicit consent. During the latter years of his tenure at the War Office, Haldane launched several campaigns to convince individual members of the Territorial Force to waive this right. The results of these efforts, however, were invariably disappointing. In February 1912, Haldane reported that a grand total of 20,629 officers and men, and thus a little more than 8 per cent of the strength of the Territorial Force, had signed the papers that made them available for service in places other than the British Isles.[27]

Haldane left the War Office in the summer of 1912. However, on 4 August 1914, the very day that the United Kingdom declared war on the German Empire, a series of unusual circumstances put him back at his old desk for two very busy days. During those days, he oversaw the embodiment of the Territorial Force, the mobilization of the Regular Army, and the decision to send the lion's share of the Expeditionary Force to France. He also attempted, without success, to convince Horatio Herbert Kitchener, who was about to become the new Secretary of State for War, to use the Territorial Force as the chief means of increasing the size of the wartime British Army.[28]

The Kitchener reforms and birth of the New Army

On 6 August 1914, Kitchener took formal charge of the War Office. The next morning, he made public, in the form of announcements to the press, newspaper advertisements, and posters, his intention to expand the Regular Army by 100,000 men, each of whom was to be enlisted 'for a period of three years or until the war is concluded'.[29] Soon thereafter, Kitchener informed his senior subordinates at the War Office of his plan to use these recruits to create a 'New Army'. Also known as the 'New Expeditionary Force', 'Second Army', 'Second Expeditionary Force', and 'Kitchener's Army', this body was to consist of six complete infantry divisions and seven spare infantry battalions.

While the New Army was often described as a close copy of the original Expeditionary Force, the two bodies differed in a number of important respects. Where the original Expeditionary Force included five cavalry brigades and a robust logistics infrastructure, the 'New Army' had neither cavalry formations nor a mobile base nor a lines-of-communications organization. Where the original Expeditionary Force had no Territorial units whatsoever, the divisions of the New Army were to draw their engineer field companies, their divisional cavalry squadrons, and perhaps even their field artillery batteries from the Territorial Force.[30] (This would have represented 43 per cent of the field companies and 47 per cent of the field batteries of the Territorial Force, but less than 4 per cent of the Yeomanry squadrons.)[31]

Notwithstanding the role that Territorial units played in his original New Army scheme, Kitchener made no provision for an expansion of the Territorial Force. Indeed, during the three weeks that it took the recruiting machinery of the Regular Army to induct the 100,000 men Kitchener had called for, the War Office refrained from authorizing any increase in the authorized strength of the Territorial Force. This meant that the Territorial Force continued to operate on pre-war rules that allowed units that were below establishment to recruit new members but required units without vacancies to turn away surplus applicants. During the years preceding the outbreak of war, when most Territorial units were short of men, this limitation had been of little concern.[32] By the second week of the war, however, some Territorial units were so well supplied with would-be recruits that they resorted to the drawing up of waiting lists.[33]

On 10 August 1914, the War Office began to look for Territorial units that would be willing to complete their training in Egypt, Malta, or Gibraltar, thereby making available additional units from the Imperial garrisons there.[34] Soon thereafter, the War Office began to look for Territorial infantry battalions and field batteries to send to India, thereby making possible the repatriation, not only of most of the Regular Army infantry battalions serving with the Indian Army, but also a considerable amount of state-of-the-art field artillery.[35] This liberation of units of the peacetime Regular Army made it possible for Kitchener to plan the creation of additional divisions, which, somewhat ironically, would have to call upon the Territorial Force for engineer field companies, divisional cavalry squadrons, and, perhaps, even field artillery batteries.

The use of some Territorial units to serve in overseas garrisons, as well as the assignment of others to formations composed largely of men of the pre-war Regular Army, was made possible by another serendipitous development of the first few weeks of the war. Notwithstanding the longstanding reluctance of both officers and men of the pre-war Territorial Force to make themselves liable for Imperial service, the first few weeks of the war saw a substantial percentage of the individual members of the embodied Territorial Force volunteer to serve overseas. An important inducement for many of these volunteers was the rule, announced on 10 August 1914, that each man who belonged to a unit in which 80 per cent of the members had waived their right to remain at home would be sent overseas with that unit. (Ten days later, this threshold was reduced to 60 per cent.)[36]

The increase in the number of Imperial service units raised a number of questions. The first was that of a mechanism to keep deployed Territorial Force units up to strength. The second was the disposition of those men who had declined to volunteer to go overseas. During the third week of August 1914, Kitchener solved both problems by authorizing each unit of the Territorial Force that had volunteered for overseas service to create a 'reserve' ('second-line') unit. With an establishment that mirrored that of the original ('first-line') unit, the reserve unit served four functions. It trained recruits, provided an organizational home for 'home service' men, formed part of the forces charged with the immediate defence of the British Isles, and provided drafts of trained men to its first-line counterpart.[37] On 31 August 1914, Kitchener ordered all remaining mobile units of the Territorial Force to form second-line counterparts, thereby completing the 'doubling' of all the infantry divisions and mounted brigades of that body.[38]

The authorization of reserve units raised the ceiling on recruiting for the Territorial Force, replacing the firm upward limit of the pre-war establishment with a maximum strength that increased by several hundred men each time an infantry battalion, Yeomanry regiment, or field artillery brigade volunteered for Imperial service. As this radical change in policy coincided with a period in which an extraordinarily large number of men sought to enter uniformed service, it led directly to a great increase in the size of the Territorial Force. A census dated 26 September 1914 found 363,666 officers and men serving with the Territorial Force. As the number of officers and men serving on 1 August 1914 had been 268,777, this meant that the first eight weeks of the war had seen the membership of the Territorial Force grow by nearly 95,000. (The first eight weeks of the war also saw a substantial portion of the membership of the Territorial Force volunteer for Imperial service. Thus, by 26 September 1914, some 263,430 officers and men had signed the document that waived their right to serve exclusively at home.)[39]

Paradoxically, Kitchener's authorization of an expanded Territorial Force coincided with his decision to relieve that body of the duty of providing field artillery batteries to the new divisions of the Regular Army. (The divisions assembled from repatriated units of the peacetime Regular Army would be provided with artillery units formed from elements of the Regular Army that had not been assigned to the original Expeditionary Force. The New Army divisions would form all of their artillery units 'from the ground up'. In both cases, the artillery establishments would be formed as understrength organizations, but would add officers, men, and weapons as they became available.)[40]

Raising a second New Army

The third week of August of 1914 also found Kitchener taking the decision to create a second New Army, one that, like the first New Army, was to consist of six new Regular Army infantry divisions. At the same time, Kitchener launched a campaign to recruit another 100,000 men for the Regular Army, one that, for the first time, permitted the enlistment of married men, widowers with children and men over the age of 30.[41] One reason for this relaxation of standards seems to have been a desire to obtain the services of former non-commissioned officers, who, even if no longer fit for active service, would be able to train recruits, thereby relieving some of the strain on the hard-pressed instructional staff at the reserve units and depots of the Regular Army.[42]

The raising of the second New Army pushed the ability of the Regular Army to accommodate new men well beyond the breaking point. At first, the authorities at depots and reserve units resorted to such expedients as the billeting of recruits in nearby towns and the sending of newly enlisted men back to their homes in order to await their uniforms, their places in barracks, and their turn on the drill field. When these measures proved insufficient, Kitchener began to encourage local authorities and civic groups to shoulder some of the burden of recruiting, clothing and housing New Army units. In most cases, the units created in this way were relatively small: infantry battalions, artillery batteries, or engineer companies. In one instance, however, a paramilitary organization in Ireland committed to raising the infantry, engineer, cavalry, and medical units of a complete infantry division.[43] In another, an ad hoc committee of Welshmen undertook the creation of two complete divisions.[44]

With their close ties to particular communities and occupational groups, the locally raised units of the New Armies shared many similarities with units of the Territorial Force. The local authorities and civic groups that supported these units had much in common, and, in some cases, considerable overlap with, County Associations. On 4 September 1914, Kitchener went so far as to formally invite the County Associations to participate in the raising of the New Armies. While the committee formed to coordinate this effort lasted for only a week, individual County Associations possessed the sort of influence, expertise, and business acumen that was needed to obtain resources that the War Office had been unable to locate, let alone acquire.[45] Kitchener's invitation was a clear sign that he had lost faith in his plan to use the administrative machinery of the pre-war Regular Army as the chief means of creating a much larger wartime army. Five days later, on 9 September 1914, Kitchener took the more radical step of adding seven complete Territorial Force infantry divisions to the list of formations earmarked for eventual service on the Continent.[46]

The roster of infantry divisions approved by Kitchener on 9 September 1914 also included two additional new armies (for a total of 24 divisions), the three 'Municipal' divisions (from Ireland and Wales), and the two divisions made up of units of the pre-war Regular Army withdrawn from Imperial garrisons. This list did a poor job of predicting the exact number of divisions of each type that were eventually formed, let alone deployed overseas. Nonetheless, it proved to be a microcosm of the great array of divisions that served, not only on the Western Front, but also in the Near East, the Balkans, and Italy. To put things another way, the compromises and improvisations of the first month of the war were a far better predictor of the methods used to provide infantry divisions for the British Army in the three years that followed than either Haldane's dream of an expanded Territorial Force or Kitchener's vision of a much larger Regular Army.

At the end of January 1915, all of the British formations (eight cavalry brigades and ten infantry divisions) serving on the Continent were largely composed of elements of the pre-war Regular Army.[47] In many of these formations, however, a handful of Territorial Force infantry units served alongside their regular counterparts. In some cases, these were 'supplemental' infantry battalions that were temporarily assigned to infantry brigades to help them deal with the particular demands of trench warfare. In others, the

Territorial Force units were permanently assigned to their parent formations. In both the 27th and 28th divisions, for example, the divisional cavalry squadron, both field engineer companies, the divisional signals company, and all three of the field ambulances were units of the Territorial Force.[48]

In March 1915, complete Territorial Force infantry divisions began to cross the English Channel. By the end of May of that year, six complete formations of that type were serving with the Expeditionary Force.[49] By the end of July, eight additional divisions had joined the Expeditionary Force. (Three of these were from the First New Army. Five were from the Second New Army.) The summer of 1915 also saw the dispatch of four divisions to the Mediterranean to take part in the Gallipoli campaign.[50] (Three of these divisions were from the First New Army and one, the 29th Division, had been formed on the pattern of the 27th and 28th divisions. That is, while most units belonged to the pre-war Regular Army, the engineer, medical, and cavalry units came from the Territorial Force.)[51]

In August of 1915, the Expeditionary Force formed an infantry division (the Guards Division) by combining units of the pre-war Regular Army with units of the Second New Army and other units of the Regular Army that had been raised since the start of the war. While this new formation contained no units of the Territorial Force, the shuffling of infantry battalions caused by its creation led to the permanent assignment of Territorial Force battalions to Regular Army infantry brigades.[52] Later that year, the provision of first-class artillery pieces to Territorial Force infantry divisions greatly reduced the chief functional difference between those formations and the infantry divisions of the Regular Army.[53] (Early in 1916, the remaining differences were eliminated when New Army artillery batteries were used to fill gaps in divisional artillery establishments of Territorial Force infantry divisions.)[54]

In the course of 1915, as Territorial Force units serving overseas became increasingly hard to distinguish from their counterparts in the Regular Army, those remaining in the United Kingdom evolved in a very different direction. At the end of the queue for weapons, and continually deprived of their best men, these home defence units were chronically understrength, badly equipped, and poorly trained.[55] In other words, by the end of 1915, the distinction between 'Regular' and 'Territorial' had become far less significant than the distinction between 'home service' and 'general service'. Nonetheless, the Territorial Force and the Regular Army retained much of the administrative autonomy that each had exercised in the years before the war. Indeed, for most of the first two years of the war the transfer of a man from a unit of the Territorial Force to an otherwise identical unit of the Regular Army required that he be formally discharged from the former and then enlisted into the latter.[56]

The effects of conscription on the Territorial Force

The first Military Service Act of 1916, which came into force on 27 January 1916, simultaneously ended direct enlistment into the Territorial Force and, paradoxically, respected its status as a separate body. The act replaced voluntary enlistment of all types with the compulsory call up of all single men of military age. Thus, rather than joining either the Territorial Force or the Regular Army, a man subject to the act registered with the authorities and waited to be called. At the same time, the act called for the discharge and subsequent conscription into the Regular Army of unmarried members of the Territorial Force who declined to volunteer for Imperial service.[57] The second Military Service Act of 1916, which was implemented on 25 May 1916, included married men in the list of those liable to conscription into the Regular Army. At the same time, it made all members of the Territorial Force both available for service outside of the borders of the United Kingdom and subject to involuntary transfer to a unit of the Regular Army.[58] This latter provision did much to facilitate the thoroughgoing reorganization of the field artillery of the Expeditionary Force that took place in the second half of 1916.[59] It also dealt a mortal blow to the administrative independence of the Territorial Force.

It took some time for the effects of conscription to erode the particular identities of those parts of the Territorial Force that were serving overseas. While field artillery units serving on the Western Front lost their traditional designations in the course of the great reorganization of 1916, those serving elsewhere, as well as all infantry battalions and Yeomanry regiments, held on to their old names until the end of the war.[60] Moreover, while overseas units were often obligated to accept drafts from sources other than their own reserve units, all concerned with the personnel replacement system seem to have placed a high value on the maintenance of the traditional relationship between units at the front and their affiliated reserve units.[61]

During the first week of May 1916, the overall strength of the Territorial Force was 1,017,763. Of these million or so officers and men, about a quarter had been members of the Territorial Force at the start of the war. (On 4 August 1914, some 270,859 were serving with either drilling units of the Territorial Force or the Territorial Force Reserve.)[62] Thus, in the first twenty-two months of the war, the Territorial Force had enjoyed a net increase of some three-quarters of a million men.[63] These figures compare favourably with the figure of 900,000 mentioned by Haldane in the early public discussions of the Territorial Force. Moreover, as more than nine-tenths of the officers and men of the Territorial Force had volunteered for overseas service before the onset of conscription made such declarations obsolete, Haldane's prediction in that regard proved to be accurate as well.[64] The one area in which Haldane was less than prescient was the overall size of the land forces that the United Kingdom would put into the field. The 1 million members of the Territorial Force represented about a third of the nearly 3 million officers and men serving in the British Army in May 1916 and a little more than a quarter of the almost 4 million soldiers of all ranks who were with the colours when, in March 1918, the British Army was as large as it would ever be.[65]

From the point of view of individual arms, the Territorial Force provided both the lion's share of the horse cavalry regiments (57 out of 91) and a substantial proportion of the front-line infantry battalions (486 out of 1,051).[66] It did not, however, contribute nearly as much to the new arms that played such a large role in World War I. Thus, while many men who had entered the British Army through the Territorial Force served with the units that employed siege artillery, tanks, aircraft, poison gas, and tunnelling techniques, nearly all of those units belonged to the Regular Army. The exception that proves this general rule is provided by the many cyclist battalions and bicycle-mounted Yeomanry regiments of the Territorial Force, most of which spent the war on coast defence duties.

In the recent popular literature on World War I, the Territorial Force gets much less attention than the New Armies, and Haldane is all but eclipsed by the figure of Kitchener. However, there is much evidence that the contemporaries of both men realized that Kitchener's failure to make better use of the framework for expansion provided by the Territorial Force was a mistake. Chief among these was Winston Churchill. While serving as Secretary of State for War in the months after the armistice, Churchill took the first steps towards the reconstitution of the Territorial Force, rechristened it the 'Territorial Army', and made it the chief means of expanding the British Army in the event of another major war.

CHAPTER 4
WORLD WAR I AVIATION
From Reconnaissance to the Modern Air Campaign
Dr James S. Corum

When World War I began the aeroplane was already recognized as an important weapon of war. However, the concept of airpower was that of a specialist supporting branch of the army that could enhance ground operations through reconnaissance and artillery observation. By the end of the war aviation in all major powers had developed into a separate branch of the armed forces, not yet equal to the army or navy, but capable of mounting large-scale operations independent of the armies and potentially a war-winning service in its own right. By the mid-point of the war aviation forces had become much more than a supporting weapon. In the eyes of senior commanders of both sides the employment of large air forces and control of the air over the battlefield had become an essential part of any formula for military success. In the latter half of the war, both sides conducted strategic bombing campaigns with the aim of striking a decisive blow against the enemy homeland.

The rapid evolution of airpower from 1914 to 1918 is one of the most dramatic examples in military history of rapid technological change decisively changing the conduct and nature of war. Airpower was used on every front and in support of all types of operations. Navies developed air arms to support the battle fleet and to conduct anti-submarine operations. In Germany, France, and the UK extensive homeland defence systems were created to protect key cities and industries from enemy bombers. Along with homeland defence came civil defence organizations, ground-based anti-aircraft guns, and fighter units – all tied into a centralized control system. Airpower played an important role from the Eastern Front, to Macedonia, to the Austro-Hungarian Alps, to Palestine. However, the primary focus of air operations in World War I, and the focus of this chapter, is the use of military aviation in support of the great land battles on the Western Front between Germany and the Allied Powers.

The pre-war concept of military airpower

The military development of the aeroplane made rapid progress in the 11 years since the aeroplane's invention and the advent of World War I. After the 1910 Reims Air Show dramatically demonstrated the capabilities of aeroplanes, all major powers moved to create air services as branches of the army and navy.

The priority mission of the pre-World War I aircraft, and the one most in line with the capabilities of the aircraft of the time, was aerial reconnaissance. The major powers believed that a future war would be short and sharp, involving large armies moving quickly to strike and annihilate their opponents. In such a war reconnaissance to locate the enemy's troop movements could mean the difference between victory and defeat. Thus, the first military aircraft to be developed were simple and rugged two-seat planes that carried a trained observer as well as the pilot. Per the military doctrine of all the great powers, ground armies would have detachments of aeroplanes to serve as the eyes of the commander.

Powered airships, which had been developed before the aeroplane, had an important role to play in pre-war aviation. Airships had the advantage of long range and a large carrying capacity, and found their strongest advocates in navies which needed the airship's capabilities for long range and endurance to scout the large expanses of the ocean for enemy ships. But airships had significant disadvantages. They were very expensive, difficult to manufacture, very vulnerable to bad weather and high winds, and they needed to be based in huge hangars to protect them from the weather. In contrast, aeroplanes were comparatively cheap, easier to mass produce, less vulnerable to high winds, and could operate from any level field close to the army. Thus, while navies still clung to the airship, armies turned to the aeroplane as the preferred aerial vehicle.

In the period from 1909 to 1914 France and Germany emerged as the leading airpower nations, and both countries made substantial investments to create a military aviation infrastructure. In addition to developing reconnaissance units to support army operations, several major powers began to explore the other potential missions of airpower.

The Italian Air Service showed the way in 1911 when it deployed an aeroplane detachment to Libya during the Italian-Turkish War of 1911. The Italians carried out the world's first bombing missions and proved that aeroplanes could serve as highly mobile and lethal long-range weapons in support of ground troops. The lessons of the Libya campaign were noted, and the French equipped their air detachment in Morocco to carry bombs and successfully used aeroplanes against rebel forces in May 1914.

The French, with the most developed aircraft industry of the major powers before the war, conducted a variety of experiments to include building heavily armoured aeroplanes to serve as close air support for the army. This failed due to the inability of the engines of the time to carry such a heavy load. But the general staff was aware of the potential of the aeroplane.[1]

In Germany the Chief of the General Staff, General von Moltke, took an active interest in military aviation, directing the army's Transportation Inspectorate (then responsible for the army's aviation) to conduct experiments in dropping bombs and in mounting machine guns on aircraft. Moltke also pushed the development of aerial photography as a tool for the commanders.[2] The first German aviation doctrine manual of March 1913 listed the missions of aircraft as: 'Strategic and tactical reconnaissance, artillery observation, transmission of orders and information, transport of people and objects, dropping bombs, fighting aircraft.'[3]

In Britain one of the leading pre-war advocates was First Sea Lord Winston Churchill who believed that aviation could play a large role in naval operations. Churchill initiated the development of long-range naval aircraft and directed experiments in dropping torpedoes and bombs from aircraft as well as mounting radios in aeroplanes. The British Army also created an aviation arm, the Royal Flying Corps, but was behind the navy in terms of innovation.[4]

The other great powers also recognized the importance of aviation and formed air services. Italy, Russia, and Austria-Hungary all had highly capable engineers and aircraft designers, but those nations suffered from a weak industrial base and little capacity to design and manufacture engines. In Russia in 1913 the brilliant designer Igor Sikorsky built a four-engine transport, the Ilya Muromets, with an impressive range and load capacity. But his plane relied on German Argus engines, as the Russian engine industry could only manufacture copies of older French engines. Although Russia poured money into buying aeroplanes before the war and, on paper, had a military air arm of over 200 planes, it was almost completely dependent on importing aircraft and its small industrial base could only produce licensed copies of French aircraft. This was also the case for the Italians and Austro-Hungarians whose aviation industries were mostly dependent upon respectively French and German aircraft designs.[5]

The reconnaissance mission was vitally important for obtaining the operational edge over the enemy in the expected grand campaigns, and almost all the German Army's aircraft were assigned to support armies and army groups. The priority for good information for the ground armies in turn pushed the development of suitable aircraft for the mission. The reconnaissance aeroplane favoured by Germany in 1914 was a sturdy, fairly fast (100mph), manoeuvrable two-seat biplane with moderate range. Such aircraft could take off from rough landing fields near the army headquarters, fly up to 40 miles behind the enemy lines, observe enemy troop deployments, and return to army headquarters with the information. Such light aircraft could be fitted with a few light bombs dropped by the observer, but had little capability to contribute directly to combat operations.

The first battles – airpower shows promise

At the outbreak of the war in August 1914 the Germans had the lead in military aviation with 250 reconnaissance aircraft organized into small units to support the army. France was next with an air service of 200 aeroplanes available in early August. The British Royal Flying Corps had fewer than 80 aircraft available. The war's first campaigns proved the value of the pre-war investment in aircraft. In the Tannenberg campaign German reconnaissance aeroplanes tracked Russian troop movements and brought back information that the Russian 1st and 2nd Armies were widely separated and that the Russian troop dispositions were open to a devastating envelopment by the Germans. After the battle, General von Hindenburg, commander of 8. Armee, gave the aeroplane the credit for the overwhelming German victory.[6] On the Western Front French reconnaissance planes discovered the gap that had opened between the German armies advancing on Paris, and this information gave the retreating British and French armies the opportunity to strike a powerful blow against the exposed German flanks and halt the German advance.[7]

By autumn 1914 it was clear to all the powers that the war would be a long one and that the role of aviation would be a big one. So the combatant powers rushed to pour resources into the aviation industries and to increase the size of the air services. The general staffs began to look at how aviation could be used in other roles.

The birth of bombers and fighters, 1915

The year 1915 saw the rapid expansion of the aircraft and engine industries of the major powers as well as the creation of new types of aircraft. With the fronts largely stabilized the general staffs looked to the air as a means to strike vital targets behind the enemy lines. In autumn 1914 the British and Germans created bomber units using two-seater reconnaissance planes that could carry a small bomb load. Both the Germans and British carried out small bombing raids against key targets behind the lines. The value of bombing the enemy was clear; what was needed was large, multi-engine planes that could carry a large bomb load far behind the enemy lines.

In Germany several companies began developing heavy bomber planes. In summer 1915 the Germans successfully tested their first multi-engine bombers and the army ordered them into production.[8] The first German bomber was the AEG K I, a two-engine biplane powered by 100hp Mercedes engines and carrying 220lb of bombs. The next version carried a 440lb bomb load.[9] The Germans created their first heavy bomber units in 1915 and in that year creation of heavy bomber forces became a high priority for all the powers. By 1917 heavy bombers had five hours' endurance and carried bomb loads of over 1,000lb.[10] The French developed some heavy bombers, but were less successful than the Germans. However, the French light bombers developed in the latter half of the war proved highly successful.

The other great innovation of 1915 was the fighter plane. It was clear that control of the air gave the ground forces an enormous advantage. Artillery was the great killing weapon of World War I with more than two-thirds of all casualties inflicted by artillery shells, and the effective use of artillery largely depended on the air services. Accurate targeting required aerial reconnaissance photos. Observation planes could also spot targets and provide the artillery with immediate information on enemy troop concentrations and artillery positions during the battle. A plane capable of sweeping the skies of enemy observation planes and protecting one's own observation provided a significant edge in battle. So both sides raced to develop fighter planes.[11]

The Germans fielded the first purpose-built fighter in 1915, the Fokker E-1 designed by Dutch designer Anthony Fokker. The Fokker E-1 was a monoplane with no great performance (speed less than 100mph), but was equipped with a forward-firing machine gun able to fire through the propeller by use of a mechanical interrupter gear. This meant that the pilot merely had to aim the plane to shoot down the opponent. This was better than the British solution of fielding two-seater 'pusher' aeroplanes (propeller in back) with the observer in front firing a Lewis gun, or the French solution of armouring the propeller, which resulted in the occasional ricochet into one's own engine.

In 1915 the Germans formed fighter units manned by aggressive and experienced pilots. Airmen Oswald Boelcke and Max Immelmann took the lead in developing tactics that enabled the pilot to outmanoeuvre his enemy and put the plane into position for a kill. Armed with new fighters and new tactics the Germans freely shot down Allied observation planes over the front until the British and French developed fighters of their own and also equipped them with interrupter gear. By early 1916 both the British and French had adopted the German fighter tactics and developed fighter units.

Throughout the war fighter plane development was an on-going race. Relatively minor changes in manoeuvrability, armament, and engine capability could provide a clear advantage to one side. With the introduction of a new fighter model, the advantage would shift. In the World War I literature great attention is given to the fighter aces, the 'knights of the air', who seemingly revived the image of the noble lone combatant in a war that mostly featured massed infantry and massed firepower. However, it must be remembered that fighter pilots were a minority of the air forces and that the fighter's primary mission was to support the observation and bombing mission. While lone fighter duels between aces occurred in 1915 and 1916, by 1917 the fighter pilot's war had evolved to large operations as air forces flew missions in squadron and wing strength.

Total aerial war – the revolution in organization

By autumn 1914 the military leaders of all combatant powers understood that airpower would play a key role in deciding the war. Large sums were invested to quickly build up the aviation industries. Building air forces was much more than just planes and pilots. Large-scale training programmes had to be organized to train not only pilots, but also the large number of mechanics and technical support personnel. Air units required an extensive logistics network to repair aircraft, and supply fuel and parts. Command systems had to be developed to coordinate large air operations in support of the army. Intelligence services had to analyse and process thousands of aerial photos per day and quickly feed vital information to the army commanders. Anti-aircraft guns made their appearance on the battlefields. Homeland defence forces had to be created to provide protection from enemy bombers.

The requirements of total war that transformed aircraft manufacture from workshops to mass production required close coordination between industrial and military leaders to ensure that the needs of the front were translated into research and development and the rapid fielding of better planes and engines. Each nation created new organizations to coordinate the manufacture of aircraft among dozens of airframe and engine manufacturers. In 1915 the French created the Undersecretariat for the Air Service inside the War Ministry with control of aircraft production, logistics, and training.[12]

In April 1915 the German Army created the post 'Chief of Field Aviation', and control of aircraft and engine development and production were placed under command of the Aviation Inspectorate of the army. From 1914 to 1916 in Germany the authority over air units at the front was diffused among various army commands with unsatisfactory results. So in 1916 the (Imperial Air Service) *Luftstreitkräfte* was reorganized to reflect the importance of air power in all facets of combat operations. The new organization placed all the aviation assets of the army under a single command with its own headquarters and general staff. These aviation assets included not only the flying units but also observation balloons, flak units, support services, communications, and training units. The new law established a single commander for the *Luftstreitkräfte* who answered directly to the High Command.[13]

The British had serious organizational problems in the first half of the war as responsibility for aircraft development and procurement was spread among the army, navy, and competing industrial boards. It took time to sort out the production issues. Britain lagged in aircraft production in the first half of the war, and the industry only hit its stride in 1917. During the war Britain produced 55,092 aeroplanes and 41,054 engines. But even in the latter half of the war the British required French engines and aircraft to keep the Royal Flying Corps (RFC) up to strength.[14] At the front, the Royal Flying Corps served as the command element of the British aviation forces in France. The RFC and Royal Naval Air Arm were consolidated into one force when the Royal Air Force was established in April 1918.

France was the powerhouse of Allied aviation production, and the French aviation industry was the biggest single contribution to the Allied aerial superiority in the second half of the war. The French produced 51,700 aeroplanes from 1914 to 1918 as well as 92,368 aircraft engines. At key points the French were able to supply the British, Italians, and Americans with high-quality aircraft. In the course of the war France supplied 9,480 planes to its allies. Indeed, the US could not have fielded an air force at the front without the French contribution. More importantly, France was able to provide 24,550 aircraft engines to its allies, a great part of these going to power British aeroplanes.[15]

Germany had many excellent aircraft firms but began the war behind the French in terms of manufacturing aircraft engines and never caught up. During the war the Germans produced 41,000 aircraft. Germany failed to match the Allied production levels due to the policy of building too many aircraft prototypes and models, more than 600 during the war, which diffused the production effort. In contrast to the Allies, Germany had to fight a war on two huge fronts, and the German war industry suffered from serious shortages of everything from raw materials to skilled labour. Although the German High Command in 1917 placed a top priority on aircraft production when formulating their plan to defeat the Allies before America could effectively intervene (Amerika Plan) and set a goal of delivering 2,000 aircraft a month to the army in 1918, German industry could not come close to that figure.[16]

Fighting a war in the air demanded technical training and skills far beyond those required of the ground war. To meet the challenge of fielding large air forces the major powers had to develop programmes to train thousands of aircrew and support personnel capable of operating high-tech machinery. The infantry might get by with partially trained troops, but air forces could not.

The Germans had the best aerial training programme of the major powers and this gave the *Luftstreitkräfte* a decided advantage even when flying inferior aeroplanes. German pilot training was thorough and systematic, and pilots went through a basic flying course that required 65 flight hours before assignment to the front. In 1916, as fighter aviation evolved into a specialized branch of air warfare, the Germans set up a special fighter school in Valenciennes where pilots detailed to fighter units underwent a three- to four-week course in fighter tactics.[17]

France came next in terms of effective training programmes with a ground course much like that of the Germans and a step-by-step process in training pilots. The Americans came into the war with only a small aviation branch and thus had to rely mainly on French instructors to train their airmen – which proved a good thing. In contrast, RFC pilot training was very informal and haphazard. Indeed, the biggest cause of death for British airmen in World War I was training accidents. A total of 8,000 British aircrew were killed while training in the UK – a record of casualties per training hours that exceeded those of the Germans, French, and Americans by several times.[18] From 1915 to 1917 British pilots were routinely sent to the front with fewer than 20 hours' total flight time (a fraction of the experience of a new German or French pilot), and consequently the British suffered far more battle casualties than the Germans.[19] Only in the latter half of 1917, when the casualty rates grew extreme, did the RFC revamp its training programme.[20]

The first air campaigns – Verdun and the Somme

By 1916 the aviation forces were ready to play a major role in the ground campaigns. In their plan for the Verdun Offensive in February 1916 the Germans massed 168 aircraft with the major part of their new fighter arm to win air superiority over the battlefield. The Verdun front was divided into five sectors, each patrolled by fighter units to maintain an 'aerial blockade' of the battlefield. The German plan aimed to give their observation planes complete freedom to operate. Observation planes were the key to success because the German plan emphasized the destruction of the French Army by means of massed artillery fire. The French quickly countered the Germans by committing six fighter squadrons and eight observation squadrons to the Verdun front and organizing their fighters into elite units equipped with their new Nieuport 11 biplanes, which were far superior in performance to the obsolete German Fokker monoplanes. While the Germans had great fighter leaders in Boelcke and Immelmann, at Verdun the French had their top aces Georges Guynemer and Charles Nungesser, who further developed fighter organization and tactics.[21] Using several fighters to escort their observation planes the French fought their way through the German fighter screen to accomplish the reconnaissance mission, and by April the French had the upper hand in the skies over Verdun. By the end of the campaign both sides had learned a great deal about coordinating large-scale air and ground operations.[22]

In summer 1916 the British massed the Royal Flying Corps to support their offensive at the Somme. The RFC, supported by the French Air Service, was able to overwhelm the German defence by sheer mass of numbers, and under fighter cover British observation planes were able to do their job as British artillery inflicted heavy losses on the Germans. The British plan not only included aerial observation but also sustained bombing of the German rear area to include rail yards and supply depots. But success in the air came at a tremendous cost. Royal Flying Corps aircrew losses were three times that of the Germans (900 dead to 300 dead), despite British advantages in aircraft quantity and quality. The Germans, though inferior in numbers and aircraft, had the advantage in better trained pilots and better tactics and were supported by a good communications system.

In autumn 1916 the Germans redressed the Allied technological superiority by fielding the new Albatros D I and D II fighter biplanes, which were fast, highly manoeuvrable, and carried two forward-firing machine guns. In January 1917 the Germans introduced the Albatros D III, which was superior to the British FE 2a and De Havilland DH 2 in British service.

Aerial campaigns

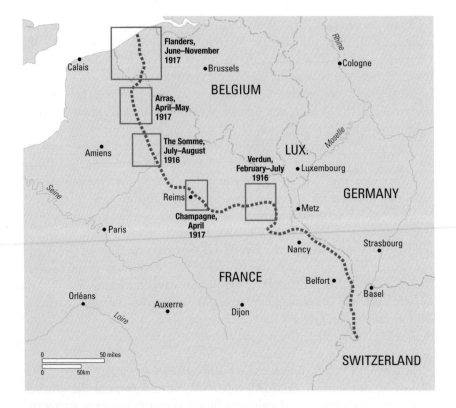

The operational air war matures, 1917

In 1917 air services played a major role in every operation. Conducting offensive or defensive operations now required massing air units to gain air superiority, which was considered essential to ensure success on the ground. Detailed staff planning was now required to coordinate ground and air and artillery forces. The 1917 campaigns saw extensive use of bombers to attack enemy logistics centres behind the front to include ports, rail yards, and supply depots. A major new innovation appeared in 1917 with the appearance of specially trained light bomber units assigned to close air support of the ground troops. Anti-aircraft guns appeared on the front in large numbers.

In spring 1917 the French massed their airpower in Champagne to support the Nivelle Offensive, which turned out to be a disaster. Bad weather prevented the effective employment of aircraft and the attack collapsed against highly effective German defences. The Germans' new Albatros fighters provided a significant edge in the air battles over the front.[23]

At Arras in April the British attacked and the RFC units, with poorly trained pilots and equipped with obsolescent aeroplanes, proved easy prey for the German fighter squadrons as the British lost 151 aircraft to 66 German planes lost.[24] The debacle, called 'Bloody April', proved that better training and equipment could beat superior numbers. The British were forced to reform their training and waited for the arrival of new aircraft that would soon prove superior to that of the Germans.

In mid-1917 the British initiated a major offensive to break through the German defences in Flanders.[25] The battle began in June 1917 and the offensive continued until the British halted short of their objectives in November. In contrast to the spring, the RFC now had superior aircraft with the highly manoeuvrable Sopwith Camel and the fast SE 5. The Bristol two-seat fighter had just come into service and equipped several of the British squadrons. The excellent French Spad VII and Nieuport 17 were now available in quantity and equipped some British as well as French units. The British Royal Flying Corps and Royal Naval Air Service and supporting French air units began the campaign in June with 748 aeroplanes opposing 300 German planes in the sector. The Germans rushed air reinforcements to the endangered sector, and by July the Germans had 600 planes in Flanders opposing 840 Allied planes.[26]

Both sides had developed sophisticated doctrine and tactics by this time. The RFC developed a standard system for observation and artillery spotting that allowed air observers to switch support from corps to corps as the situation developed.[27] For their part, the Germans initiated major changes in tactics and organization. In June 1917 the Germans organized four fighter squadrons into a single wing placed under command of Germany's top ace, Rittmeister Baron Manfred von Richthofen. When Allied planes crossed the front they would be met by several squadrons operating at different heights, with the top squadron flying at 15,000 feet and ready to bounce on lower-flying Allied fighters escorting observation planes. With the success of Richthofen's Jagdgeschwader 1, more wings were organized. From 1917 on the air war centred on large-scale operations.

In Flanders the Germans massed more than 200 anti-aircraft guns, supported by a ground observer corps, and all were wired into direct communication with the army air headquarters and the fighter units.[28] The new anti-aircraft guns were far more lethal than the improvisations that characterized the first half of the war, and new rangefinders and better shell fuses improved accuracy.[29]

One of the most important German innovations was the creation of specially trained and equipped ground-attack units. Two-seat fighters such as the Hannover

CL III and the Halberstadt CL II were well suited to the role as they were fast and rugged and carried two forward-firing machine guns and one machine gun fired by the observer. Ground-attack planes also carried four or five 22lb bombs.[30] These planes were employed in squadron strength to provide immediate support for the German infantry by attacking enemy troop concentrations and suppressing the enemy's forward artillery. In Flanders radios were used to direct ground attack squadrons onto targets during the battle.[31] Close support planes proved highly effective in supporting attacks and counter-attacks.

Strategic bombing campaigns

An important side-line of the war was the use of the bomber as a strategic weapon to strike the enemy's homeland. In 1915–16 the Germans used their only available heavy aircraft, the Zeppelin airships, to strike London in an attempt to demoralize the British population. In 1917–18 the Germans struck England again, this time with Gotha bombers. The Germans also bombed the key industrial centre of Nancy in 1917 with the aim of damaging French war production. The Allies responded to German attacks in kind and in 1918 the British created the Independent Bomber Force under General Hugh Trenchard and equipped it with Handley Page heavy bombers. Trenchard's objective was to strike vital industrial regions in western Germany with the additional objective of demoralizing the German population. Both German and British bombing campaigns hoped that air attacks against the enemy homeland would strike a decisive blow, panic the civilian population, and force a quick end to the war. Both sides were to be very disappointed.

In terms of damage and casualties inflicted bombing campaigns accomplished very little. Bomber forces were small and the bomber capabilities were minimal compared with the standard of World War II. The German Zeppelin campaign against Britain in 1915–16 dropped only 155 tons of bombs and killed 500 and wounded 1,200 Britons. On the other hand, Zeppelins were very expensive and highly vulnerable to the weather, not to mention the enemy fighters. Airship attacks were soon abandoned as too costly.[32] Still, the German General Staff believed that stronger attacks might have a significant impact on British national morale. So in the summer of 1917 the *Luftstreitkräfte* organized 40 Gotha bombers into a special wing with the mission of attacking London. As in the first Zeppelin raids of 1915, the Gotha attacks caused some outbreaks of panic, but the morale effect of bombing declined as the British created an extensive defence system that made the German bombing increasingly dangerous. The 1917–18 bombing campaign inflicted little damage, with British casualties of 836 dead and 1,982 wounded, and in spring 1918 the Germans abandoned the effort.[33]

Britain's bombing campaign against German cities and industries had no more success than the German operations against Britain.[34] Indeed, night bombing raids often could not find the target city, much less hit a specific factory. While defences were rarely lethal the operational problems of flying large planes long distances at night resulted in heavy losses. Between June and November 1918 the RAF dropped 543 tons of bombs on Germany for a loss rate of 352 planes badly damaged or destroyed – a wastage rate of one plane for every 1.54 tons of bombs dropped.[35]

The most important thing about World War I strategic bombing was not the operational or strategic effects but the huge impetus that bombing gave to the advancement of aviation technology. Designing and manufacturing a small single-engine fighter employed for short range and duration was relatively easy compared with designing a large multi-engine aircraft capable of several hours' duration, a range of several hundred miles, and a bomb load of one to three thousand pounds. Since the large and slow bombers were highly vulnerable to fighters, most strategic bomber missions were flown at night. The requirements to fly long distances at night spurred the development of an array of navigation aids. In 1915 the Zeppelins attacking England first used radio direction finding to fix their position. Night flying required both sides to create a system of lighted beacons and lighted runways for safe operations. Extended high-altitude flying required the development of oxygen systems and electrically heated flight suits for aircrew. All these innovations were developed and fielded in a brief time.[36]

Direct attacks on their homelands forced the British and Germans to develop large and sophisticated air defence organizations to locate and engage the bombers. The Germans developed an extensive system of air defences, with western Germany divided into five air defence zones, each with its own commander observation and communications service. By 1918 the German home air defence forces had 896 heavy flak guns, 454 searchlights, and nine fighter squadrons to repel Allied bombers.[37] In the UK the measures in southern England and around London were even more extensive. The British built a centralized air defence organization that could spot and track German bombers and get the fighters in the air within minutes. By 1917 the British London air defences included signals intelligence as well as 200 ground observer posts to track German bombers and support hundreds of anti-aircraft guns and 17 fighter squadrons. It was an exceptionally effective organization, and the core of it remained after the war as the air defence system of Great Britain.[38]

In addition to strategic bombing raids both the Germans and the Allies used heavy bombers to attack key enemy logistics centres behind the lines. Rail centres and ports were some of the major targets attacked in 1917 and 1918. The interdiction attacks were considerably more successful than the strategic bombing raids in inflicting damage to the enemy.[39]

America enters the war

When America entered the war on the Allied side in April 1917 it possessed tiny army and navy aviation arms and had few aeroplanes that met the combat standards of the Western Front. Realizing that airpower had changed the nature of conflict, in May 1917 the US Congress voted an aviation bill of $640,000,000 to enable the US Army to quickly build an air arm equal to that of the other major powers. It was up to that time the largest single appropriation ever made by the US Congress. That investment, plus a request from France for large-scale American aircraft production, enabled the US to quickly create a large aircraft industry and military aviation organization.[40] Although few American-made aeroplanes made it to the front, and the US Army Air Service remained dependent upon French aircraft and training, America would end the war with a large air force and aviation industry.

As the Americans planned their own operations for the 1918 counter-offensives, American Expeditionary Forces commander General Pershing approved a plan for an American Air Service of 202 American squadrons, of which 101 would be observation squadrons (also capable as light bombers), 60 fighter squadrons, and 41 bomber squadrons. The US Air Service would be committed to close support of the armies in the field.[41]

High-intensity air war, 1918

With the United States expected to send large forces to the Western Front by late 1918, the Germans saw a major offensive in the spring as their last chance to defeat the Allies. America's entry into the war also spurred the German High Command to initiate a major expansion of aircraft production in anticipation of major battles to come. By early 1918 the German Air Service grew to approximately 4,500 aircrew at the front.[42] But despite German efforts the Allies now had the advantage in numbers and aircraft quality as they readied themselves for the 1918 battles. Thanks to new aircraft and better training and doctrine, the French and British air forces were far more effective than in 1917.[43] France trained 5,608 pilots in 1917 and was able to train 8,000 pilots in 1918. Moreover, the French were training thousands of American pilots.[44] The newer Allied fighter planes, such as the French Spad XIII, the SE 5a and the Sopwith Snipe, were excellent machines and extremely deadly in the hands of capable pilots. At the start of the spring 1918 German offensive the Allies on the Western Front had 4,500 combat aircraft to Germany's 3,668.[45] The French and British aircraft production was in high gear and the Allies could absorb heavy losses. Moreover, the Americans were preparing a large air force, mostly equipped with French aircraft, which would be ready for battle by autumn 1918. The Germans could only hope that their spring offensives resulted in a quick victory, as the Allies had all the advantages in a war of attrition. Allied aircraft industries had hit their full stride by 1918 and both the British and French aircraft industries delivered more aeroplanes than the Germans every month. British, French, and American training programmes were turning out large numbers of aircrew who were far better trained than the pilots of 1916–17.

The year 1918 saw intensive aerial combat along the whole front. From March to July 1918 the German Air Service supported a series of huge army offensives against the centre of the Allied lines. After the initial collapse on the British front in northern France in March 1918, Allied defences stiffened and each successive German attack cost the Germans more casualties for small gains on the ground.[46] In the air the Allies massed their aircraft and threw them aggressively against the German forces. In the non-stop intensive combat along the whole Western Front from March 1918 to the war's end in November all sides suffered from heavy attrition of aeroplanes and aircrew. The *Luftstreitkräfte* declined from 3,668 front-line aircraft in March 1918 to 2,709 combat aircraft on 11 November 1918.[47] In 1918 the Germans faced increasingly unfavourable odds as the German aviation industry and aircrew training programme were unable to replace lost planes and pilots. In contrast, the Allied aviation industries and training programmes were able to increase the air forces despite the heavy losses in 1918. By autumn 1918 on the Western Front the Allies fielded 7,200 combat aircraft for a three to one superiority over the Germans.[48]

At first the Germans could only temporarily gain local air superiority by massing the *Luftstreitkräfte* over specific sectors of the front. But the Allied air services responded and soon had the upper hand over the Western Front. The Germans redressed the Allied advantage in numbers in May 1918 when they fielded the Fokker D 7 fighter plane, regarded as the best fighter of the World War. The Fokker D 7 was fast (124mph), highly manoeuvrable, and had superb handling characteristics.[49] The appearance of the Fokker D 7 changed the conditions of dogfighting to the German's favour, and on 8 May 1918 the RAF experienced the heaviest single-day casualties of the war.[50] But such momentary advantages were lost to the Allied numerical superiority.

On 8 August 1918, the day the British attack at Amiens broke the German lines wide open, the British and French managed to mass 1,904 aircraft to cover a 25-mile sector of the front. To oppose the Allies in that sector the Germans had only 365 aircraft.[51] In September to November 1918 the American Air Service supported the US Armies in the St Mihiel and Meuse-Argonne offensives. In September 1918, in America's first major offensive, Brigadier-General Billy Mitchell commanded 1,418 aeroplanes (one-half of them French) to support the attack. The American performance demonstrated that American airpower had matured as a capable combat force.[52] The final battles of 1918 saw the air forces of both sides used effectively in a variety of missions. Unlike the German Army, the *Luftstreitkräfte* remained an effective fighting force to the end and, although greatly outnumbered, still managed to inflict heavy casualties on the Allies.

Conclusion

Where air services had been small supporting arms of the armies and navies in 1914, by 1918 they had developed into true air forces in the modern sense with their own headquarters and general staffs and complex organizational infrastructure that included vast enterprises ranging from aircraft research and development to training and specialized logistics. If air services were not yet equal in status to the armies and navies they were getting close. At the end of the war the French Army and naval air services had a total of 3,437 planes on the Western Front with more than 101,000 total military personnel. The RAF had large forces on several fronts with 2,690 total aircraft. The American Air Service had grown in less than two years from one operational squadron to a force of 740 combat aircraft in France.[53]

The use of airpower in World War I fundamentally transformed modern warfare. Between 1914 and 1918 almost all the current missions of airpower were developed and used extensively to include reconnaissance, strategic bombing, close air support, ground-based air defence, and the air superiority battle. The only modern mission that was not a major part of World War I operations was air transport. As early as 1916 air support had become a key consideration in the planning of all ground operations. By 1918 all major powers had an extensive body of doctrine to direct the employment of airpower in various operations. Military planning was revolutionized by the need to coordinate hundreds of planes in offensive and defensive operations. Although some aspects of airpower, notably strategic bombing, had not lived up to expectations, the foundations were set for the evolution of a highly deadly form of war that would culminate in the strategic bombing campaigns of World War II.

CHAPTER 5

THE GLOBAL WAR AT SEA, 1914–18

Professor Dr Michael Epkenhans

The main feature of the two decades prior to the outbreak of World War I in August 1914 is the build-up of navies by many countries. Following the teachings of the American naval theorist Captain USN Alfred T. Mahan – who argued that, as Britain's history in the 18th and 19th centuries had shown, sea-power was the most important means of achieving the status of a world power and of securing national wealth – all major and many minor powers had begun to build up fleets in the mid-1890s. Building navies to defend one's own interests, however, also meant, directly or indirectly, interfering with the interests of rival powers sooner or later. Though the Anglo-German naval race between 1908/09 and 1914 is probably the most well-known aspect of this development, other nations also competed with their rivals: Austria-Hungary with Italy in the Adriatic despite being allies since 1882; both of them with France and Britain in the Mediterranean; Russia and Turkey in the Black Sea; Turkey and Greece in the Aegean Sea; and even Brazil and Argentina in the South Atlantic. Last but not least, Japan and the United States had also built up powerful navies, which sooner or later would become rivals in the Far East. The number of warships these navies possessed in 1914 clearly shows their importance in the mind of politicians, admirals, and, not to forget, leading opinion-makers (see overleaf). Even though the military value of these ships,

The naval balance of the Great Powers at the outbreak of war in 1914

	Britain	Germany	France	Russia	Austria-Hungary	Italy	Turkey	USA	Japan
Dreadnoughts	22	15	2	5 Baltic 5 Black Sea	3 dreadnoughts 3 semi-dreadnoughts (Radetzky-class)	3	-	10	2
Dreadnoughts under construction	13	5	2 (on trials)	-	-	-	-	4	2
Battle-cruisers	9	5	-	-	-	-	-	-	1
Battle-cruisers under construction	1	3	-	-	-	-	-	-	3
Pre-dreadnoughts	40	22	14	-	6	6–8	2	23	10
Coast-defence ships	NA	8	1	1 Black Sea	3	-	1	-	4
Armoured cruisers	34	7	19	6 Baltic	2	7	-	12	12
Protected cruisers	52	17	9	4 Baltic 2 Black Sea	3	11	2	22	15
Scout cruisers	15	-	-	-	-	-	-	-	-
Light cruisers	20	16	-	-	2	3	-	-	6
Destroyers	221	90	81	21 Baltic 4 Black Sea	18	33	8	50	50
Torpedo boats	109	115	17 (large) 170 (small)	48 Baltic 24 Black Sea	21–30 high sea 40 coastal	71–85	9	-	-
Submarines	73	31	67–75	15 Baltic 7 Black Sea	5	20–22	-	23	12
Gunboats	-	-	-	7 Baltic 5 Black Sea	-	-	-	-	-

All figures according to Paul Halpern, *A Naval History of World War I* (London 1994), pp. 7–19.

built in an era of rapid technological change, differed greatly, the sheer number of warships in the arsenals of the most important powers was indeed impressive.

However, navalism on a global scale and, more importantly, naval races between rival powers, did not necessarily result in war. Both contributed to an increase of political tensions only, if, as in the case of Germany, the build-up of navies was a means to achieve more far-reaching aims, such as a revolution of the international system.[1] In early 1900, the Austro-Hungarian ambassador in Berlin described this attempt at revolutionizing the existing balance of power in Europe in a long memorandum to his political masters in Vienna:

> The leading German statesmen, and above all Kaiser Wilhelm, have looked into the distant future and are striving to turn Germany's already swiftly growing position as a world power into the dominating one, expecting to become England's successor in this respect. However, people in Berlin are well aware that Germany may not be in the position to take this step in the near future and for this reason a speedy collapse of English world power is not desired. It is fully recognised that Germany's far-reaching plans are at present only castles in the air. Notwithstanding this, Germany is already preparing with speed and vigour for her self-appointed future mission. In this connection I may permit myself to refer to the constant concern for the growth of German naval forces… England is now regarded as the most dangerous enemy which, at least as long as Germany is not sufficiently armed at sea, must be treated with consideration in all ways… but because of the universally dominant Anglophobia, it is not easy [to convince public opinion of this] [2]

Of course Imperial Germany had the same right to demand its 'place in the sun' as other great powers in the age of rival imperialisms. To be taken seriously with its claims, this also included the build-up of a fleet to either defend or even fight for German interests overseas.[3] However, the demand for *Gleichberechtigung* (equal entitlement) – never clearly defined – and the fact that naval planners in Germany tried to achieve their aims by putting the dagger at the throat of its neighbour, Great Britain, eventually contributed to an increase of political tensions not only between the two nations but in Europe in general. This, in return, eventually strengthened the ties between those powers, which had signed political agreements since 1904 though for more complex reasons and with different aims. Soon, instead of a multi-polar system, two political camps watched each other with increasing distrust, both of them accusing the other of wanting war. Though in 1911–12, an arms race on land had begun to supersede the naval race, which had so far dominated European politics as well as public opinion, this did not mean that navies would not feature a future great encounter.

Naval war plans

But what role were navies to play in the war? For the *Hochseeflotte* (German High Seas Fleet) in the years immediately preceding the outbreak of war, the outlook was bleak. In early 1914, even Tirpitz admitted that the Royal Navy under the leadership of the newly appointed First Lord of the Admiralty, Sir Winston S. Churchill,[4] had won the naval race despite the enormous financial strain that this entailed. Tirpitz admitted that he was unable to finance the vessels the navy was supposed to build according to naval law.[5] More importantly, whereas the army had its Schlieffen Plan, which determined the deployment as well as the movement of troops according to a timetable and which had been carefully worked out as well as updated in the years before, the navy obviously did not have such a plan.[6] Since the German Navy had been built up only in order to help overcome Great Britain and its naval supremacy at almost any cost, one would have expected a planned strategy that promised success or that at least instructed the Commander-in-Chief of the *Hochseeflotte* exactly what to do in a war against its most dangerous enemy: the Grand Fleet.

What had happened? Since 1898 the German Admiralty staff, the Command of the *Hochseeflotte*, the Imperial Navy Office, and the Kaiser had discussed a number of operations plans against Great Britain. These plans were all based on the assumption that the Royal Navy would impose a close blockade against the German coast and that, sooner or later, a decisive battle would take place in the wet triangle off Heligoland.

This scenario, however, seemed very unlikely on the eve of war. In 1912, the German Navy had concluded from a number of observations that the Admiralty was beginning to change its strategy against Germany. Battleships had become too vulnerable to submarine attacks as well as to the damage caused by torpedoes and mines to risk them in a battle which seemed unnecessary for one important reason: geography. As a result the idea of establishing a close blockade or at least an observational blockade was dismissed, which sooner or later would have forced the German Navy to break it by challenging the Grand Fleet. Instead, a distant blockade of cruisers between the Orkneys, Shetlands, and Faroes covered by the Grand Fleet from its new war base at Scapa Flow seemed sufficient to achieve the Royal Navy's main aim, namely to cut off Germany's lines of communications. Many officers in the Royal Navy had difficulties coping with this change in naval strategy; it not only forced them to renounce a decisive Trafalgar-like battle right after the outbreak of war, but also to accept that – as Churchill put in September 1914 – the navy's main role would be to provide 'the cover and shield' that would allow Britain to create an army 'strong enough to enable our country to play its full part in the decision of this terrible struggle'.[7] In this they hardly differed from their enemy on the other side of the North Sea, who, for lack of hard knowledge about the operational implications of the new technology at sea the and more complex ideas of sea control and trade protection, still also clung to traditional ideas of naval warfare, which were no longer feasible.

The German naval leadership had only very slowly realized the consequences of this change in Britain's strategy for its own war plans, and it was stunned. When first asked what the *Hochseeflotte* would do 'if the Grand Fleet did not come', the Chief of the Admiral staff, Admiral August von Heeringen, answered in 1912, 'Then, our submarines will have to make it.'[8] Two years later the Imperial Navy still had no idea how to solve this dilemma. In May 1914, during the last manoeuvres of the *Hochseeflotte* before the outbreak of war, its Commander-in-Chief, Admiral Friedrich von Ingenohl, only shrugged his shoulders when Tirpitz asked the same question.

These reactions are in fact easy to explain: in 1912, in 1913, and, once again, in spring 1914, the Imperial Navy had looked for alternatives in manoeuvres and war games. The results were disappointing: the party representing the *Hochseeflotte* had always lost. Due to the disadvantages of geography the German Navy had no chance of breaking such a blockade or of forcing the Royal Navy to offer battle close to the German coast without risking total disaster.

With regard to Russia, due to the overall importance of the North Sea theatre of war as well as Russian numerical and *matériel* superiority, the Imperial German Navy had no option but to stay on the defensive. However, the Kiel Canal, which had become operational on 30 July 1914 after many years of reconstruction made necessary by the bigger size of the new German capital ships, enabled German naval planners to reinforce its forces in the Baltic to either meet Russian challenges or even to launch offensive strikes itself. This possible scenario had, in return, prompted the Russian Navy to stay on the defensive. Though Russia had begun to rebuild its fleet in 1912, its forces were still too weak for an offensive role even against a smaller German fleet. More importantly, still suffering from the traumatic experiences of the Russo-Japanese War in 1904–05, the prospect of losing the new fleet in a sudden encounter with numerically far superior German units caused the leadership of the Russian Baltic Fleet to be cautious. A German strike against Russia's long coastline and in the back of its armies, not to speak of a direct attack of its capital, St Petersburg, could have a disastrous impact upon the future course of war.

For the French Navy the Mediterranean was the most important theatre of war. Without secure lines of communication with its colonies in North Africa and the safe and fast transport of colonial troops to the South of France, the French Army would have great difficulties in meeting the expected German onslaught on its eastern border. Though there was no formal alliance, the British government, worried about the protection of its most important lifeline to its possessions in the Far East, had, in late 1912, at least morally obliged itself to protect the French Channel coast in a war between Britain, France, and Germany. In return the French had promised to defend British interests in the Mediterranean, which had come under severe pressure due to both the challenges of the German fleet in the North Sea and that of the combined Austro-Hungarian and Italian navies in the Mediterranean.[9]

These fears were not unfounded, for in 1913 the navies of the Triple Alliance had signed a naval convention aimed at securing 'the naval control of the Mediterranean through the swiftest possible defeat of the enemy fleets'.[10] Using Messina as a base, German forces were to operate against French troop transports after the outbreak of war before uniting with the fleets of its Italian and Austro-Hungarian allies to fight the Royal Navy.

The Great War at sea: the North Sea

Many contemporaries, who, following the speeches and writings of naval officers before 1914, had expected a great and decisive battle in the North Sea were soon deeply disappointed. Instead, the Grand Fleet as well as the *Hochseeflotte* restricted their actions to watching each other, waiting for an opportunity to strike under favourable circumstances for one's own forces. Due to its overwhelming superiority in modern as well as pre-dreadnought battleships and battle-cruisers, the Grand Fleet with its new Commander-in-Chief, Admiral Sir John Jellicoe,[11] could afford a wait-and-see-attitude. Safeguarding the transport of the British Expeditionary Force to the Continent after the outbreak of war proved successful. Implementing and keeping up the blockade was a more difficult problem. First, the strain of war service experienced by smaller craft of the Northern Patrol as well as by many modern ships in the rough waters of the North Sea was indeed great, as deficiencies in machinery and the need for repairs soon showed. Second, as long as the British government hesitated for political reasons to force neutrals like the Netherlands or Norway not to re-export contraband, all efforts to cut off Germany's lifelines proved at least partly in vain.[12]

The *Hochseeflotte* was in a more difficult position. Due to the change in British naval strategy, operations plan number 1 – which finally became effective on 31 July – offered no alternative but simply to order to wear down Britain's naval strength first, and to seek battle only under favourable circumstances.[13] Anything else would have been suicidal. Accordingly, submarines and smaller vessels were to attack the Grand Fleet and to infest the North Sea with mines.

As a result the *Hochseeflotte* remained on the defensive in the North Sea, leaving the initiative to the Grand Fleet in the vague hope that an opportunity might arise to be successful. This guerrilla war or, as the Germans called it, *Kleinkriegs*-strategy, suffered a severe blow only a few weeks after the beginning of hostilities. On 28 August, three German small cruisers and a torpedo boat were sunk, after they had been surprised by superior British forces off Heligoland.[14]

The impact of this outcome of the first encounter between the two fleets was far-reaching: for many months to come, the German naval and political leadership would discuss alternatives to the navy's operations plans, a problem, which, as it soon turned out, was closely related to the question of leadership in particular.

What alternatives did the German Navy in fact have? As far as the North Sea was concerned, the number of options was indeed limited. It simply amounted to a kind of hit-and-run-strategy against the British east coast that aimed at enticing parts of the Grand Fleet to come out and offer battle under more favourable circumstances than in the open or even the northern parts of the North Sea, where the risks of meeting superior forces were simply too great.

In September 1914, the first of these strikes was planned but cancelled at the last minute. German naval intelligence had received reports about the location of the Grand Fleet, which made it appear too dangerous to leave port.[15] In the following months German battle-cruisers raided the British east coast several times, without, however, achieving any strategic successes. Though both fleets came close to each other and eventually exchanged fire, either poor visibility or Admiral Franz von Hipper's conclusion – that it would be wiser to run for home instead of running into a trap – prevented any bigger encounter. Moreover, the battle of the Dogger Bank in January 1915 clearly demonstrated the risks of this strategy: while the Grand Fleet reached home without the loss of any vessel, the *Hochseeflotte* lost the armoured cruiser *Blücher*.

As a result of this disaster the *Hochseeflotte* remained on the defensive for more than a year. It would, however, be wrong to assume that only the *Hochseeflotte* was dissatisfied with this development. In Britain, important voices time and again also demanded a more active role for the Royal Navy in the North Sea by suggesting the occupation of one of the Frisian Islands, Heligoland, and of the Danish port of Esbjerg.[16]

Only as late as April 1916, Admiral Reinhard Scheer, who had been appointed Commander-in-Chief of the *Hochseeflotte* in January 1916, again ordered more offensive strikes into the North Sea. Scheer thus hoped to find an opportunity to challenge smaller parts of the Grand Fleet, which he hoped to annihilate. For reasons of morale as well as political considerations, namely the justification of the navy's existence, a more active role seemed of the greatest importance after two years of fighting in which the navy had not yet proven that it was worth the money that had been spent on it. It was one of those strikes that, more or less by accident, led to the battle of Jutland on 31 May 1916 – almost two years after the outbreak of the war.[17]

Whatever the German naval officers later said or wrote about this 'Glorious First of June',[18] as Kaiser Wilhelm II first wanted to call this battle, it was no German victory, although British losses of men and materiel were higher.[19] Strategically, the battle had changed nothing, as Admiral Scheer frankly admitted in a memorandum to the Kaiser in early July.[20] After the repair of his vessels, which had been severely mauled at Jutland, Scheer nevertheless twice left Schillig Roads again, hoping to meet and annihilate parts of the Grand Fleet. These hopes were, however, not fulfilled. Despite great disappointment about the outcome of the battle of Jutland, which had been no Trafalgar, the Grand Fleet saw no use in offering a battle, which even if it resulted in a great victory would not change anything strategically. Neither its Commander-in-Chief, Admiral Jellicoe – transferred to the post of First Sea Lord in 1917 not for his merits but as a result of the loss of confidence in his leadership qualities – nor his successor, Admiral David Beatty, was willing to risk too much for nothing. Like the Grand Fleet, which nevertheless was in a much better position, the *Hochseeflotte* stayed in harbour, only to leave again in April 1918 in order to make a raid into the northern North Sea to attack Allied convoys. For this it paid rather dearly, for one of its most modern battle-cruisers, *Moltke*, was hit by a torpedo fired by a British submarine; the Grand Fleet or parts of it, however, did not come into sight. Subsequently, the Imperial German Navy again restricted its own role to that of a fleet-in-being which protected Germany's coast from invasion, and which backed the increasingly more difficult task of sweeping mines in the German Bight to allow submarines to exit into the North Sea for operations against Britain's merchant fleet.

When the German Empire was on the verge of collapse in October 1918, the newly established Naval Command under Admiral Scheer, the *Seekriegsleitung*, again made plans for an offensive strike against the Grand Fleet. Fully aware that such a strike was both politically an unnecessary provocation of the Allies and strategically useless, the *Seekriegsleitung* nevertheless hoped that the attempt to gain victory in a last great battle would help save the honour of the naval officer corps and thus pave the way for the build-up of a new powerful navy after the war. This was, of course, pure nonsense. Hardly surprising, the sailors of the vessels, which were doomed to sink if they left port in the last days of October, mutinied. Angry about the way they had been treated by their officers in many respects during the war, they saw no purpose in sacrificing their lives for a system which had denied them equal rights in politics, not to speak of the increasingly disastrous situation with regard to the provision of food and other goods. Starting at Germany's main naval bases at Wilhelmshaven and Kiel, mutinying sailors, who quickly united with soldiers from the army and workers, brought down the existing political and social order.

The naval war in the Baltic

Geography, special hydrographic conditions, and climate had a deep impact upon naval operations in the Baltic. Unlike the North Sea, the Baltic was nothing but a large lake with only one narrow entrance in the west. Hydrographic conditions and climate, however, had advantages and disadvantages for both sides. Whereas the former were favourable for the deployment of submarines and the use of mines, long nights and ice made operations very difficult, especially in the eastern parts of the Baltic between October and March. Since no modern means of reconnaissance were available at that time, enemy forces could advance and strike without being detected early, if ice allowed any operations at all.

In contrast to the North Sea, where German forces were in an inferior position, the situation in the Baltic was, by and large, nevertheless advantageous for the Imperial German Navy. Though the number of vessels stationed at Kiel and other forward positions such as Danzig or Pillau (eight mostly old light cruisers, eight torpedo boats, and three submarines) was fewer than the Russian Baltic Fleet, which consisted of four older pre-dreadnoughts, five armoured cruisers, four light cruisers, 63 torpedo boats, and 12 submarines (as well as four modern capital ships, which would become operational within less than a year), the Imperial German Navy could always rely upon the *Hochseeflotte* for support for either defensive or offensive operations.[21]

It was precisely this situation that caused the German Baltic Fleet to start an offensive right after the outbreak of war. First, to prevent the Grand Fleet from entering the Baltic, the Commander-in-Chief of the German Baltic Fleet, Prinz Heinrich, the Emperor's younger brother, ordered to mine the entrance into the Baltic. This measure was, however, only at first glance advantageous for the German Navy. Of course, it could thus prevent its direct enemy, the

Russian Baltic Fleet, as well as, indirectly, the Grand Fleet, from forcing the Danish Straits. This notwithstanding, the closure of the Danish Straits also had serious repercussions on Germany's naval grand strategy. By limiting the possibility of a raid of the *Hochseeflotte* out of the Kattegat into the North Sea, the German naval leadership thus carelessly renounced a strategic option that would have kept the Grand Fleet in suspense and that would have complicated their defence measures. Second, in order to discourage the Russian Baltic Fleet from offensive strikes against the long German coast, German cruisers and torpedo boats were dispatched into the eastern parts of the Baltic to show force. Unfortunately, this strike turned out to be a disaster with far-reaching consequences. The small cruiser *Magdeburg* ran aground in the Gulf of Finland and had to be given up while the rest of the squadron made a narrow escape. It was, however, not the loss of the *Magdeburg* itself that proved disastrous, but the fact that the Russian Navy found the top-secret signal book of the Imperial German Navy in the wreckage. Handed over to the British immediately, this signal book enabled the Grand Fleet to detect the movements of the German fleet at a very early stage and to thus remain 'master of the situation'[22] in the North Sea until the end of the war by taking precautionary measures.

Though the Russians refrained from openly attacking its enemy, they were nevertheless quite successful. In autumn 1914, several German warships were either severely damaged or lost after running into Russian minefields. For the German Baltic Fleet the situation became more complicated when, after the end of the winter, it successfully moved east with the victorious German armies. The scouting forces of the Baltic Fleet, established in April 1915 and based on the Russian port of Libau conquered in May, were now in a better position to try to secure the lines of communication in the Baltic, especially the important sea-routes to Sweden. This task, however, soon proved more difficult than expected. The Russians were masters in mine-laying, and, supported by British submarines, they launched a successful campaign during which, from the German point of view, an alarming rate of merchant vessels and warships were sunk. The failure of German attempts to force the entrance into Riga Bay in 1915 and the sinking of seven torpedo-boats which, advancing into the Bay of Finland in December 1916 had run onto a minefield, illustrate that the Russian Baltic Navy knew how to fulfil its task. However, the Russian Baltic Fleet was soon on the verge of collapse after the outbreak of revolution in 1917. Thus it paved the way for a combined amphibious operation of both the German Army and Navy to conquer the Baltic islands in October 1917, only weeks before the outbreak of the Bolshevik Revolution. Though successful, the navy's losses – two modern capital ships were hit by mines – were an unnecessary, high price for an operation, which, as some commanding officers rightly assumed, had only been ordered for two reasons. The first was to prove to the army that the navy was capable and willing to strike successfully if necessary, and, the second was to divert attention from the first mutinies which had seriously affected morale in the summer of 1917. The German naval expedition to Finland, following the request of the new government of this former part of the Russian Empire and intended to support Finnish forces in their attempts at preventing Bolshevists from invading the country, saw no combat action. Nevertheless, the damage of the battleship *Rheinland*, which had hit a rock, was another severe and also unnecessary loss in a situation that was already difficult for the navy.

The naval war in the Mediterranean and in the Adriatic

For Britain and France as well as the navies of the Triple Alliance the Mediterranean was, as described above, a very important theatre of war. However, when war broke out, things soon turned out to be different from what had been anticipated before. Due to Italy's declaration to remain neutral, at least for the time being, the German Mediterranean Squadron, consisting of the battle-cruiser *Goeben* and the small cruiser *Breslau*, had no choice but to try to escape instead of waiting to be caught by superior British and French forces. After shelling French positions in Algeria, they ran for the Dardanelles to seek refuge. The failure of British forces to deal with these ships eventually proved one of the greatest shortcomings of the war.[23] By supporting the Turkish Navy after the signing of a German–Turkish alliance treaty in early August, these vessels contributed enormously to the defence of the Dardanelles as well as of the Bosphorus against Allied attempts to open a new front against the Central Powers.[24]

For the Austro-Hungarian Navy this development was fortunate in some ways. Like its main ally, Germany, the Austro-Hungarian Navy also had to fight in narrow seas, the Adriatic.[25] Though the Austro-Hungarian naval command first thought of sending the whole fleet to Turkey, where it might play an important role in fighting the powerful Russian fleet in the Black Sea, it eventually remained in the Adriatic. With respect to its two main tasks – protecting Austria's long coastline and acting as a deterrent to Italy – it seemed more important to stay in home waters than to wage a naval war in a far distant theatre.

The Austro-Hungarian Navy fulfilled its first task in a remarkable way. Of course, after Italy's entry into the war on the side of the Allies in May 1915, the Entente navies closed the entrance into the Adriatic with a blockade, consisting of trawlers and anti-submarine nets, backed by more powerful warships, which the Austro-Hungarian Navy proved unable to break despite several efforts.[26]

Within the Adriatic, the Austro-Hungarian Navy defended its supremacy successfully, either through offensive strikes or the increasing use of submarines against enemy shipping in close collaboration with the Germans. Continuing confusion, division, and jealousy among Allied commanders, who proved unable to agree upon a common strategy against the Austro-Hungarian Navy, further contributed to this favourable situation.[27]

Right from the first days of the war, the Austro-Hungarians conducted offensive strikes against the Italian coast. Moreover, actions of sabotage helped to intimidate the Italian Navy. In the end, despite setbacks such as the sinking of the dreadnought *Szent István* through an Italian motor torpedo boat attack in 1918, the Austro-Hungarians could be quite satisfied with the performance of their navy, which, unlike the Imperial German Navy, never aspired to achieve more than it could actually perform.

The naval war in Turkish waters

The Turkish Navy, small and old anyway, was nothing but an appendix to the German Navy, for its core consisted of the two vessels of the German Mediterranean Squadron, the battle cruisers *Goeben* and the small cruiser *Breslau*.[28] These vessels finally led the Ottoman Empire into war in October by shelling Russian ports. By and large, surprise strikes of this kind were all they could perform, for the Turkish Navy was inferior to its Russian as well as its British opponents. Accordingly, strategically the Turkish Navy remained on the defensive.

This defensive strategy was sufficient to achieve Turkey's main aim: to prevent both the Russian as well as the Royal Navy from forcing the Bosphorus and the Dardanelles. In these attempts they were also supported by German submarines, which operated successfully off the Dardanelles as the remarkable loss of several British and French warships in 1915 made clear. Similarly, minefields and coastal defences also made clear that despite heavy bombardment from the sea even a superior naval force was unable to pave the way for successful land operations. The attempt of the Allies to bring down the Central Powers through the back door by attacking the Dardanelles proved one of the war's greatest military disasters.[29]

With respect to Turkey's long lines of communication, especially in the Black Sea, the Turkish Navy failed to achieve its aims. Thus the Russians were able to interdict Turkish coastal traffic, which was of great importance for the supply of coal and other goods as well as the support of Turkish troops on the front in Eastern Turkey. However, the collapse of Russia in 1917 helped establish German as well as Turkish naval supremacy in this theatre of the naval war.

The war on distant oceans

In naval history cruiser or commerce warfare has always been a strategy implemented by numerically weaker navies in order to inflict losses upon an overwhelming enemy. By destroying enemy merchant vessels and thus causing serious problems for trade, industry, and the provision of food, or by destroying vessels transporting troops and war materials from distant parts of the British and French empires to the main theatre in Europe, fast cruisers could help force a powerful opponent to sue for peace. Subsequently, it would have been natural for the Imperial German Navy to work out plans for cruiser warfare. Such a strategy would not only have seriously threatened Britain's and even France's lifelines, but also would have forced the numerically far superior Royal Navy to disperse its ships. In the event, the number of British vessels available for a decisive battle in the North Sea might have been much smaller than it actually was in 1914.

Remarkably enough, due to the great impact of Mahanian ideas on naval warfare, cruiser warfare had, however, played neither an important role in preparing for the war at sea nor did it after the war had actually broken out. The lack of bases and coaling stations had been one reason why Tirpitz had always emphasized the need to build a battle fleet and not a fleet of cruisers waging commerce warfare on the oceans. On the eve of war Tirpitz seems to have toyed with the idea of forming two 'flying squadrons' consisting of battle-cruisers to wage cruiser-warfare in the Atlantic.[30] He even picked up this idea again in mid-August 1914; however, he dismissed it soon. After the unexpected success of *U9* against Royal Navy ships in the Channel, the Secretary of State of the Imperial Navy Office was convinced that submarine warfare would deliver results more quickly than old-fashioned cruiser warfare.

Against this background Germany's cruisers, scattered over distant parts of the world, were doomed to be sunk sooner or later. Although the German Admiralty Staff had issued orders to the German East Asiatic Squadron in spring 1914 recommending an attack on the British forces in East Asia immediately after the war 'if circumstances for the Cruiser Squadron... are particularly favourable',[31] Vizeadmiral Reichsgraf Maximilian von Spee, the commander of Germany's most powerful squadron overseas, consisting of two armoured and four small cruisers, decided to try to reach his home base. Of course, on the way back he defeated an inferior British squadron under Admiral Sir Christopher Cradock off the coast of Chile in November 1914. However, the Admiralty, which had at first underestimated the potential dangers of a powerful German squadron menacing important British trade routes in the South Atlantic and had let the German ships escape from its naval base on the Chinese coast, struck back by dispatching superior forces to hunt them down.[32] Only a month after the battle of Coronel Spee's squadron was sunk off the Falkland Islands when preparing for an attack on Port Stanley. The remaining German small cruisers, including the famous *Emden* (sunk in November 1914), the *Dresden,* and the *Königsberg,* waging commerce warfare in the Indian and Pacific Oceans and off the coast of East Africa, were all hunted down until spring 1915.

Whereas the Royal Navy had had no apprehensions about the impact of Germany's cruisers overseas upon Britain's lifelines, the prospect of fast German passenger and merchant vessels converted into auxiliary cruisers had increasingly worried the Admiralty. Due to their great speed and their number these vessels were supposed to pose a much more serious threat to British trade routes than any German warship. In the event, these fears proved largely unjustified. Though most of Germany's auxiliary warships were sunk in the first months of the war, they could claim some successes. For example, one of Britain's newest dreadnoughts, *Audacious,* fell victim to a mine laid by the German auxiliary cruiser *Berlin* in the Irish Channel in October 1914. After an interlude of almost two years the lack of success in the main theatre of war eventually caused the German naval leadership to resume the war against Britain's trade routes with auxiliary cruisers. Hoping to thus force the Admiralty to weaken its forces in the North Sea, the German Navy again sent out several converted merchant vessels such as the old steamships *Möwe* and *Wolf* or the *Seeadler,* a slow sailing ship. Whereas *Seeadler* was soon hunted down and sunk, *Möwe* and *Wolf* successfully waged commerce warfare in the Atlantic, Indian, and Pacific Oceans for almost two years before returning to Kiel in early 1917 and 1918, respectively.[33]

New forms of war: the submarine challenge and naval aviation

The only serious threat to British superiority in the Mediterranean, the North Sea, and, of course, in the Atlantic was submarines. Realizing that a Mahanian blue-water strategy would bring no success, in late 1914 the German naval command at least partly reverted to a completely different strategy: submarine warfare. The submarine had been invented in the mid-19th century. In a slow process of trial and error entailing many accidents and setbacks, by the turn of the century all navies had developed this new type of vessel, with Britain having the largest submarine fleet – 72 vessels on the eve of war – whereas the German Navy had only 28. As early as 1904 Sir John Fisher, the British First Sea Lord, convinced of the need to revolutionize British naval warfare by implementing his ideas of flotilla defence,[34] had written:

The submarine is the coming type of war vessel for sea fighting. And what is it that the coming of the submarine really means? It means that the whole foundation of our traditional naval strategy … has broken down! The foundation of that strategy was blockade. The Fleet did not exist merely to win battles – that was the means not the end. The ultimate purpose of the Fleet was to make blockade possible for us and impossible for the enemy… Surface ships can no longer maintain or prevent blockade… All our old ideas of strategy are simmering in the melting pot![35]

Despite this statement submarines were still not regarded as an important weapon in future wars at sea. Though submarine warfare remained a question of trial and error for all navies throughout the war due to manifold technical problems either of the boat itself or of its armament, the success of the German submarine *U9* was something of a turning of the tide, in spite of many reservations by the adherents of battleships. Under very favourable circumstances, *U9* had sunk three old British armoured cruisers within one hour off Dover in September 1914. In 1915 and 1916, attempts to introduce submarine warfare on a larger scale and more effectively by sinking Allied ships without warning, however, met with severe opposition from Germany's political leadership. Until 1917 the risks of the entry of the United States into the war on the side of the Allies outweighed all prospects of a quick and decisive success against Allied shipping by the Admiral Staff. Only in February 1917, when victory on land was still not in sight and when hunger as well as the lack of raw materials had become a serious domestic problem threatening political and social stability, Germany's leadership unanimously decided to put everything on one last card to force Britain onto its knees – and it lost everything. Though German submarines inflicted heavy losses upon Allied shipping in the first months of 1917, the introduction of the convoy system soon helped to improve the Allies' situation. Moreover, new forms of anti-submarine warfare and a large-scale mining offensive effectively blockading their exit-routes proved successful in fighting German submarines, which soon suffered increasing losses totalling 178 out of 335 vessels in service and 4,474 men.

However, not only the German Navy increasingly made use of submarines. From the outset Royal Navy coastal submarines, despite their limited range, poor endurance, and questionable habitability patrolled the North Sea – though with little success. With much greater success British submarines supported the Russian Baltic Fleet in its war against the German Navy in 1915. In the same period the Royal Navy even managed to send submarines into the Marmora to destroy Turkish vessels. Nevertheless, due to manifold reasons – technical problems, the unsuitability of British E-class submarines for the role they were supposed to perform, and the shortage of men and materiel to build them, not to mention the fact that the *Hochseeflotte* seldom left port to thus offer a target – the submarine never played as important a role for the Royal Navy as it did for the German Navy.[36] In the Mediterranean Austro-Hungarian submarines, supported by German submarines transferred from Germany, successfully waged submarine warfare against Allied merchant vessels and even warships, causing serious problems for the Allies.[37]

Naval aviation, which, like the submarine, had been in its infancy at the outbreak of war, also played an increasingly more important role in naval operations. Though all navies had experimented with different types of planes, their tactical use was limited due to technical problems. For example, launching and recovering planes, especially in the rough waters of the North Sea, proved difficult. Moreover, their armament was insufficient to really harm a big ship or to inflict more than psychological damage, as in the British attack on German airship stations in late 1914 as well as in later years. Subsequently, planes were mostly used for reconnaissance and messenger purposes. This, however, gradually changed. When the war to came to an end, aviation had become a weapon that had to be taken seriously. Though technical problems had eventually thwarted British plans to attack the *Hochseeflotte* from the air with more than 100 torpedo planes, the *Hochseeflotte*, in return, had proved its ability to strike from the air, when seaplanes sank several British coastal motor boats in August 1917 off the Dutch coast.[38] In the Adriatic, with its shorter flying distances, naval aviation played a more important role right from the beginning. Here attacks from the air were soon a constant means of fighting the enemy at sea as well as on land. While the Allies attacked Austro-Hungarian positions on the Pola Peninsula, Austro-Hungarian seaplanes bombed Venice until the last days of the war.[39]

The German airship, however, proved a total failure from a technical as well as a strategic point of view. Though much dreaded at first by the inhabitants of British towns, because airships took the war directly to the British Isles, the psychological effect of airship attacks was much greater than the actual damage they caused. In 1917, due to increasing losses as a result of better air defences as well as the capability of British aeroplanes to attack high-flying airships, the German Admiralty Staff eventually realized that losses did not justify such attacks anymore.

Conclusion

On 21 November 1918 the end eventually arrived, though in a different form as expected when war broke out. In a humiliating procedure, from the German point of view, the Grand Fleet and vessels from its Allies, in total more than 370 ships, met the disarmed *Hochseeflotte* in the North Sea in order to accompany it into custody at Scapa Flow. Allied success on all fronts in the West, the South, and the South-East, as well as the outbreak of revolutions in Austria-Hungary and Germany, had brought the Central Powers and their navies respectively down onto their knees. During this great struggle, navies had played their part, though in a different way than expected. No Trafalgar-like battle had taken place; instead, different kinds of warfare, such as the blockade (even though it was a distant one), the commerce war conducted by submarines difficult to detect, and the war from the air, had become more important. The era of powerful battleships fighting for naval supremacy thus seemed over; the aircraft carrier, capable of projecting power across much farther distances and of controlling and defending important sea-lanes from the air with its planes, seemed, despite its limitations, apt to replace the capital ship. Moreover, as the fate of the German, Austro-Hungarian, and Russian navies showed, only a system that gave the sailors of its navies the feeling that they were treated fairly and that their interests were considered as seriously as those of the so-called upper classes, could successfully rally the rank-and-file behind its leaders. Last but not least, the enormous costs of the armaments races prior to 1914, with all their repercussions on domestic politics as well as their impact upon international relations, made it imperative to look for solutions to prevent a repetition of this fatal development in the future. Unfortunately, as events were to prove only a generation later, many people had either forgotten or simply denied to learn their lesson from history.

CHAPTER 6

THE FRENCH ARMY BETWEEN TRADITION AND MODERNITY

Weaponry, Tactics, and Soldiers, 1914–18

Professor Dr François Cochet

The French Army of 1914 was not a stagnant mass frozen in the defeat of 1870. Indeed, rarely has an army reformed as well as the French did following the humiliation of the Franco-Prussian War. Both officers and men had benefited from new training regimes, while modern equipment had also been introduced. However, on the outbreak of World War I some old principles still prevailed when it came to the deployment of men and weapons, and this proved to be fatal to the hopes of the French Army. With the consolidation of the Western Front into over 500 miles of trenches from the North Sea to the Vosges Mountains, the situation changed radically. The onset of trench warfare saw the end of '*furia francese*', exemplified by the power of the bayonet, with artillery and aviation taking an increasing role on the battlefield.

New weapons emerged, often in response to those implemented by the Germans such as poison gas or flamethrowers. Throughout the war the French innovated significantly in several key areas, which had a lasting effect for decades to come – the use of the Renault FT-17 tank, for example, marked a fundamental change in land warfare. The growing shortage of manpower provoked other fundamental changes in fighting techniques, and the French Army of 1918 barely resembled that of just four years before. Never had so many Frenchmen been engaged simultaneously in war operations. Five French armies took part in the fighting of 1914 and 12 in that of 1918. This shows the scale of the national effort during World War I.

The situation in 1914 – equipment and beliefs

The phrase 'arms race' is a term often used to describe the military spending spree that most developed states were involved in during the last years of the 19th and the early years of the 20th century. In fact this 'race' was almost exclusively focused on the maritime rivalry between Germany and England, especially the growth of naval power following the introduction of HMS *Dreadnought*. However, land forces also underwent significant changes during this period, and nowhere was this clearer than in the French Army. Two weapons symbolize the technical developments and deployment principles of the time. The 75mm gun was a technological marvel that outperformed all equivalent weapons. Thanks to its hydraulic brake it did not need re-aiming between shots and thus could maintain a high rate of fire. Developed in 1897 the '75' was extremely versatile – so much so that when the Germans captured a large number in June 1940 they successfully reused them as anti-tank guns on the Eastern Front from June 1941. Although powerful, the '75' had too direct a line of fire to target enemy trenches buried once the war changed from one of manoeuvre to the stalemate of trench warfare.[1]

While the Germans used a variety of different calibres of artillery, each adapted for a specific purpose, the French were convinced that the '75' was the only calibre required for all purposes. This had an adverse effect, as it led to an institutional belief that there was no need for heavier artillery. It was ultimately the French parliament that cancelled the development of heavy artillery planned before the war.

Infantry firepower had also changed beyond all recognition. In 1914, a French battalion of 1,100 men armed with Lebel rifles could send a 'wall of fire' of 22,000 rounds per minute against enemy troops. This was three times the firepower available to a battalion equipped with the 1866 Chassepot rifle in 1870. All of these developments in weaponry relied upon an increasingly sophisticated industrial base.

The adoption of machine guns, on the other hand, was more problematic. The Russo-Japanese War in Manchuria had revealed the potency of the machine gun in a defensive battle, particularly when associated with the use of barbed wire. However, the fear of an excessive consumption of ammunition delayed its mass adoption, except in the case of the German armies. The French, who invented an early machine gun known as the *canon à balles* before the Franco-Prussian War of 1870, made limited use of it, as did the British, because they thought it to be inappropriate for offensive combat due to the large amount of ammunition it required.

Along with the changes in weaponry came developments in strategy and tactics. Among the French, there is a widely held stereotype of Lieutenant-Colonel Louis Loyseau de Grandmaison as the author of the so-called 'doctrine of the offensive at all costs'. Because he gave three lectures at the War College on this subject, this modest lieutenant-colonel is seen as the man responsible for a military principle that caused the deaths of thousands in the summer of 1914. Anti-military pacifists and the military, shamed by the losses of the summer of 1914, joined in an uneasy alliance to stigmatize this officer. This is a misunderstanding of de Grandmaison and his teachings, as well as of the way the French military hierarchy functions. Lieutenant-Colonel de Grandmaison was placed in charge of the third section of the French General Staff[2] on 24 October 1908. Like many officers of his generation, he analysed the causes of the French defeat in 1870 and tried to take into account the lessons of Clausewitz. For de Grandmaison, in order to defeat the enemy one had to advance. He became convinced – as was his 'superior' Ferdinand Foch – that victory depended first and foremost on moral dominance over the enemy. This does not make de Grandmaison the irresponsible murderer that he is often portrayed as. De Grandmaison recommended making an offensive effort in specific directions rather than in a linear way: 'The main force will be divided into very unequal columns whose only concern will be to meet their goal at any price, no matter what, for their own account, and do not fear that one doesn't worry enough about one's neighbours: one worries only too much about them.'

De Grandmaison, whose only crime was to be 'up to date' with current beliefs, delivered three lectures on the subject in February 1911. To claim that he had a decisive role would be to undue importance to a mere lieutenant-colonel, however avant-garde his beliefs. It is by no means de Grandmaison who designed the French offensive principle. The official regulations of the period show an undercurrent of these beliefs amongst the *jeunes turcs* ('young radicals'), supported by Joffre.

Concepts of mobility – the best guarantee to escape fire – are apparent in the official literature of the regulations. Indeed, the *Service en campagne* field manual of 1913, for example, shows a real evolution in the roles of artillery and infantry: 'The action of the artillery cannot be independent of the infantry. Because the artillery fire has only limited effectiveness against a sheltered opponent, attacking with infantry enables exposure of the enemy.'

A number of French military experts who analysed various conflicts before World War I stressed the devastating effects of the gun, especially in the context of the fighting in Manchuria. However, others had differing opinions, and although their concerns were known, they were not necessarily heeded by those responsible for military planning. Following the Russo-Japanese War of 1904–05, observers commented most frequently on the offensive spirit of the Japanese, which led them to victory despite defensive combat around Port Arthur, already marked by the prevalence of trench warfare.

In fact, in 1914 the French were far from being the only ones to adhere to the cult of the offensive. The main European armies all followed the same thinking. 'In contrast with the former, the new text makes an undeniable progress. It is animated by the purist of offensive spirits from one end to the other', says the Austro-Hungarian army New Field Service Regulations of January 1913,[3] while its Russian counterpart, released in May 1912, argues that 'only the offensive can impose its will on the opponent'. 'Bullets rarely decide upon victory but pave the way for the bayonet charge… This is the most important part of the instruction of infantry', adds the British regulations of 30 May 1911. The Germans, of course, were no exception, as shown by the Schlieffen Plan itself. On the eve of World War I, the German cavalry arm was reinforced with 13 regiments of mounted infantry.[4] In France, Plan XVII was in place from April 1914 in case of war. This was not an operational plan but a plan for the mobilization and concentration of troops. The first such plan was devised in 1875, relying on the assumption that the Germans would accept Belgian neutrality. This mainly enabled the protection of the industrial centres of the Massif Central, including the city of Saint-Etienne and its arms industry. Various plans then followed from 1878, as the violation of Belgian neutrality was taken into account (Plan III), and also because of the development of railway infrastructure (Plan V). From 1887, the progress of the railway enabled the more rapid concentration of troops, leading to the adoption of further ideas related to more offensive operations.

Général Victor Michel was the new vice-president of the *Conseil Supérieur de a Guerre*. He anticipated a German attack through Belgium and wanted to move French reserves to the north of Lille. His plans were rejected by the Conseil in 1911.

Général Gallieni was the main cause of this refusal because he wanted to replace Michel with his former subordinate Joseph Joffre. The latter became

Chief of the General Staff on 28 July 1911. At first Joffre, always the technician, developed his plan in terms of transportation, particularly to ensure the movement of the British Expeditionary Force. In 1912, Joffre adopted parts of Michel's ideas and intended to wage war in Belgium, but was dissuaded by Raymond Poincaré who wanted to preserve the alliance with England.[5]

The general staff developed plans based on several hypothetical German actions.[6] Starting with a frontal attack on Lorraine, more or less forceful secondary operations were considered in Alsace, Verdun, and Belgium. Plan XVII was applied on 15 April 1914 and did not include an Alpine front, proof that the Italians were not perceived as a threat.

The transportation plan was particularly efficient, and the general staff had ten independent railway lines available in order to place cavalry into action on the fourth day after mobilization.

The operational plan foresaw the French Army having 'all combined forces to attack the German armies' to the north of the Verdun–Metz line and between the Vosges and the Moselle. Each of the five active armies was given precise objectives.

It is on the basis of Plan XVII that the Lorraine Offensive was launched on Sarrebourg and Morhange. The political implication is clear: the attack was intended to regain the 'lost provinces' of 1870. But the Germans prepared carefully and the French, despite their heroism, were stopped by heavy artillery and German machine guns. After this came battles in Belgium that followed the same logic, with offensives being given little artillery preparation, relying solely on the will of the soldiers. In Belgium and the Ardennes, the figures speak for themselves. No fewer than 80,000 French soldiers were killed, including 40,000 in the Belgian Ardennes between 22 and 25 August 1914.[7] These early clashes reveal the horror of both sides' belief in the ability to defeat the enemy quickly by a violent assault. On 24 August the French plan had totally failed but the French did not collapse. Joffre kept a firm grip on his men and began a methodical retreat, interspersed with repeated short, violent counter-attacks to protect the retreat. In the meantime, he sacked a hundred generals. In autumn 1914, in the battles of Artois and the Yser, a particular form of warfare disappeared, leaving room for other, more industrialized forms.

The adaptation of principles, equipment, and men to the new system of trench warfare

The French tradition of an army of movement and the traditional principles of troop deployment all had to be abandoned to fit into the new form of 'static war' in deep trenches from the end of 1914. This did not happen overnight and offensives in Artois, Champagne, and Woëvre in 1915 still attest to an adherence to old ways of thinking. French strategists, along with the English and Germans, quickly realized that artillery had become the queen of the battlefield, if only because it alone was capable of destroying the network of enemy barbed wire that blocked any possible hope of advance. The French therefore began to manufacture 105 and 155mm heavy guns in large numbers, while at the same time developing even larger calibres such as the 400mm. In 1917, generals Buat and Nivelle develop the idea of a 'general reserve artillery', in which many pieces of all sizes of weaponry are grouped together at a specific place on the front. By the end of the war, the French had 5,000 75mm guns and 5,500 pieces of heavy artillery. In 1914, there were already 4,200 75mm guns, but only 308 pieces of heavy artillery.

The secret of victory lay in French industrial capacity, a point Joffre had understood by the end of 1914.

Some examples of manufacturing

	August 1914 (Index)	September 1915 (index)
75mm guns	100	1,000
75mm shells	100	500
Machine guns	100	4,500
Aircraft	100	1,300

This growth in manufacturing output continued beyond 1915. In August 1918 alone, 191,000 75mm shells, 32,000 155mm shells, and 132,000 infantry cartridges were produced for French troops.[8]

However, artillery was not the only new weapon introduced in World War I. The new style of siege warfare brought about by the 'trench system' led to the use of technologies and other new weapons that were in many ways reinventions of ancient processes. There was a need for weapons with a high trajectory and plunging fire in order to reach the buried opponent. The Germans had the great *Minenwerfer* in their possession, but the French were compelled to improvise.

Under General Sarrail, in the Meuse, one Capitaine Benoist designed a tube to launch a box filled with anti-personnel nails. Mortars were also reused from the period of the July Monarchy (1830–48), including 15cm tubes from 1839, before real trench artillery was invented. In December 1914, Commander Duchene, Chief Engineer of the 20eme Division d'infanterie designed a 58cm mortar that was able to reuse 75mm shell casings, found in large quantities on the battlefield. This machine, quickly nicknamed the *crapouillot* because it looked like a frog, is the most obvious example of the French ability to improvise in wartime what had not been planned for in peace.[9]

Mine warfare also made a comeback following its heyday in the 17th and 18th centuries. In 1628, Antoine de Ville formulated the first principles of this style of warfare, which were later developed by the experiments of the great military engineer Vauban. In the French Army, various documents reveal how these techniques were reintroduced. A Practical Manual for Mine Devices had been published in 1880 and in 1915 this was republished, updated by the early experience of World War I, with the title Instructions for Field Works. From the moment the front becomes static, and heavy artillery is not yet as widespread as the army would like, the technique of mining becomes a logical method of war. Ideally, it is a way to breach a crack in the enemy's front, to take advantage of the confusion and assault the enemy. On 21 December 1915 GHQ set out a methodology for this form of warfare: 'When you are in the presence of a part of the enemy front of which possession would provide significant benefits, but that would prove too costly to acquire by the usual methods (attack by force, by grenade, attack on foot), one must, if the terrain is appropriate, be ready to use mine attacks.'[10] Mine warfare, involving engineers, sappers, and miners, develops into a nervous race against time. The enemy hears a knock digging under his trench and hastens to build a counter-attack mine – a snub (or *camouflet*) – to blow the opponent's gallery before the charge is ready, which contains hundreds of pounds of explosives. By 1915, mine warfare had extended along the entire Western Front.

Even though the technique continued to be used throughout the war – and the British exploded 19 mines during the assault of the Australians and New Zealanders on the Messines Ridge on the Ypres front on 17 June 1917 – mine warfare reached the height of its horror in 1915. The peak of the technology was achieved in the battles of Vauquois, in the Meuse region. On the German side, sappers dug a total of 14 mines, two of them 100 yards below the surface of the Vauquois Ridge. The French opened 12 mines at least 50 yards deep. A total of 519 explosions took place around Vauquois throughout the war for almost no territorial gains.

Other techniques were developed during trench warfare. The use of poison gas prevailed in violation of the Hague (1899) and Geneva (1907) conventions. If it was the Germans who innovated on this point, assisted by a highly developed chemical industry, others had thought of it well before. Thus, during the uprising in the Vendée in 1793–94 Bertrand Barrere had supported the use of toxic substances against the Royalists. It is probably only the impossibility of production at the time that had stopped him. In Germany in 1915, the chemist

Fritz Haber, head of the Research Institute of Organic Chemistry in Berlin, suggested the use of gaseous chlorine against the Allies to the German General Staff. On 29 October 1914, the Germans had already bombed Neuve-Chapelle in Artois with shells containing an irritant substance.[11] On 22 April 1915 in the area of Ypres, 150 tons of chlorine were released to the wind from steel cylinders. The technique of drifting gas led to considerable panic amongst front-line troops and the front gave in locally, but the Germans were unable to continue.

The Allies responded of course. On 23 April 1915, after the first use of gas on the Western Front, the French sent André Kling, director of the municipal laboratory of Paris, to conduct an investigation. Committees succeeded one another in April and May at the Ministry of War and the Technical Section of Engineering. These committees brought together chemical scientists, manufacturers, and the military. In August 1915, General Ozil had the mission of coordinating the combined efforts of these participants in three areas: the front, the offensive means, and the means of protection.

Also in 1915 the flamethrower appeared on the German side. The holder of the weapon must have had great courage. The canisters of flammable liquid that he carried on his back were of significant risk to him. An enemy bullet in the metal containers would cause an explosion. The French and the British, initially reluctant, developed the weapon, just as they did with gas shells. For 75mm shells alone, the proportion of gas shells rises from 2.5 per cent in 1917 to over 6 per cent in August 1918.

But the real star of trench fighting, also rediscovered in 1915, was the grenade. In its many forms – offensive, defensive, flammable, rifle – it proved to be extremely versatile. The defensive 'grid' grenade enabled the soldier to stop the assault of the enemy with sharp projectiles once he had reached a distance of 20 yards and was sheltered in his trench. The offensive grenade, with a limited blast, silenced the opponent, especially in mine trenches. The French possessed a defensive grenade as early as 1914, but in the battles of the Argonne in particular, they relied on homemade gadgets such as 'firecracker rackets', simple wooden boards wired and loaded with dynamite or melinite. Later, they developed more reliable grenades.

Advances in aviation were also a visible indication of the move towards total war.[12] In 1914, the French Army had dozens of aeroplanes, all dedicated to observation. In 1918, there were thousands, specializing in hunting, bombing, and observation. The first aerial combat took place over Jonchery-sur-Vesle, west of Reims, on 5 October 1914. The French aviators Frantz and Quenault shot down a German aircraft using a self-assembled machine gun. It was the discovery of the principle of firing through the propeller which allowed the development of real air-to-air combat. Invented by the Frenchman Roland Garros, it was then copied by the Germans after his capture (and that of his aircraft) in April 1915.

During the battle of Verdun the French adopted the organizational and fighting structure of the squadron thanks to Major Charles de Tricornot de Rose and also to a new type of aircraft, the Nieuport 11, fast and easy to manoeuvre. While the Germans had been in a position of superiority over the Allied air forces at the beginning of the war, this position had reversed in the spring of 1916. The war now also had a vertical dimension. Not only was there a battle between aircraft, but also with other arms. Contact between forces in the air and troops on the ground became increasingly important. Aerial forces needed to clear the sky of enemy planes so that the enemy could not be informed. They could also restrict the movement of the opponents on the ground by air-to-ground operations. We are thus quite far from the image of the valiant knight aviator of modern warfare. As stated by the French aviator Alfred Heurtaux, shooting down an aircraft was much like 'shooting a cow in a corridor'.[13]

The first use of tanks was another notch in the technological transformation of the war. It was the same deadlock on the Western Front that led to the conception of this new weapon. The idea of a powerful shockproof weapon had been well established. The tank integrated the power of penetration with firepower. In 1916, the tank was one solution among others for crossing enemy trenches. The English used tanks for the first time on 15 September 1916, during the battle of the Somme, between Courcelette and Flers, where 49 tanks tried to break through the enemy front. The French also conducted studies leading to the construction of two types of tanks, the Saint-Chamond and Schneider. Eighty of them were launched on 16 April 1917 during the Chemin des Dames Offensive against the German lines in Berry-Áu-Bac. 'Special artillery' tanks under Major Louis Bossut certainly weakened some German positions but were quickly stopped with the loss of half of the tanks, including Bossut's.

The first experiments in the use of tanks in combat, therefore, had mixed results. However, in a few months, when the principles of deployment were better understood, their use became increasingly successful. When Foch ordered the counter-attack after the failure of the last German offensives on 18 July 1918, more than 700 tanks were involved, while 600 more were launched against the Germans by the British in Picardy, on 8 August. On 25 August 1914, Colonel Estienne, the true 'father' of French tanks, addressed the officers of his regiment: 'Gentlemen, the victory of this war belongs to the warrior who manages to place a 75mm gun on a vehicle capable of moving off-road.'[14] The tank becomes truly effective with the French Renault FT-17. Operated by only two men, a driver and a gunner, it already had all the characteristics of a modern tank, in particular its 360-degree rotating turret. It could be equipped with a Hotchkiss machine gun for use against individuals or a 37mm cannon for use against machine-gun nests. Launched in large numbers against the German lines in the battle of Metz, during the summer of 1918, the small FT-17 deployed a tactic that is evocative of that used in 1940 by the German Panzer divisions.

In many respects, the French spontaneously invented deployment principles – including the Blitzkrieg principle – and this symptom of victory is found in other areas too. Indeed, the 75mm anti-aircraft weapons mounted on trucks and stabilized by jacks by De Dion-Bouton in 1918 are surprisingly modern. But they paid for this modernity, as some of these arms were still in service in 1940 because of a lack of will among the politicians to invest in new equipment.

In 1918, the mechanization of the French Army was very advanced. While the army had only 220 motorized vehicles in 1914, and had to rely on the seizure of 80,000 civilian vehicles, sometimes with their drivers, by 1918 the army had hundreds of thousands of vehicles of all types – cars and especially trucks, tanks, and armoured cars.[15]

Changes to command and control, and the organization of the men in the front line

When the war moved into the trenches, army and divisional staffs of armies worked hard to produce new doctrine and manuals to support it. Their aim was to find a way to avoid as many unnecessary casualties as possible. The staff were not the bloodthirsty monsters described by the anti-militarist propaganda of the 1920s and 1930s, particularly in the wake of the emergence of the French Communist Party.

The field manuals issued on 3 January 1915, developed by those around Joffre, are full of eminently sensible instructions. They recommend meticulous artillery preparation and strong cooperation between the artillery and the infantry, in particular the posting of artillery observers to the front line so they are able to accurately observe the fall of shot and correct accordingly. This practice was first developed by Lieutenant-Colonel Samuel Bourguet, a gunner and an expert on combined arms warfare and liaising with the infantry, who was killed in the Champagne Offensive of September 1915. However, it took time for these principles to come down the chain of command and they were slow to be implemented. The attacks on Perthes (February–March 1915) on the Éparges and further east on the Hartmannsweilerkopf (January–May 1915) were carried out in the old manner and not according to the new manuals, which was partly due to the difficulty in changing set attitudes and partly due to a lack of resources.

The army's high command also developed considerably over the course of the war. By the end of the war, the General Headquarters was controlled by Major-General Buat, assisted by five generals. Since the spring of 1918, he had been stationed at Provins with 354 officers and 3,300 NCOs and men under his command. Throughout the war a number of new command functions were created within General Headquarters, such as the Bureau of the Health Service or the Bureau of Aeronautics.

By the end of 1917 Philippe Pétain, now head of the French Army, having restored the army's morale following the unfortunate April offensive on the Chemin des Dames, realized that it was essential to remove the stricture, more political than military, not to lose a metre of 'sacred Fatherland soil'. He believed it was better to lose ground than unduly sacrifice men. His instructions on 'defence in depth', which first emerged in 1915, were applied with success at the onset of the German offensive of March 1918.

As for the men, in 1918 the French infantry battalion, the unit that actually led the fight on the ground, had little in common with its 1914 counterpart. Its numbers were reduced, with barely 600 men compared with 800 in 1914. But it had gained in tactical complexity. The objective in 1918 was to expose as few men as possible to enemy fire when they advanced. Along with this came the rise of the small tactical unit, the half-platoon, composed of two sections, one consisting of grenadiers and the other one the machine-gun section that provided the necessary fire support; weapons had taken on the role of men. The infantrymen represented only 45 per cent of soldiers in 1918, while they were 67 per cent in 1914. In 1914, all infantrymen had the same role, but there soon emerged grenadiers, machine-gunners, 37mm gunmen, signallers, and telegraph operators. These men were all trained differently and specifically.

The growth of artillery also led to a corresponding increase in the number of gunners. While they represented 16 per cent of the French Army in 1914, they comprised 26 per cent in 1918. In contrast, the traditional cavalry horse was practically unheard of in 1918. A directive of Pétain at the end of 1917 states, 'The methods of fighting of dismounted cavalry are identical to those of the infantry.'[16]

It was not only in terms of weaponry that the French Army changed. Logistics and transport evolved considerably, so much so that in January 1917, as well as the three traditional staff functions of the French Army,[17] a fourth was added dedicated to issues of transport and supplies.

The year 1918 was both a return to the roots as well as a synthesis of the lessons learned in the war. Infantrymen left the trenches once more and regained the possibility of manoeuvre as in 1914, though in a much more cautious way. The heavy losses of the first summer of the war were still bitterly remembered. Offensive operations were lighter and there was no more striking in tight columns as before. Soldiers, more heavily armed than in 1914, now knew how to infiltrate instead of advancing by units of aligned men. However, there were no longer hasty assaults. The French infantryman, as is true of the English, American, or German, was now burdened down by the weight of his arms and especially his ammunition, of which he used far more than in 1914.

Soldiers could not be commanded in the same way in 1918 as in 1914. In 1915, Joffre continued to launch offensives to liberate the territory, but more importantly, to 'maintain the morale' of the army. New tactics and techniques were trialed which resulted in high blood loss. Finally, mutinies broke out that affected as many as one-third of the army. These rebellions were now seen as reflections of the complex developments occurring both in the French military and society. Since the 1789 revolution, the army had been experiencing contradictions that were difficult to resolve. The democratic principles asserted by the revolution were difficult to apply to an army at war. An army must be controlled and orders must be executed immediately and without discussion, or else any military operation will fail. Patriotism and a sense of obedience, long inculcated by French institutions – schools and the army – worked together on the eve of the war to promote obedience without hesitation as the most sacred duty of citizenship. But at the same time, the revival of egalitarianism was expressed, especially against leaders whose decisions were queried in the trenches. In 1914, Joseph Joffre led an army mainly composed of conscripts, more than 2 million men, with an iron fist. This grip saved the situation in August 1914 by preventing the retreat from becoming a debacle. The human cost was very high as about 500 men were executed by firing squads between 1914 and 1915.[18] However, this form of command was not possible in 1918. Military justice was radically reformed in 1916, and accused soldiers were given more opportunities to defend themselves for faltering in front of the enemy. Most death sentences were commuted to prison sentences. The vast protest movement of spring 1917 was related to the failure of the offensive on the Chemin des Dames. The high morale of the French Army preceding the offensive was destroyed by its comprehensive failure, leading to mutinies or perhaps more exactly what has been described as 'trench strikes'. Although recent research has shown that many more units of the French Army were involved than previously thought, it should be noted that almost no platoon or company commander – second or first lieutenant or captain – was attacked by the angry soldiers. Some generals were, however. The aim of the mutineers was to renegotiate the terms of acceptance of the war. Without going as far as accepting a negotiation – incompatible with operational military principles – French soldiers at least wanted to know what was asked of them. They wanted to be ordered more intelligently. Philippe Pétain, who succeeded Robert Nivelle, understood this although he also knew how to handle a discreet but firm repression. Thus, in four years, the citizen-soldier had changed into a soldier-citizen, agreeing to fight again and again, as long as his commanders explained to him what they wanted from him – something that they were not always able to do at the beginning of the war.

Even his appearance had changed. The soldier wearing a canvas kepi (cap), dark blue overcoat, and red trousers from 1914 to 1915 gave way to another, protected by a metal helmet thanks to the Superintendent-General Adrian, inspired by Burgundian helmets of the Middle Ages. His overcoat was 'horizon blue' for metropolitan troops and 'khaki' for colonial troops.

By the end of World War I, the French Army had found a new coherence, built gradually in the trenches. It had positioned itself clearly as the best army in the world. It endured the largest impact of the war on the Western Front and was able to provide reinforcements where necessary, both to the Americans during the operations of St Mihiel in September 1918, as well as to the British troops attacked in the spring of the same year. The 1918 army barely resembled that of 1914, whether in its administrative structures – its regiments had three battalions instead of the four of 1916 – in its arms, or its equipment. It had evolved tremendously in terms of its mentality. It learnt to waive its 1914 convictions, through blood, sweat, and tears. It was able to implement the means of victory through innovation and new tactics. But the French Army was also exhausted at the end of the war as, apart from the Serbians, it was the army that had experienced the greatest losses as a percentage of its total manpower. And above all it was convinced at the end of the war that it had invented ways to win any war in the future. In the words of General Robert Doughty, a true 'ideological straitjacket' reigned in the 1920s and 1930s that froze French military beliefs in the same state that they were in during 1918, making the triumph of the Great War a Pyrrhic victory.[19]

CHAPTER 7

GERMAN TACTICAL DOCTRINE AND THE DEFENSIVE BATTLE ON THE WESTERN FRONT

Dr Matthias Strohn

On 3 August 1914 the war in the West began when German troops crossed the borders into Belgium and Luxembourg. The troops were full of hope and confidence that the war would be won quickly and that the 'boys would be home again by Christmas'. However, problems soon became apparent. Logistics proved difficult and the enemy's resistance was stronger than anticipated. After the withdrawal from the Marne and the failed offensives in Flanders the Germans had to acknowledge that the war would not be won in a swift campaign.

As a consequence, and to release troops for the endangered Eastern Front, the Chief of the General Staff, Erich von Falkenhayn, ordered the taking up of defensive positions along the entire front line in the West on 25 November. In his memoirs, Falkenhayn stated that this was the moment when 'Trench warfare in the real sense, with all its horrors, began.'[1] Falkenhayn realized that the new form of warfare imposed different fighting conditions on the soldiers. He accepted that trench warfare in the West was not a temporary measure owing to the exhaustion of both sides, but a logical consequence of modern military equipment and technology. Despite pre-war beliefs, morale had not prevailed over machine guns. Accordingly, Falkenhayn concluded that a major breakthrough would be possible only after the introduction of new military equipment. In November 1914, he told the Italian military attaché:

> We were all blind. The Russo-Japanese War presented an opportunity for us to learn about the tactical consequences of the new weapons and combat conditions. Instead we believed that the trench warfare that was characteristic of this war was due to logistical problems and national traditions of the belligerents... The force of the defensive is unbelievable.[2]

However, this did not mean that Falkenhayn was the driving force behind the changes that now occurred. Rather it seems that only he accepted and acknowledged an unchangeable situation and that the development was driven from the bottom of the command chain upwards. This meant that the orders to prepare for the defence had different consequences for different units. For instance, VII Reserve-Korps was almost not affected, since it had hardly participated in the 'war of movement in the real sense of the word'.[3] Other units, like III Armee-Korps, which had formed the right flank of 1. Armee, had adopted trench warfare as a necessity before Falkenhayn ordered the changes. On 20 November, General von Lochow, the corps commander, issued a directive to his troops saying, 'The overall situation forced us to establish positions here. Now, we are expected to hold out in the enemy artillery fire and to wring every foot of ground from a tough enemy ("*einem zähen Gegner jeden Fuß breit abzuringen*").'[4]

Nevertheless, Falkenhayn's order clarified the situation for the soldiers on the ground. Until now, they had been unsure about the further conduct of operations and this had impacted negatively on the tactical situation of the troops. The war diary of 4. Pionierkompanie, which was attached to XII Reserve-Korps, stated as early as 20 September 1914 that 'simple obstacles – trip wire – have been constructed. Further obstacles cannot be built, because not even the division knows whether the position has to be defended or whether an attack will be launched.'[5] Similarly, the regimental history of Infanterie-Regiment Nr. 13 from the Westphalian city of Münster complained about the defensive positions which the regiment occupied in the vicinity of Neuve-Chapelle in early December 1914. These positions had remained unchanged since late October. They were unfavourable for the troops and 'had not been chosen in accordance with the rules of the art of war', since it had been believed that these positions would only have to be manned for a short period of time before the next offensive.[6]

Once Falkenhayn had accepted the situation in the West, he enforced the construction of defensive positions, and the troops began to feel an increasing pressure from the top to speed up the erection of defensive works. Hand in hand with this went the establishment of a more permanent infrastructure that could support the new defensive layout. In the early days of trench warfare, the men of Infanterie-Regiment Nr. 13 had been forced to take the needed materials from destroyed houses, but in January 1915, the battalions established artisans' workshops that provided the units with obstacles, sand-bags, and the like. When these facilities could not meet the ever-increasing demands from the front-line troops, the division, the brigade, and the regiment established similar workshops, and in April 1915 the regiment began incorporating concrete shelters into the defensive line.

Falkenhayn ordered that not a single inch of territory won was to be ceded to the enemy – even if doing so would result in better placed positions. He argued that any loss of territory, which had been conquered by the troops, was bad for the soldiers' morale, and a propaganda victory for the enemy.

In compliance with the 1906 infantry manual, which was used as the tactical training manual in the early stages of the war, it was ordered that only one defensive position with little depth had to be erected.[7] Concentrating the bulk of the troops in only one trench would ensure that the defender's maximum firepower could be brought into effect when the enemy attacked. At this stage of the war, the overall firepower of the infantry still rested with the individual soldier; the real effect of the machine gun would be felt only later in the war, when these weapons became increasingly available. Additional strongholds in the rear were acceptable, mainly to assemble reserve troops. Positions forward of the main line of resistance were, however, seen as pointless or even harmful. Troops deployed in these positions would make it harder for the soldiers in the main line of resistance to bring their full small-arms fire into effect, because they could hit their own troops deployed in front of them. Moreover, these positions would sooner or later be overrun by the enemy; this would lead to 'partial defeats' that would weaken the defender's strength and would have a negative effect on morale.

Offensive spirit was very much at the centre of the doctrine and it advocated local attacks on the enemy lines in regular intervals. This would not only keep up morale, but Falkenhayn also reckoned that the danger of possible German attacks would force the enemy to deploy large numbers of troops in the trenches, thereby reducing the number of reserve units that the enemy might otherwise be able to deploy in an offensive action. These troops could then be engaged by the German artillery, causing casualties among the enemy. The fact that this approach also worked the other way round was obviously not a reason for Falkenhayn to change his attitude towards the conduct of the defensive battle.

In 1915, the strategic point of main effort was shifted to the East and the Germans achieved victories in Poland and the breakthrough at Gorlice-Tarnów while fighting defensively in the West, trying to hold the front against several Allied offensives. It became obvious that modifications and improvements to the defence system were necessary. In particular, the autumn battle in the Champagne, in which the French came close to breaking the German defences, had a considerable impact on Falkenhayn and the *Oberste Heeresleitung* (supreme army command or OHL). In October 1915, the general staff issued the *Gesichtspunkte für den Stellungskrieg* (Aspects of Positional Warfare).[8] Here, Falkenhayn stated that the defensive systems had to be expanded, so that they could be defended with a minimum of soldiers, at least in theory a radical shift from the initial 1914 orders and guidelines. To achieve this, a second line of defence had to be erected behind the first one, each of which had to be defendable independently. On certain sectors of the front, which were highly likely to be attacked, three or more lines might be suitable. Every line had to consist of two trenches, so that four to six trenches had to be defended altogether. The second line of defence should be erected so far to the rear that the enemy would not be able to hit it with concentrated artillery fire and that an attack on the second line of defence demanded a new deployment of the enemy's infantry and artillery.

Nevertheless, the first line of resistance was still regarded as the main line of defence (*Hauptkampflinie* or HKL) which had to be held against the enemy. It was here that, in a perfect scenario, the enemy's attack should be beaten back. To achieve this, Falkenhayn still demanded that the first line of resistance be strongly manned in order to achieve the highest concentration of firepower possible. This makes clear that Falkenhayn still believed that establishing defensive positions in the rear would have a negative impact on the soldiers' morale, and that, eventually, the first line of defence was still the most important one. Only if the troops managed to hold on to this line would they avoid giving up ground that had been paid for by the lives of many German soldiers.

In 1916, the OHL put the emphasis of operations on the Western Front again and the Germans launched the offensive at Verdun. However, this battle did not achieve its strategic aim of 'bleeding the French to death',[9] or of breaking the deadlock of trench warfare by forcing the British to launch a premature offensive in the northern sector of the front which, as the Germans hoped, would eventually lead to mobile warfare and the defeat of the British Expeditionary Force. The battle of the Somme, which was launched by the British and French forces on 1 July 1916, quickly deteriorated into trench warfare in its most horrible form. The Allies could not breach the German defensive line, but the losses sustained by the Germans forced them to rethink their guidelines for combat in positional warfare. It was obvious that the changes introduced in the *Gesichtspunkte* were not sufficient to prevent high casualties. The principle that ground should not be surrendered and that immediate counter-attacks were seen as crucial resulted in a dense deployment of forces in the main line of defence. General von Below, commander of 1. Armee on the Somme, summed up his experiences of the fighting on the Somme:

> In spite of 'defended area', the fighting must take place in the foremost line… During the battle of the Somme … every man was obliged to fight at that point at which he was stationed; the enemy's line of advance could only lead over his dead body. Army Headquarters believes that it was owing to this firm determination to fight with which every leader was inspired, that the enemy, in spite of superior numbers, bled to death in front of the serried ranks of our soldiers.[10]

As a result of this approach, casualties were very high, nearly 500,000 men, and the OHL realized that Germany could not cope with such casualty rates for long.

The lessons of trench warfare and the defence in depth

When Paul von Hindenburg took over command from Falkenhayn on 29 August 1916 and Erich Ludendorff became *Generalquartermeister* of the army, the high casualty rates were the most pressing problems for the German Army. As Ludendorff stated in his memoirs:

> The loss of ground to date appeared to me of little importance in itself. We could stand that; but the question how this, and the progressive falling-off of our fighting power of which it was symptomatic, was to be prevented, was of immense importance. It was just as necessary to have a clear idea of our fighting capacity as to know whether our tactical views were still sound. The first was an easy matter, the second of extreme difficulty.[11]

Hindenburg expressed his concerns in a memorandum on the future conduct of war which he issued on 22 November 1916.[12] War had developed into a stalemate, he argued, for which the army had not been trained. Moreover, Hindenburg had to acknowledge that the French and the British had improved their fighting skills a great deal and he stated that they were actually becoming superior to the Germans in the conduct of war. One reason for this was, according to Hindenburg, that the infantry had suffered heavy casualties and that it was doubtful whether the infantry's fighting power could be sustained. The only solution for the numerically inferior German troops was the increased use of materiel and the adoption of a more flexible approach to the conduct of the defensive battle. The question of whether an operation could be regarded as a success or a failure had now to be measured by the proportion of losses in men and materiel rather than the gain or loss of territory.

To adapt battle tactics to these realities of warfare the OHL issued the regulation *Grundsätze für die Führung in der Abwehrschlacht im Stellungskriege* (Principles of Leadership in the Defensive Battle in Position Warfare) on 1 December 1916.[13] The manual provided general guidance for the conduct of the defensive battle and, together with subsequent editions and adaptations, it would remain the German doctrine of defensive warfare for the rest of the war. The use of *matériel* instead of soldiers was the main principle of the new directive: the aim was to exhaust the enemy and to bleed him to death while Germany's forces were to be spared. The increased importance of *matériel* becomes clear when one looks at the amount of machine guns available in the German armies. In 1915, the armies comprised 8,000 machine guns, 1,400 of which were weapons captured from the enemy. In 1918, it is estimated that 100,000 machine guns were available.

The new doctrine advocated a more flexible defence. For this, the battlefield was now divided into two zones. The first was the forward zone, which would usually be surrendered to the enemy after a short period of resistance. This area stretched from the enemy lines to one's own main defensive positions. Under certain circumstances, this zone could also be evacuated without any resistance, so that the enemy would quickly enter the second zone, the area of main resistance. This zone was a deep area into which the enemy would be dragged and in which he would exhaust himself. Within this zone, often several kilometres deep, neatly created trenches had given way to dugouts and concrete strongholds which served as the corset-bones of the defence. Resistance was to be conducted in a flexible manner, and it was expected that some defensive positions would be lost to the enemy in the course of the battle. This was not a major threat, as long as the German forces were able to keep the initiative and to mount counter-attacks which would eventually drive the enemy forces out of these positions.

Diagram of a defensive position

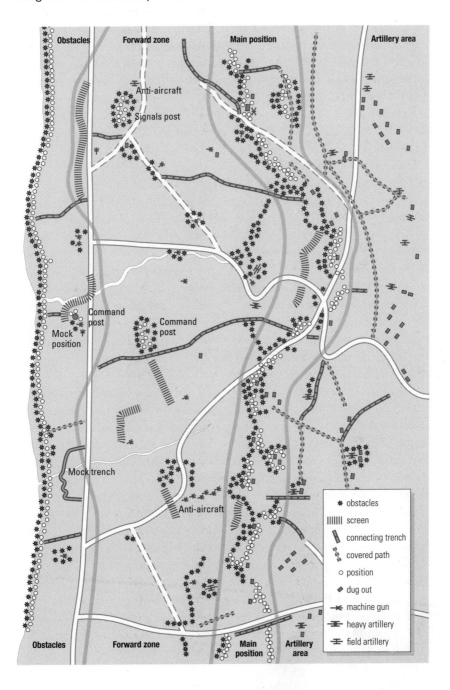

Obstacles Forward zone Main position Artillery area

Anti-aircraft

Signals post

Command post

Command post

Mock position

Mock trench

Anti-aircraft

Obstacles Forward zone Main position Artillery area

✳	obstacles
‖‖‖‖	screen
▨	connecting trench
⋮	covered path
○	position
◆	dug out
⊣⊢	machine gun
⊨	heavy artillery
⊨	field artillery

The reality of trench warfare had shown the high importance of artillery fire. Previous doctrine had caused the Germans to strengthen that part of the battlefield that was within the range of Allied artillery and where the enemy applied their maximum power to achieve a penetration or breakthrough – that is, on the forward edge. With the new German doctrine, the Allied concentration of firepower missed its purpose as the forward edge was held by relatively few German troops. By defending a deep space rather than only the first trench-line, the infantry disappeared from the enemy's line of direct sight, which led to the so-called 'emptiness of the battlefield'. Moreover, the enemy artillery had to shell the whole space of German defence, thus decreasing its effectiveness and increasing the amount of shells needed for adequate support of the infantry attack. Additionally, the enemy artillery had to move forward across the devastated battlefield during the attack to support the infantry in its ongoing attack. While the artillery was moving forward it was not available to support the infantry in its ongoing attack and to soften up the German defences. Moreover, target acquisition would become more difficult in this part of the battle, further decreasing the effectiveness of the artillery. All this would contribute to the enemy's strength being absorbed as the attack progressed. The attacker's relative power would deteriorate and the advance would become increasingly confused and weak. German resistance, on the other hand, would strengthen, because more and more units would be available in the rear areas of the defensive zone and because the Germans would be able to bring up more reserves to the endangered front line.

The experience of fighting against numerically superior enemy troops had shaped the general staff's views, and the *Grundsätze Abwehrschlacht* stressed that it was not numerical superiority that was crucial for this new method of defensive warfare, but 'the energy of the will', the cooperation of all branches of the army, and quick decisions and actions. Thus, when the enemy soldiers approached the defensive zone the German artillery was expected to lay down a barrage between the first enemy wave and the following enemy troops, trying to isolate the former from the rest of the forces. If this was achieved it was expected that the German troops would launch immediate hasty and local counter-attacks, without waiting for explicit orders from superiors. If necessary, the soldiers were expected to cross the enemy's artillery fire before engaging the enemy in hand-to-hand combat. However, if the soldiers within the battle zone were not successful in pushing the enemy back, a full-scale deliberate counter-attack with reserve troops would have to be carried out. This had to happen as quickly as possible, while the enemy was still busy organizing its defence in the unknown network of trenches, strongholds, and dugouts. Every soldier who was still fighting in the combat zone had to be conscious of the fact that his resistance would hinder the enemy's advance and would therefore contribute to the successful counter-attack. This applied especially to individuals or groups of soldiers that had been surrounded by the enemy and who were expected to continue the fight instead of surrendering.

The new doctrine was put to the test in 1917, when the British started their offensives near Arras, attacking Kronprinz Rupprecht's army group. After the usual preparatory bombardment, the British and Empire forces went over the top on 9 April. In spite of the new doctrine and the organization of the German forces in depth, things did not go very well for the Germans that day. Obviously, it took much time for the leaders to understand the new principles and some of them were not willing to adapt to the new form of defence, as it stood in contrast to traditional views concerning the importance of holding ground.

Moreover, the Germans experienced difficulties in coordinating their defence and fighting a combined arms battle. Artillery did not always manage to provide timely support for hasty and local counter-attacks, and counter-attack divisions had not been moved up close enough to the battlefield. Ludendorff was outraged and feared that the training conducted during the previous months had been futile. He sent for officers who had taken part in the battle, and by talking to them and telephoning front-line units he gained the impression that the principles laid down by the OHL were sound. It was not the new doctrine that had caused the crisis, but the inadequate training of the troops in flexible defence and the consequent failure in the application of the new doctrine's principles. Ludendorff insisted that the new regulations were adopted and put into action without any further delay.

He was to be proven right. On 14 April, the British launched further attacks to expand the salient created by their initial assault. This time the Germans were prepared. Ludendorff had sent Oberst Fritz von Loßberg, an expert on defensive warfare, to the endangered front and he had used the scarce time to reorganize the German defence. Thus, the fighting of 14 April resembled a perfect scenario for the new German concept of defence. In the sector of VII British Corps, British battalions attacked at 0530hrs behind the usual creeping barrage that was supposed to suppress the German defenders. However, German artillery became active, too, and hit the attacking soldiers, who were forced to take cover. This slowed down their advance and separated the infantry from the creeping barrage. As a consequence the German defenders had enough time to get into position once the British creeping barrage had gone over them. The Germans met the attackers with a shower of bullets and the British troops were surprised to encounter small-arms fire from German reverse slope positions and strongholds that had not been destroyed by the British artillery. German counter-attack units closed in on the confused remainders of the British advance. By 0800hrs, after having lost two-thirds of the strength from their lead units, the British were back at their starting line.

Only two days after this failed attack, the French launched an offensive at the Chemin des Dames as part of the Neville offensives. Again, the outcome was disastrous. The infantry was unable to keep up with the 'insane pace of the barrage',[14] because French commanders had tried to outdo each other during training for the offensive in establishing the fastest creeping barrage. Just like on 14 April against the British, this enabled the Germans to prepare themselves for the attacking infantry once the creeping barrage had passed. As the French infantry advanced into the battle zone, well-concealed German machine-gun strongpoints opened fire on the French from all directions, even from the rear. The German artillery was prepared as well. The Germans had captured a set of orders that described the French offensive plan, a document that contained 'matter of extraordinary value', as Kronprinz Wilhelm put it.[15] Thus, the Germans knew about the French preparatory firing plans and the German guns kept silent during the French artillery bombardment that was supposed to soften up the German defences. Not encountering enemy artillery fire, the French wrongly concluded that they had silenced the German guns and French assault units, amassed in the front areas, often did not take the precaution of digging in. The German artillery suddenly opened fire on the French forces, causing heavy casualties. The offensive developed into a disaster for the French: during the first weeks of the offensive, the French suffered 35,000 dead and, during the entire campaign, casualties reached the number of 270,000 killed, wounded, or taken prisoner. Other battles had resulted in similar blood-tolls, but the high expectations put into this offensive meant that the failure resulted in great disappointment and led to mutinies in some units of the French Army in 1917.

The major British campaign after Nivelle's failure was the Third Battle of Ypres, 'probably the most controversial campaign in British military history'.[16] Once again, Oberst von Loßberg was sent to the centre of action. Under his guidance, the German defence did not break, even though the terrain in Flanders did not favour the use of the elastic defence in depth. Moreover, the high level of groundwater made it impossible to dig in deeply. The German answer to these problems was concrete, and they built thousands of concrete machine-gun and artillery positions. These could only be destroyed by direct artillery hits, but Allied reconnaissance, which would have been necessary for this, was hampered by fog, rain, and clouds, which were also responsible for the fact that the battle took place in a 'viscous, muddy element', as Ernst Jünger, a war volunteer and arguably the most famous German writer of World War I, called it.[17]

However, the British managed to achieve some success. They introduced a more flexible infantry tactic, which was based on so-called all-arms platoons. These small units incorporated machine guns, rifle-bearing soldiers, and experts in explosives. These flexible and independent units attacked the German concrete positions, causing high casualties among the Germans. Moreover, the staff of Second British Army under the command of General Plumer had studied the German elastic defence and had come to the conclusion that only methodical attacks for limited objects stood a good chance of success, and, having observed the qualities of defensive firepower, they argued for the adoption of the 'bite and hold' tactic. The aim of this tactic was to 'bite out' a piece of the enemy's front line and 'hold' it against the enemy's counter-attacks. Thus, the defenders would become the attackers and vice versa. By letting the Germans attack, the British believed that they would be able to inflict heavier casualties on the Germans than they themselves would have to suffer. One big problem for the British was that they tended to bite off more than they could chew, thus making it easier for the German counter-attacks to succeed. Nevertheless, the new approach adopted by the British seemed to outwit the Germans at first. From 20 September 1917 until 4 October, Second British Army managed to launch successful limited attacks, inflicting heavy casualties on the Germans, and Ludendorff had to admit: 'The enemy managed to adapt himself to our method of employing counter-attack divisions. There were no more attacks with unlimited objectives, such as General Nivelle had made in the Aisne-Champagne Battle. He [the enemy] was ready for our counter-attacks and prepared for them by exercising restraint in the exploitation of success.'[18]

As a consequence of the new British method of attack, the Germans started placing more troops in the forward positions again, and they were able to repulse the last British attack at Poelkapelle on 9 October which became a disaster for the British. However, the deployment of more forces in forward positions again resulted in the usual high casualties among the defender.

Overall, the introduction of a new defence doctrine resulted in the Allies gaining very little ground in 1917, while suffering very high losses in men and materiel. The Germans had suffered considerably, too, but they had preserved enough strength not only to continue the war into 1918, but also to knock Russia out of the war. The German elastic defence in depth on the Western Front had proven its value, and, without it, it seems at least doubtful whether Germany would have had enough reserves to achieve victory in the East and to launch offensives in the West in 1918. Kronprinz Wilhelm was convinced that had the German Army not changed its defensive doctrine, it 'would not have come victoriously through the great defensive battles of 1917'.[19]

The final act: defeat in the West

Having fought defensively on the Western Front for most of the war, the defeat of Russia made it possible for the Germans to take the offensive in the West again. A quick victory was needed, because US troops were arriving en masse in the European theatre of war, and Ludendorff knew that time was not working in favour of the Germans. After several month of preparation, the Germans launched the Michael Offensive on 21 March 1918.

At first, Ludendorff's plan seemed to succeed. German forces shattered the British Fifth Army near St Quentin and broke through the British lines into open country on the first day of the offensive. By 23 March, the Germans had achieved a 40-mile breach in Allied lines. However, high casualties and the exhaustion of the troops slowed down the offensive. On the first day of the offensive alone the Germans lost approximately 40,000 men. Moreover, it proved difficult to move reinforcements, artillery, and supplies to the new battle line. Consequent attacks in different sectors of the Western Front resulted in a further exhaustion of German troops, but not in the much hoped for defeat of the enemy forces. Moreover, after nearly four years of trench warfare, the offensives revealed deficiencies in the training for mobile warfare, although Ludendorff had tried to remedy this by intensive training behind the front. In particular the young non-commissioned officers and junior officers did not have enough experience with mission-oriented battle tactics and were lacking basic tactical knowledge for mobile warfare. Contact between infantry and artillery was often broken, the artillery was not able to follow the infantry over the devastated battlefield fast enough, and the infantry still often attacked in line or in dense, rather than in open, formations.

When the offensives in the West had failed, the power of resistance began to decrease. On 21 July 1918, Loßberg, now promoted to *Generalmajor*, sent a report to Ludendorff stating that the German forces had been weakened considerably by Allied attacks. In some sectors of the front, the companies were 20 to 30 men strong when the nominal strength stood at 150. The artillery had hardly any shells left, so that the infantry could not expect much support from the sister arm in the following defensive battle. Moreover, the *Sturmtruppen*, the elite of the army that had been deployed as the first wave in the attacks, had suffered heavy casualties. The remaining troops were of considerably lower quality, and it was clear that these units did not have the same will and ability to fight as the young and experienced *Sturmtruppen*. Finally, the fact that the offensives had failed also had a deep impact on German morale. The soldiers had been told that one last effort was needed to bring about victory in the West, but they had to realize that this was not the case, and that the casualties had seemingly been suffered in vain. Describing the mood among his soldiers after the failed offensives, Ernst Jünger stated that they 'fight with the old reliability, but without expectations, I would like to say without hope and only because it is their duty… One can observe an exhaustion in expression and posture, which is also visible in the style of dying.'[20] The overall grim situation was made worse by the occurrence of the influenza epidemic, which hit the weakened German soldiers particularly hard. The first epidemic that occurred in June and July infected over half a million German soldiers with the virus, basically making them unfit for any military duty. The company of Ernst Jünger was also affected, and to him the virus was more alarming and dangerous than enemy artillery fire. He stated that the influenza made 'its victim unable to fight and it wears him down over night. Almost every morning we have to send back two or three men, who sit in their dug-outs apathetically and feverishly, and who we will not see again in the near future.'[21]

Despite these problems, the German Army did not collapse until late October or early November. The fact that wide parts of the army fought on can be seen in the estimate of Generalleutnant von Kuhl, who stated that the army lost a further 420,000 dead between 18 July and the armistice.[22] Nevertheless, these losses, combined with the inadequate reinforcements sent from Germany, resulted in a massive deterioration of combat power. XXXXXI Armee-Korps, part of 2. Armee that fought in the Le Quesnoy area, reported on 12 October 1918 that the infantry combat strength of the entire corps amounted to 2,683 men with 83 heavy and 79 light machine guns.[23] The corps consisted of seven and a half divisions, each of which had a nominal strength of between 11,000 and 13,000 men (even though the infantry combat strength would have been somewhat lower). The corps had reserves of 2,050 men and covered a front line of 4 miles. In early November, information supplied by the units to the OHL revealed that along the entire Western Front scarcely a dozen divisions could be classified as fully or partially combat ready. The then Major Ludwig Beck, later Chief of the General Staff of the Wehrmacht, summed up the situation by saying that the front line was a mere 'spider's web of fighters'.[24]

These factors caused immense problems in the defensive battles that now occurred. In early July, Ludendorff had still deemed it important to point out to the commanding officers that the defence in depth had to be upheld and that the soldiers should not be deployed in one single trench.[25] However, this perception now changed. The heavy casualties suffered during the offensives and decreasing morale and quality of the troops made it seem more appropriate to return to the more traditional – and, importantly, easier – form of defence.

On 4 September Ludendorff issued an order that made the changes clear to the troops. The main line of resistance had to be held again at all costs, and counter-attacks had to be launched only if they had good prospects of success.[26] In contradiction to earlier doctrine from before the war, Ludendorff stated that sealing off the occupied territory and isolating the enemy troops would normally be the preferable solution. These changes were clearly borne out of desperation, but Ludendorff tried to see the positive in this development as well. He argued that standing fast and not surrendering ground would have a devastating effect on the enemy and his morale, since he had got used to occupying some ground before encountering strong resistance.

The new tactical guidelines were reinforced by a number of orders issued by the OHL in the following weeks. The character and the intention of these are clear: it was of paramount importance to preserve one's own fighting power on both the physical and psychological levels. 'Economy of force' and 'morale of the troops' became the centres of gravity around which fighting on the tactical level had to revolve. All these points and latest developments were clear indicators for the decreasing fighting power and morale of the German armies. By November 1918, Germany was truly beaten even though no Allied soldier had set foot on German territory. Despite this outcome the lessons of the war reinforced the army's belief in the superiority of its flexible and mobile approach on both the tactical and the operational levels, which they would put to the test again in just over 20 years.

CHAPTER 8

THE ROLLERCOASTER OF AUSTRIA-HUNGARY'S WORLD WAR I EXPERIENCE

Professor Dr Lothar Höbelt

Austria-Hungary's war experience differs significantly from the stalemate on the Western Front. It was characterized by dramatic shifts and often somewhat paradoxical developments.

The Third Balkan War

Austria-Hungary's part in unleashing World War I was obviously crucial. All the other powers had their own reasons to join in or at least let it happen, but the initiative clearly was an Austro-Hungarian one. Contrary to interpretations that see the war as the apogee of 19th-century nationalism, Vienna's declaration of war was directed against nationalism – and perfected by a group of aristocratic diplomats who were as cosmopolitan as possible. Among top decision-makers the only clear-cut nationalist, Hungarian Prime Minister Graf István Tisza, was the only war sceptic.[1] In summer 1914, the decision to go to war seemed almost inevitable, for a paradoxical reason. Austria-Hungary opted for war because it could no longer afford costly mobilizations – both in terms of money and prestige – that ended in hollow diplomatic victories (as had twice happened in 1913). Tisza's alternative to 'keep your powder dry and bide your time' until Serbia's Balkan rivals, the Bulgarians and Albanians, were ready to tear Serbia to pieces, offered no ready-made solutions to an immediate crisis. Considerations of prestige forbade the Empire from reacting with a stiff upper lip to an act of terrorism like the assassination of the heir apparent. This time it was going to be all or nothing.

To some extent the Austro-Hungarian declaration of war was born of desperation. Franz Conrad, the Austro-Hungarian Chief of Staff, had been famously trigger-happy during previous crises. In 1914 he saw only a 50-50 chance of victory but felt that he was simply unable to argue against war now. In military terms, Austria-Hungary was ill-prepared for a big, and above all, a long war. In terms of wealth and per capita income, Austria-Hungary lagged behind Germany and France, if not Russia and Italy. For once, though, it was not money that was the limiting factor in the arms race that Austria had only joined at a very late date. Two decades of domestic political gridlock had left their mark on the Habsburg armed forces. Between 1889 and 1912, despite massive population growth, the annual contingent of recruits had never been augmented. As a result, unlike all the other warring powers (except Britain), Austria-Hungary had trained less than half of its manpower and could not rely on any cadres for reserve divisions. As a result, brigades of barely trained so-called *Ersatz* reservists were fed into battle as cannon fodder. Thus, if the Austro-Hungarians held fast to the concept of a short war, they did so instinctively because this was the only war they were equipped to fight.

In 1914, the war plans of all the great powers failed. Yet, Austria-Hungary had the dubious distinction of being the only one to mismanage the basics of the mobilization plan: get there 'firstest with the mostest'. Military logic dictated a concentration of forces in the decisive theatre of war against Russia; political imperatives pushed for a show of strength in the Balkans. The result was a far from tidy compromise. Because of a last-minute change of plan, one army out of six was left idling while the supposedly crucial first battles were fought.[2] Austria's operations against Russia were supposed to be a holding action until the Germans had beaten the French. During those first few weeks, Austro-Hungarian morale was high, suicidally so. Austria even won a few battles in Poland, notably at Komarow, where they claimed to have almost surrounded the opposing Russian army. Yet, in Eastern Galicia, a lack of rail links or fortified defensive positions prevented the Austro-Hungarians from using interior lines the way the Germans did in East Prussia. British military historian and strategist Sir Basil Liddell Hart sums it up rather well in his judgement of Conrad as

Planned concentration areas in Central Europe, 1914

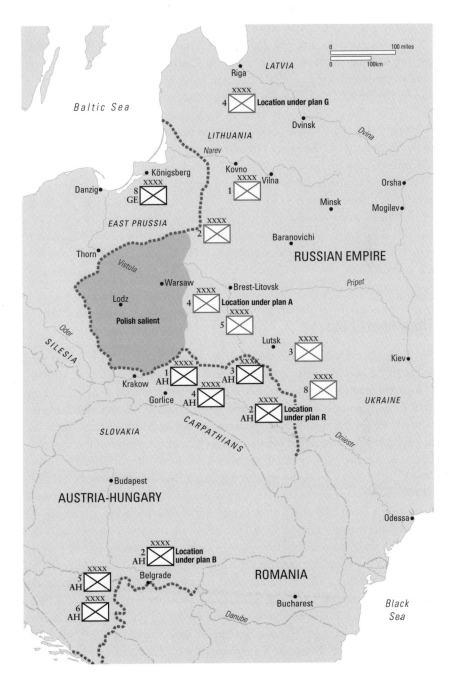

'The Man who juggled with armies – and broke them.'[3] Sooner or later, Russian pressure from the East forced a hurried retreat from Lemberg on 11 September – two days after the German retreat from the Marne.

According to the pre-war models, with no big flow of reinforcements coming in from the West, this is when the Central Powers should have been crushed between France and the Russian steamroller. Tactical and logistical factors combined to provide the first of many unexpected turns during the Great War. The machine gun gave an unexpected boost to the defence. In the West, the advancing Germans had found it more difficult than the French to use the railways to shift forces from one wing of their armies to the other; in the East, those were the difficulties the Russians faced. After a crisis of nerves in late October, the Austro-Hungarians managed to stabilize their front, even extending a protective screen in front of Prussian Silesia. Pilsudski, the leader of the Polish volunteers fighting with the Austro-Hungarians, took part in a battle (Limanowa–Lapanow) that stopped the Russians in front of Krakow in early December. The battle also probably saved Conrad – of all the chiefs of the general staffs of 1914, Conrad, who faced the worst crisis, was the only one to keep his job until 1917.[4]

Their finest hour

Yet, the political outlook remained bleak. In the South, with a background of rough numerical parity against Serb and Montenegrin forces, the Austro-Hungarians had briefly captured Belgrade on 2 December but were pushed out of Serbia again the week after.[5] In the North, even if Vienna and Budapest seemed safe for the time being, almost all of Galicia had been lost. Above all, the wounded giant attracted predators eager to make the most of the situation. Foremost among the potential aggressors were two formal allies, Italy and Romania. Already during the crisis in autumn 1914, Romania was supposed to have been close to declaring war. Unless Austro-Hungarian fortunes revived dramatically, both Italy and Romania were certainly expected to do so once the campaigning season started in May. In the short term at least, Turkey's entry did little to improve Austria's position. For the Germans, the events of 1914 meant that they did not win outright; for the Austro-Hungarians, it looked like defeat.

The impending crisis of the expected Italo-Romanian *coup dê grace* in the spring also threatened to poison relations between the two partners. Germans pleaded with the Austro-Hungarians that they should not content themselves with bribing individual politicians but buy off their neighbours with wholesale offers of territory. If Trieste or Transylvania were considered sacrosanct, parts of the Tyrol or of the Bukovina could still be ceded. Austria was clearly reluctant to follow that sort of advice. If anything, Vienna was willing to reward active collaboration, not mere neutrality. But the Germans insisted the Austro-Hungarians had to start bidding. If concessions would help the Austro-Hungarians survive the war, they were well worth the price. After all, once the Central Powers had won, the Austro-Hungarians could always try to punish their unfaithful ally. That possibility, however, was not lost on the Italians, either. Thus, it is unlikely that earlier and more generous offers could have averted the Italian declaration of war.[6]

In the meantime, though, Germany increased its pressure on the Austro-Hungarians by all means fair or foul. But the old emperor remained stubborn. It was during this period that he muttered that Austria would go down honourably rather than stoop to treacherous bargaining. In January 1915, Foreign Secretary Graf Leopold Berchtold, who was prepared to go along with German hints, was replaced by Graf István Burian, who earned a well-deserved reputation for long-winded intransigence. The maximum he was prepared to offer was the Trentino – to be handed over after the war, though. He took the fatalistic view that the neutrals would only enter the war once they were certain of Austro-Hungarian defeat. Starting from the assumption that the Italians saw through the dubious nature of the Austro-Hungarian offers, that was not a mistaken view in itself. Yet, the unfortunate result of Burian's insistence on a stiff upper lip was a series of counter-productive Austro-Hungarian offensives during the winter, undertaken for no other reason than to impress the neutrals with Austria's continued prowess.[7]

On 22 March, the fortress of Przemysl – sometimes called the Stalingrad of World War I – surrendered, with 120,000 Austro-Hungarians being taken prisoner. Gloom set in. Once the Italians entered the war, they could be in Vienna within six weeks, the German Chief of Staff Falkenhayn predicted. In return for the Austro-Hungarians finally agreeing to go through the motions of humouring the Italians, Falkenhayn released eight divisions from the Western Front, equipped with the sort of know-how acquired by an experience of warfare that was far more high-tech than anything yet witnessed in the East. Thus, the Central Powers made good use of the 'window of opportunity' until Kitchener's 'New Armies' arrived on the Continent. On 2 May the offensive of Gorlice-Tarnów started. In military terms, it turned into the most successful single campaign of the war: within three months, the Central Powers had conquered all of Poland. In political terms, Tarnów came too late to influence the Italian decision for war but sufficed to scare off the Romanians, who were at loggerheads over war-aims with the Russians anyway.

On 23 May, Italy declared war on Austria-Hungary. Once more, conventional wisdom had it that Austria-Hungary would now finally be crushed by three, or maybe even four, opponents. Once again, conventional wisdom turned out to be wrong. The Austro-Hungarian Empire would not last a thousand years, but the summer of 1915 turned out to be its 'finest hour'. The Italians were stopped right at the border; they enjoyed a two-to-one advantage in men but probably had fewer machine guns than the Austro-Hungarians. (The Italian orders from Britain had been stopped after the outbreak of war.[8]) The Balkan theatre was almost completely denuded of fighting divisions in favour of the Isonzo front; the Serbs, hit by a cholera epidemic and unwilling to help their Italian rivals, reacted by invading Albania rather than Bosnia. In the North, though, after briefly flirting with all the possible alternatives, Conrad and Falkenhayn decided to continue their thrust into Russian Poland rather than send more than a couple of divisions south. That decision paid off: on 22 June Lemberg was recovered; on 5 August Warsaw fell. If the Germans provided the cutting edge of the advance, the Austro-Hungarians could still claim the majority of the troops involved were theirs.

Euphoria, part I: Bulgarian arms and Romanian grain

Military success in the East was followed by a diplomatic triumph in the Balkans. If the Austro-Hungarians had complained about blackmail by the Italians or Romanians, the bidding was nowhere more intense than in the case of Bulgaria. It came close to a public auction when Prime Minister Radoslavov declared the rival offers during a press conference. As the victim of the Second Balkan War, Bulgaria was a potential camp follower of the Central Powers, but then it also had claims against Turkey. If given an extra inducement by the cession of Greek or Serb territory, Bulgarians might yet throw in their lot with the Allies. A British breakthrough at the Dardanelles might have clinched the case. As it happened, Gallipoli turned out to be a failure, Tarnów a spectacular success. In the East, that combination set the stage for the next three years. On 22 July King Ferdinand of Bulgaria, a Coburg with estates in Hungary, sent an emissary to German Headquarters. On 6 September, a military convention was signed between Bulgaria and the Central Powers.[9]

The accession of Bulgaria also brought extra benefits in relations with Romania and Greece. The monarchy kept the Romanians happy with an offer to buy the grain surplus they could no longer export through the Straits; in Greece King Constantine (the Kaiser's brother-in-law) sacked his pro-French Prime Minister Venizelos on 5 October just as the Allies were landing their

Army of the East in Salonika. The army came too late to save Serbia from the concentric attack launched 48 hours afterwards. The remnants of the Serb Army had to retreat into the snow-bound mountains of Albania where they were evacuated to Corfu in a sort of Balkan Dunkirk. Conrad wanted to go on and crush the Orient army but the Germans insisted on respecting Greek neutrality; thus, the Bulgarian Army kept a dozen Western divisions locked up around Salonika, who suffered disproportionate losses from malaria and used a disproportionate share of shipping.[10] Conrad had to content himself with overrunning Montenegro and most of equally malaria-infested Albania, where warfare was carried on by rival clans who might switch sides at the appropriate moment, with cattle-rousing if not worse going on between Italian and French clients just as between Austro-Hungarian and Bulgarian ones.[11]

Thus, far from the prospect of almost certain defeat in the spring, by late autumn 1915 Austria-Hungary was looking back on a series of successes. All that remained was to deliver a knockout blow to Italy. In the Italian theatre of war, the Isonzo River had acquired a reputation similar to that of the Somme in the West; however, trench warfare had to adapt to Alpine conditions – flint-like rock rather than soggy Flanders mud. Even though the Austro-Hungarians were still inferior in overall numbers, Conrad did launch an attack from Tyrol on 15 May 1916 that was successful enough to frighten the Italians, but did not result in a breakthrough. Just as that offensive was winding down, disaster struck. On 4 June, in a surprise attack, the Russians under Brusilov overran the lines of the complacent Austro-Hungarians on a wide front south of the Pripyat marshes. It took the Central Powers weeks to stabilize the front up to 70 miles to the rear;[12] once again, a sizeable part of Galicia was occupied by the Russians. The Austro-Hungarians lost 400,000 men in POWs. Even worse, Brusilov's unexpected success tempted the Romanians to enter the war, after all – even though, as it turned out, delays caused by supply problems deprived their advance of much of their impact.[13]

The German–Austro-Hungarian partnership, part I: leverage of the weak?

Up to mid-1916, Conrad and the Austro-Hungarian High Command had prickly defended their independence from their German allies; the separate attacks against the Italians and at Verdun in early 1916 provided ample proof of the dangers of this attitude. After the Brusilov disaster when only German help (and, later on, even an Ottoman corps) saved the Austro-Hungarian front from collapse, Conrad was told in no uncertain terms that henceforth he would have to submit to a unified and obviously German-directed command of the

Eastern theatre of the war ('Oberost'). Much ink has been spilled about the ambivalent feelings among the Central Powers. Once the Germans did not deliver on their promise of a speedy victory in the West, the Austro-Hungarians thought they had a grievance. Once the lesser fighting potential of Austria's under-gunned and multi-ethnic troops showed, the Germans thought they had a grievance, too. Yet, on second thought, most of those turf wars between the two allies involved players from both sides fighting each other.[14]

To take the most famous example, the creation of 'Oberost' was no simple takeover bid by the Germans. Rather, it was a move in the perennial tug-of-war between frock-coats and brass-hats. The politicians in the Habsburg monarchy wanted to get rid of Conrad the way Lloyd George later on tried to tame Haig by putting him under a Supreme Command. In fact, as early as November 1914, the Austro-Hungarians held out the carrot of a unified command in the East under a German chief of staff if only that would lead to bigger reinforcements for the Eastern Front. In crucial situations, Austro-Hungarians exercised the leverage of the weak: the Germans simply could not afford to let the Austro-Hungarians go down to defeat. On the German side, the Chancellor Bethmann tried to play off Hindenburg and Ludendorff against Falkenhayn who had made a nuisance of himself by insisting on unrestricted submarine warfare. Thus, Hindenburg was appointed Commander-in-Chief for the Russian theatre; a few weeks later, Romania's entry into the war gave his career a further boost: Falkenhayn had to resign and Hindenburg became Chief of the General Staff as well. During the Romanian campaign, the Germans even strove to establish a Supreme War Leadership (OKL) to coordinate the activities of all four Central Powers. Fears of Austria's loss of independence were exaggerated, though. Franz Joseph retained a power of veto; the Italian front remained outside of Hindenburg's remit. More than anything else, the OKL was supposed to harmonize Bulgarian and Turkish sensibilities. With all four powers cooperating for once, the Romanian crisis ended in a triumph of the Central Powers. Bucharest was occupied in early December 1916. The all-important grain supplies for starving Vienna started flowing again in spring 1917.

In one way, though, Hindenburg's appointment turned out to be a cure worse than the malady. Bethmann thought he could use Hindenburg's prestige as a shield against the 'submarine fanatics'. The victorious team from the East was supposed to win the war on land without recourse to such extreme measures. But when Ludendorff – the power behind Hindenburg's throne – started to lean towards unrestricted submarine warfare at the end of 1916, Bethmann's strategy turned out to be self-defeating. Austria-Hungary had been a prime mover in the July crisis. It was a mere bystander in what has sometimes been called 'the second declaration of war'. Vienna leaders fought a rearguard action against 'unrestricted submarine warfare' but could not reverse the decision (quite apart from the fact that their own military advisers sided with the U-boat lobby, too). Austria's U-boat ace Korvettenkapitän von Trapp (of *The Sound of Music* fame) had been the first to sink an enemy cruiser at night; but in terms of cruiser warfare against commerce, the Austro-Hungarian contribution simply did not matter, even if Kapitän Miklos Horthy laid the foundations of a spectacular career, both military and political, with a successful foray against the Allied blockade of the Straits of Otranto in May 1917.[15]

Germany had saved the Austro-Hungarian monarchy from its enemies in 1914–16; in 1917–18 it sacrificed the monarchy by its untimely provocation of the US, a few weeks before Russia started to withdraw from the war. This reliance on wonder weapons, coupled with an underestimation of a capitalist economy's flexibility, ushered in the turning point of the war. For a few months, the U-boats actually did sink the projected amount of tonnage, but quicker loading and unloading of ships made good much of the shortfall. Pushing a reluctant Wilson and a Wall Street that had tired of subscribing to Allied war loans into the war saved the Allies from bankruptcy. Germany 'was snatching defeat from the jaws of victory'.[16]

Euphoria, part II: Caporetto and Brest-Litovsk

If spring 1917 witnessed an escalation of the war, it also saw the famous first peace-feelers when Karl I, who had succeeded Franz Joseph as Emperor in November 1916, was secretly visited by his brother-in-law, Prince Sixte of Bourbon-Parma, who happened to serve in the Belgian Army. Charles genuinely desired peace: at a pinch he was even willing to bribe Germany with cessions of Austro-Hungarian territory (Galicia or the rest of Silesia), if in turn Germany were willing to return Alsace and Lorraine to France. (Significantly, Karl was far less willing to be generous to Italy.) Yet, neither the Sixte mission nor the subsequent meetings of an Austro-Hungarian aristocrat, Graf Nicholas Revertera, with a French emissary in Switzerland, produced any real opening.[17] Revertera thought the terms the French offered were such as Napoleon might have offered after Austerlitz but not with 'the Germans at Noyon' (to use Clemenceau's famous phrase), that is, but not with the Germans less than 50 miles from Paris.[18] The French were only interested in detaching Austria from Germany; Karl's Foreign Secretary, Graf Ottokar Czernin, was thinking in similar terms when he told the Germans, if only the French were willing to make peace, 'we have won'.[19]

Karl has been variously accused of (or praised for) trying to detach Austria from the German alliance. In fact, he did nothing of the sort. He wanted to find a formula for a compromise peace – only if the Germans refused to accept that formula would they have to continue fighting on their own. After all, as Bismarck himself had often remarked, the dual alliance was a defensive alliance, not an association for profit. However, the French did not see fit to provide Karl with such a formula. Slightly more promising hints were contained in the conversations the old Boer general Smuts, as the representative of the British Empire, had with Austro-Hungarian diplomat Graf Mensdorff, a cousin of George V, in Switzerland in early 1918, but even those suggestions were purely hypothetical. Once the escalation of 1917 had started, there was no turning back: the Germans waited for the U-boats to work their miracles; the Western powers saw no need to compromise if they were going to be bailed out by the US anyway.

By autumn 1917, both the U-boat war and Austro-Hungarian peace feelers had clearly failed to produce the desired results. Even worse, the Austro-Hungarians suffered their worst crisis yet on the Italian front. It was only in 1917, after the successful conclusion of the Romanian campaign, that Austria-Hungary finally shifted its main effort to the South-west (in terms of artillery, though, the Italian front had already drawn ahead in late 1915, even if the Austro-Hungarians were slow in developing mine-throwers and light, more easily mobile machine guns).[20] Yet, during the 11th battle of the Isonzo, the Italians came close to achieving a real breakthrough on 22–23 August. (One wonders what might have happened if his generals had followed Lloyd George's advice to transfer a few more heavy guns to the neighbourhood of Trieste rather than to Passchendaele.[21]) The crisis galvanized the Germans to take the Italian front seriously, for once. They sent half-a-dozen divisions (including a lieutenant by the name of Erwin Rommel) to help the Austro-Hungarians. The result was Caporetto (24 October), the battle that probably saw the most effective use of poison gas during World War I. Caporetto was Italy's equivalent to the shock of the Brusilov Offensive – what had been designed as a mere stop-gap move to help the Austro-Hungarians stave off disaster and hold on to Trieste, unexpectedly led to the near collapse of the Italian Army, which lost 300,000 POWs and thousands of guns. Thus, the Western Allies were compelled to send almost a dozen divisions to prop up the Italians.[22]

With the Italians in full retreat, news of Lenin's 'Red October' reached Vienna on 8 November. Two weeks later a Russian picket crossed the German lines, waving white flags and proposing an immediate armistice. The war on two fronts was about to come to an end. The formula of a peace without annexations was complemented by the mock-Wilsonian slogan of self-determination in one country (as the concept was, of course, off-limits for Austria-Hungary where the Czechs kept asking questions why self-determination was good only for Estonians and maybe Greenlanders[23]). The Soviets were prepared to let go of all their non-Russian territories which would form independent states – states independent from Russia, that is, but of course dependent on the Central Powers. If Czernin insisted that peace had to be signed at almost any price and opposed any German expansion in the Baltic that might endanger that prospect, he still saw eye to eye with Ludendorff as far as the Ukraine was concerned. With the first treaty of Brest-Litovsk (9 February 1918), Austria rushed to recognize the biggish but disorganized new state and shower the Ukrainians with promises not just to weaken Russia, but – faced with wild-cat strikes and food riots at home – above all as a short-term expedient to get its hands on 1 million tons of Ukrainian grain.

For Austria-Hungary, the early weeks of 1918 were characterized by a meeting of extremes: with strikes shutting down the railway system, the Austro-Hungarian war economy threatened to go into a downward spiral. This crisis was followed by a near-revolt on the part of the Poles once they learnt about Czernin's deal with the Ukrainians. But while the domestic situation threatened to get out of hand, Austria-Hungary scored its foreign policy triumph. Flushed with their recent victory over the Italians, the Austro-Hungarians witnessed the disintegration of the Russian Empire. They were shocked at the Bolshevik takeover, and yet relieved at the disappearance of the one enemy they had never hoped to defeat. The Russian collapse also pulled the carpet from under the Romanians who signed a preliminary peace on 5 March. Czernin – and even more so, Karl I – realized the Romanian king with his beguiling English queen would never become a reliable ally but decided against replacing the dynasty as they did not want 'to turn the baisse of monarchy on the European market into a deroute'.[24]

As far as the European market was concerned, Czernin realized there was no chance for the Germans to deliver a knock-out blow to the Anglo-Saxon powers, but he hoped a successful drive in the West (to, say, Calais or Paris) would suffice to bring the Allies to the negotiating table on fairly favourable terms. On the Italian front, the Austro-Hungarians themselves would try their luck with a push across the Piave.[25] In fact, it was the Austro-Hungarians who staged the last offensive of the Central Powers, in Albania, out of all places, in August 1918. For a few months, despite all the difficulties of the home front, a certain kind of euphoria reigned, once again.

The German–Austro-Hungarian partnership, part II: the 'affaire Sixte'

With hindsight, the war was definitely lost when the German armies came to a halt a few miles in front of Amiens during the first days of April 1918. At the same time, Czernin committed an egregious gaffe. During a punch-drunk speech in Vienna city hall, eager to prove that the Allies were unwilling to consider a peace on status quo terms, he indiscreetly referred to the French contacts with Austria the year before; French Prime Minister Clemenceau retaliated by publishing one of Karl's letters to his in-laws where he referred to the French claims to Alsace-Lorraine as 'just'. Fearing an explosive reaction on the part of the Germans, Czernin first forced Karl to deny the authenticity of the letter, then suggested the Emperor should take some time out and think about appointing a regency. Instead, Karl accepted Czernin's resignation on 14 April 1918 and tried to mend fences with his German allies on his own.

This so-called 'affaire Sixte' has often been regarded as the final straw in Austria's submission to her big brother. In fact, the results were far from dramatic, partly because Hindenburg was not all that interested in a close partnership with Austria, partly because Burian – reappointed Foreign Secretary after Czernin's fall from grace – warded off all danger by his usual tactic of boring everyone to death with his endless monologues: 'Impossible to get a word in', as one listener complained. As a result, all the airy talk about a military convention or a constitutional link between the two empires turned out to be just a passing fancy. As a sign of solidarity, four Austro-Hungarian divisions were sent to the Western Front where they briefly fought the Americans.[26] But there were no extra ties between the two empires except the outline of a commercial treaty that was actually rather favourable to Austria. Thus, reports about her 'vassal status' *vis-à-vis* Germany were greatly exaggerated.

However, Austria-Hungary's prestige certainly did suffer. That is why it has been argued that the Sixte affair turned the Allies away from the idea of considering Austria-Hungary as a possible counterweight to German power, now that Russia was gone.[27] But then, the Western powers had already signed away a lot of Austro-Hungarian territory in their agreements with Serbia, Italy, and Romania; in mid-1918, they recognized Masaryk and Benes as a Czech government in exile, not because they believed in home rule for Bohemia, but because they needed the Czechoslovak Legion, formed out of ex-Austro-Hungarian POWs in Siberia, to fight the Bolsheviks.[28] Even so, Lansing, the US Secretary of State, commented that if he were an Austro-Hungarian he would 'retaliate by recognizing the independence of Ireland, Egypt and India'. In his opinion, Britain was again trying to have 'one rule for herself and another for other nations.'[29]

True, for Austria-Hungary, the war had lost its rationale after all its enemies – except for Italy – had dropped out of the war. The monarchy had no stake in fighting the Anglo-Saxon powers. The trouble was there was no way the Austro-Hungarians could simply have ended the war, unilaterally. If anything, in 18th-century style, they might have switched sides. But such a U-turn was difficult to execute under 20th-century circumstances. On the other hand, it is unlikely the Western powers could have saved the monarchy even if they had wanted to do so. There was no way the subject nationalities could be dissuaded from founding successor states once the Habsburg monarchy had definitely lost the war. The survival or dissolution of the Habsburg monarchy was not so much a matter of sentiment, of loyalty versus treason, but a result of political constraints and options.

The home front: a multinational empire

Of course, World War I was fought by multinational empires. But most of the other players' multinational parts lay outside of Europe. Austria-Hungary did not boast a colonial empire but was composed of no fewer than 11 ethnic groups, with even the biggest of them, Germans and Hungarians, comprising no more than 23 and 20 per cent of the population respectively. Constitutional practices in Austria-Hungary were notoriously complicated. The dual monarchy consisted of two states (plus Bosnia) linked by the monarch, a common foreign policy, and a common army (whose existence did not inhibit the two states from running two small territorial armies of their own). Hungary had a functioning parliament elected by a franchise that effectively restricted voting to the upper crust of ethnic Magyars; its Prime Minister, Graf István Tisza, a Calvinist from the eastern marches of Magyardom, was a forceful figure, and his post-Liberal 'Party of National Work' could rely on a majority in parliament. Austria, on the other hand, had already introduced universal (male) suffrage in 1907; its lower house was composed of no fewer than eight different ethnic groups. Even the biggest party, the German National Liberals, held less than 20 per cent of the seats. Cabinets were usually composed of civil servants steeped in the art of *divide et impera*. Sometimes, though, tensions did get out of hand. In fact, the parliamentary session had been closed in the spring of 1914 because of Czech obstruction. Prime Minister Graf Karl Stürgkh wanted that state of affairs to last. He insisted that the ethnic bickering characteristic of Austro-Hungarian politics could only serve to give comfort to the enemy. For more than two years, Stürgkh managed to survive politically, only to be assassinated by the son of Austria's veteran Social Democratic leader, Victor Adler, in

October 1916; a few weeks later, 86-year-old Emperor Franz Joseph succumbed to pneumonia on 21 November 1916.

Franz Joseph's successor, his great nephew Karl I, was a devout Catholic who initially tended to rely on the circle of advisors that had formed around Franz Ferdinand, a coterie of mostly Bohemian aristocrats. In terms of civil-military relations, he sent troublesome Conrad packing; Conrad's successor, Arz, proved to be more of an Adjutant General than a chief of staff. In Hungary, Karl dismissed Tisza as prime minister in May 1917 but still had to work with the parliamentary majority of Tisza's party as he decided against risking a general election in wartime.[30] At the same time, in Austria, he re-opened parliament but his prime ministers (Clam, then Seidler) proved unable to find a reliable majority. Karl may have been prompted by the best of intentions but in general his cabinets only succeeded in arousing the distrust of the ruling groups, German and Poles, without winning the confidence of the supposed ethnic underdogs, for example Czechs and Slovenes. With the elites thus at least partly estranged from the establishment, the Social Democrats came into their own. It was an ironic spectacle to watch conservative Vienna authorities offer prayers for the success of the old-style Marxist leaders of the Czech Socialists lest they should fall prey to their more nationalist-minded comrades.[31]

Conventional wisdom has it that as Austria-Hungary moved closer to its German ally, the non-German groups moved away from the monarchy. A close reading of wartime politics leads to a different conclusion. No ethnic group was totally immune to the lure of self-government and independence. But politics is the art of the possible. That framework changed with the fortunes of war. Ideologues, poets and writers, drafted ringing declarations; good politicians wanted to keep all options open. Even in the Czech case, the mainstream did not throw in their fortunes with the all-out irredentists before July 1918, a few weeks before even Ludendorff admitted defeat.[32] Popular grievances were of a different sort. In every multinational state, central administration is necessarily tinged with a touch of foreign rule. Before 1914, there were few genuine Liberals any longer; but Austria-Hungary still carried on with a tradition of limited government. Politics was an elite sport. Bureaucratic decisions, even if regarded as hostile or mistaken, did not usually affect people's daily lives. However, after 1914, with a system of wartime socialism, military courts, and requisitioning of victuals, administrative chicanery became a matter of life and death.

There was also a real problem with the sociology of command. Peacetime officers (even if mostly of German extraction) had been told to acquire a working knowledge of their soldiers' languages. The same did not hold true of the reserve officers or the emergency cadets with their crash courses. Units where officers and enlisted men found it difficult to communicate could be expected to be accident-prone. In the Czech case, there does seem to have been an extra element of political awareness that was lacking in, say, Slovak regiments that faced the same problems, even if allegations of treason turned out to be mostly unfounded. The military certainly exaggerated Czech disaffection in order to be allowed to appoint a military governor for Bohemia. But whether one chooses to put the blame on unreliable soldiers or inadequate officers, some of the non-German regiments did indeed have a rather dubious fighting record.[33]

War aims: 'Poland is not yet lost'

If Czech–German relations represented trench warfare in terms of politics, Polish–Ukrainian relations provided room for manoeuvre. This was an area where domestic and foreign policy overlapped. Apart from Serbia, Austria had in fact been the first power to use irredentist movements against her neighbours. For a number of years, the Austro-Hungarian intelligence services had been supporting a Polish paramilitary force, led by noble-born Socialist Josef Pilsudski. Immediately after war broke out, Austro-Hungarians started to argue that Poland should, of course, no longer be Russian. On the other hand, Poles obviously did not want to become Prussians; thus the only solution was to merge Russian Poland with the Habsburg monarchy. Berlin agreed that all solutions to the Polish question were bad but was less than convinced that the Viennese proposal was any better.

In a convoluted story with many turns and twists, Germany tied its agreement to this so-called Austro-Polish solution to the *Mitteleuropa* ('Central Europe') concept. If an extra 12 million Poles were to join Austria, they would turn into the biggest ethnic group of the monarchy. As a counterweight, to ensure that Austria remained a reliable ally, the monarchy as a whole had to strengthen its ties with Germany by forming one coherent *Mitteleuropa* bloc.[34] In fact, the Austrian, Prussian and Hungarian elites were all split about the merits of both proposals. In Germany, the Left generally supported the *Mitteleuropa* idea; the Right was sceptical because it disliked any notion of Polish empowerment. In Austria-Hungary, the two prime ministers, Tisza and Stürgkh, were weary of entering any binding engagements. With both of them gone, in late 1917, Czernin returned to the charge: the Austro-Hungarians were willing to sign all sorts of treaties – but only if they got all of Poland in return.[35]

In 1916, the military had suddenly pushed the idea of an independent Poland. Ludendorff and Conrad wanted to create a Polish army, not a state; as it turned out, they got a state – and no army. After the proclamation of independence on 5 November 1916, step by step, a sort of dyarchy was worked out in Poland, between the occupying powers and the autonomous institutions. A regency council appointed a cabinet that ran schools and courts. Undaunted, the Austro-Hungarians continued to promote the Austro-Polish solution – as a personal union, this time, with Karl serving as king of a nominally independent Poland. Polish conservatives had been sceptical about embracing Austro-German advances as long as it seemed that the Tzar might yet return; after the Russian Revolution, the Central Powers' reputation as their only protectors against the Bolsheviks soared.

Just as the Polish regency was about to offer Karl the crown of Poland in January 1918, the storm about Czernin's concessions to the Ukrainians broke. The peace of Brest-Litovsk should have spelt the end of all Austro-Polish aspirations – but only a few weeks later, with Czernin gone and the Ukrainians unable to deliver on their promise of feeding Vienna, negotiations resumed until the very end of the war.[36] The Austro-Polish solution even enjoyed a sort of life after death: with the possible exception of Hungary, none of the other successor states was dominated to quite such an extent by networks of old Austro-Hungarian officers (and their rivalries).[37]

The Austro-Hungarian war effort in perspective

Admittedly, there was an impression that Austria-Hungary was punching below its weight. Of course, the picture is distorted when comparing the monarchy to Britain and Germany, the two leading industrial countries. Yet, compared with France, Austria-Hungary's performance fell behind, in both military and economic terms. The number of German divisions more than doubled between 1914 and 1917, from fewer than 100 to around 240. France, with a population of less than 40 million, consistently managed to put more than 100 divisions into the field; Austria-Hungary, with roughly 55 million, reached a peak of only 72 (plus a few independent brigades). Even if the army's size increased from 3.2 million in August 1914 to a maximum of 5.6 million by early 1917, the number of infantry battalions hovered between 900 and 1,100 throughout the war.

Unfortunately, reliable and comprehensive statistics are hard to come by in an empire that disintegrated as a result of the war. There is not even any agreed figure of wartime casualties, estimated at roughly 1 million altogether. Apparently, Austria-Hungary only managed to enrol about 14–17 per cent of its population in the military, compared to more than 20 per cent in Germany and France. (Only British figures, at 12 per cent, were much lower.) The Austro-Hungarian Army suffered most of its losses early in the war: the low-tech warfare in the East – including the winter campaign of 1915 – claimed far more victims than the deadly concentrations of machine guns and heavy artillery along the Isonzo. (During 1916–17, the number of machine guns along the Italian front quadrupled.) Moreover, the Austro-Hungarians lost roughly one and a half million prisoners during the war, more than any other belligerent. The growing disproportion between 'head' and 'tail' was an overall phenomenon. Occupation troops (for example, up to 40,000 men in tiny Montenegro alone) might account for part of that gap. Yet, Austria does seem to have suffered from a disproportionate number of soldiers tugged away in sick wards and training establishments at any given time (almost a million each). Between a third and a half of fatal losses were due to sickness rather than enemy action. With all these hints, Austria's (mis-)management of its human resources remains something of an enigma to be analysed more closely.

Economically, Austria enjoyed a sort of fake boom that paralleled its military fortunes in 1915–16. Production of steel actually improved, easily surpassing that of France.[38] Yet, transport difficulties created bottlenecks and wasted synergies. The second half of 1916, even if a time of troubles at the front, turned out to be the high-water mark of the war in terms of industrial output; by that time, the Austro-Hungarian artillery had been almost entirely re-equipped with state-of-the-art new guns.[39] But due to shortages of both labour and raw materials, the monarchy proved unable to further intensify its efforts. Between 1915 and 1917, machine-gun production increased from 3,700 to 15,500 in Austria-Hungary, but from 7,200 to 104,000 in Germany.[40] As far as aircraft production was concerned, Austria-Hungary consistently lagged behind Italy by a factor of more than two to one. Austria-Hungary threatened to literally run out of steam not because coal production had dropped but because lack of locomotives led to transport bottlenecks, which mean that 'the benefits of increased industrial output were not fully realized because of the transportation system's failure to deliver goods promptly.'[41] The offensive at Caporetto turned out to be a stunning victory but the effort almost led to a break-down of the Austro-Hungarian railway system.

However, Austria-Hungary experienced its biggest difficulties with food supply. These difficulties were compounded by political problems. Much of it can be traced back to the lingering illusion of a short war. Maximum prices and confiscation of grain reserves, as decreed in spring 1915, might work as a short-term expedient for one season only. In the long term they simply counted as a massive disincentive to grow more food, hard hit as farmers were by a lack of manpower, horses, and fertilizer. The recurring loss of Eastern Galicia compounded the problem. To make things worse, Hungary had always hotly defended its grip on the Austrian market; with the onset of the blockade, that right was converted into a duty. With the Hungarians' help, the Austrians held. But once shortages set in, Hungarians were loath to part with their food reserves any longer.

Hungarians apparently handled the problem better. The Austrian grain harvest declined to less than half its peacetime level by 1916–17, from over 4 million tons to less than 2 million; Hungarian production proved to be fairly stable at 4–5 million tons until 1918. Austrians compared their system of 'requisitioning down to the last village' to the free markets that still operated locally in Hungary.[42] Austrian efforts to protect urban consumers from the socially unacceptable effects of wartime inflation, fuelled by fears of working-class unrest, may have been counterproductive in the long term. A command economy might work with rent-control (established in early 1917, and not lifted until the 1980s), as flats could not be hidden, fed to the pigs, or spirited away to be sold on the black market. Results also showed in terms of black-market prices: by the end of the war, inflation in Austria was estimated at 1,500 per cent, compared with 600 per cent in Hungary.

In 1916, Tisza at least agreed to provide for the needs of the army out of Hungarian resources. Austrian civilians, however, had to rely on Romanian imports (almost a million tons in the first half of 1916). In the beginning, this proved to be a marriage of convenience as the Romanians were unable to export their grain anywhere else. Austrians even tried to use their monopoly status as potential buyers as a means to blackmail the Romanians into neutrality. But after the Romanian declaration of war on 27 August 1916, imports stopped. Austria suffered from severe shortages in the winter of 1916–17, with Vienna, the coastal districts, and the densely populated Sudeten German areas being hit hardest. Austrians had to go begging cap in hand to Germany, not just for troops and loans, but also for food. In one of those snooker-like indirect manoeuvres, the Austrians hoped the Germans would help them put pressure on the Hungarians to adopt strong-arm tactics against recalcitrant producers.[43] One year later, hunger persuaded Czernin to execute a U-turn in terms of domestic politics when he dropped the Poles and showered promises on the Ukrainians to get hold of their legendary grain reserves. Legendary was the operative word, though; with administrative chaos reigning in the newly conquered East, the so-called 'bread peace' did not live up to its promise.[44] In June 1918 – with rations of bread and potatoes having dropped to less than half their peacetime average – Viennese started to plunder the fields before the harvest had even started.[45]

Supplies and morale both started to break down. Yet, those disintegrating forces only gained the upper hand in the second half of 1918 once the war had, to all intents and purposes, been lost anyway.

Appendix I:

Percentage of Austro-Hungarian fighting troops employed on the

	Russian front	Balkan front	Italian front
January 1915	70%	27%	3%
January 1916	58%	13%	29%
January 1917	53%	9%	38%

Source: *Österreich-Ungarns letzter Krieg*, Vol. II, p. 9; Vol. VI, p. 49

In terms of infantry divisions:

August 1914	37	11	
Summer 1915	43	2	21
May 1916	37	2	25
November 1917	31	1	37
June 1918	12	2	46

CHAPTER 9

THE IMPERIAL RUSSIAN ARMY AND THE EASTERN FRONT IN WORLD WAR I, 1914–17

Dr Stephen Walsh

On 30 July 1914, Russia mobilized for a war that would destroy its monarchy, devastate the Russian Army, cause millions of casualties, and play a key role in the Bolshevik Revolution of October 1917. It led to the Russian Civil War (1918–21), communism, and Stalin. In short, for Russia, World War I was a political, social, economic, and military catastrophe. The Imperial Russian Army is associated with images of hapless, poorly trained, ill-equipped soldiers driven into battle by incompetent commanders to be slaughtered by superior German forces. It was a flawed military force, the instrument of a Tsarist state incapable of harnessing Russia's potential. However, while the Russian Army struggled against the Germans, it did inflict a series of defeats upon the armies of Austria-Hungary. This chapter will analyse the Russian Army's conduct of the war on the Eastern Front during World War I. It will explore the Russian Army's pre-war thinking, military reforms, and strategy in August 1914. The fluid operations of August 1914–April 1915 will be assessed as well as the cataclysmic defeats of May 1915–March 1916. It will analyse the Russian recovery in the summer of 1916, before exploring the period of war and revolution in 1917 that led to the collapse of the Imperial Russian Army.

The legacy of the Russo-Japanese War

In 1905, the Russo-Japanese War brought defeat in war and revolution at home. In the immediate aftermath of the war the army united in its commitment to reform but by 1907–08 unity had degenerated into recrimination. The 1908 Bosnian Crisis exposed the army's weakness,[1] and, confronted by Austria-Hungary's determination to annex Bosnia, Russia chose humiliation, not war. In response in the period 1908–14 Russian policy was dominated by the cultivation of allies, a determination to avoid further humiliation, and a desire to restore Russian military power. In July 1914, Russia feared backing down more than war. It had allies and the army appeared ready for war, a short war.

The 'Great Programme' of 1914 aimed to transform the shambling giant of the Russian Army into a massive but modern fighting force. By 1917, it would possess over 1.7 million troops, 8,358 guns,[2] greater reserves, and a rail network designed to enhance the speed of Russian mobilization. In 1914, the Great Programme was an aspiration, but Russia's recovery increased German fears that by 1917 the Russian 'steamroller' would be invincible. In February 1914, Moltke commented, 'Russia's preparedness for war has made gigantic progress since the Russo-Japanese War and is now much greater than ever in the past.'[3]

The Schlieffen Plan required a cumbersome Russian mobilization to create time for German victory in the West before turning east. Therefore, a modernized Russian Army, able to mobilize greater numbers more efficiently, was a considerable threat. Indeed, on 1 August 1914, it was a major factor in Germany's decision to go to war.

Russian war strategy

It is often forgotten that the prospect of a two-front war, with Germany and Austria, dominated Russian strategy. The 1910 War Plan committed four Russian armies – First, Second, Fourth, and Fifth – against the Germans in East Prussia but only one, Third Army, against the Austro-Hungarians in Galicia, while Sixth Army defended St Petersburg and Seventh Army the Romanian border. The 1910 plan was essentially a strategy of defence but was criticized as unduly defensive, conceding the strategic initiative, giving France little active support, not contesting East Prussia, and neglecting Poland. However, two years after the Bosnian humiliation, it was also a realistic assessment of the army's strategic capabilities, not its more fanciful aspirations.

The 1912 War Plan created two strategic variants, Plan A and Plan G. In Plan A, the main German effort would be in the west. In response, First and Second armies would advance on East Prussia while three Russian armies, Third, Fourth, and Fifth, engaged the Austro-Hungarians in Galicia. In Plan G the main German blow was in the east. Three armies, First, Second, and Fourth, would concentrate against East Prussia, while Third and Fifth confronted the Austro-Hungarians. The 1912 plan also committed Sixth Army to St Petersburg with Seventh Army on the Romanian border.

The Russians faced a set of strategic dilemmas that remained unresolved in August 1914. First, should Russian strategy be offensive or defensive? Second, how could Russia support France, confront the Austro-Hungarians, and defend the Serbs? Third, if Russia attacked should its priority be East Prussia or the Austro-Hungarians in Galicia? Fourth, should Russia aim to knock out the Austro-Hungarians but adopt a more defensive strategy against Germany or vice versa? Fifth, could Austria actually be defeated quickly, and what were the consequences of enabling Germany to concentrate against France?

East Prussia loomed over Russia but a strategy that prioritized Germany faced significant operational problems. By 1912 Germany planned only defensive operations in the east but Russian strategy could not disregard the possibility of a German attack. In addition, a Russian offensive against East Prussia had to defend northern Poland. This ruled out sustained offensive operations against the Austro-Hungarians in Galicia, leaving the Serbs isolated. Furthermore, an East Prussia offensive appeared to demand simultaneous assaults from the east and south-east while guarding the Polish salient. Operational synchronization was likely to be problematic due to the Masurian Lakes, while forests and marshes channelled Russian attacks into defences such as the Angerapp Line.

A Russian attack from Poland would seize the strategic initiative and fulfil Russia's obligations to France. However, a German attack from East Prussia towards Warsaw would sever Russian communication and supply lines. Therefore, a Polish offensive required substantial troops to secure the East Prussian border, forces taken from Galicia, and the Austro-Hungarians. In addition, Russian forces moving west on the Polish–Silesian axis risked a strategic Austro-German pincer movement.

The intricacies of East Prussia and Poland argued for an offensive against the Austro-Hungarians and a defensive strategy against the Germans. First, the Russian Army was inferior to that of the Germans but arguably superior to the Austro-Hungarian Army. Second, the terrain was better there than in East Prussia and raised the possibility that Russia might defeat Austria while the Germans were contained in the west and East Prussia. However, the Russians' ability to achieve a quick victory was debatable. Third, it would release German troops to fight the French. If Russia struggled against Austria while Germany defeated France, Russia would be isolated. In summary, for Russia to defeat Austria, the French had to survive, and if Russian strategy prioritized Austria this was less, not more, likely. Therefore, Russian strategy in August 1914 was intrinsically connected to France.

In theory, Russia could utilize its traditional strengths of manpower, time, and the depths of the Russian interior. However, a passive, defensive strategy risked French defeat and Russian isolation. If successful in the west, Germany would not fear war in the east. Indeed, it was unlikely Russia's traditional strengths would enable it to prevail in either a short or long war. Therefore, if Russia had to fight, it could not fight alone and this dictated that to support France in the west, Russia attacked in the east. In 1913, under French pressure, Zhilinskiy, Chief of the Russian General Staff, committed Russia to offensive operations in East Prussia just 15 days after mobilization.

The East Prussian operation, 17 August–15 September 1914

The North-Western Front commanded by Zhilinskiy had 400,000 men, was made up of Rennenkampf's First Army on the eastern border of East Prussia and Samsonov's Second Army, north of Warsaw. It was an impressive force crippled by the inept cordiality between Zhilinskiy and Rennenkampf but poisonous antagonism towards Samsonov. East Prussia was defended by Prittwitz's 8. Armee. Its objective, driven by the Schlieffen Plan, was to hold East Prussia and destroy the Russian forces. On 17 August 1914, First Army clashed with I Armee-Korps at Stalluponen and advanced steadily. On 20 August 1914, First Army encountered three of 8. Armee's four corps at Gumbinnen. It was an indecisive encounter[4] but later Prittwitz discovered that Second Army had crossed into East Prussia and was advancing north-west, deep into the operational rear of Eighth Army.

Prittwitz concluded Second Army's advance threatened 8. Armee with catastrophe. Strategically, it faced being cut off from Germany, whilst in operational terms 8. Armee was fixed by First Army and being outmanoeuvred by Second Army. In a notorious episode, Prittwitz recommended 8. Armee's withdrawal to the Vistula. It was a temporary aberration of mood but Prittwitz was sacked. Indeed, by 22 August 1914, it appeared the Russians had

The Eastern Front, August–December 1914

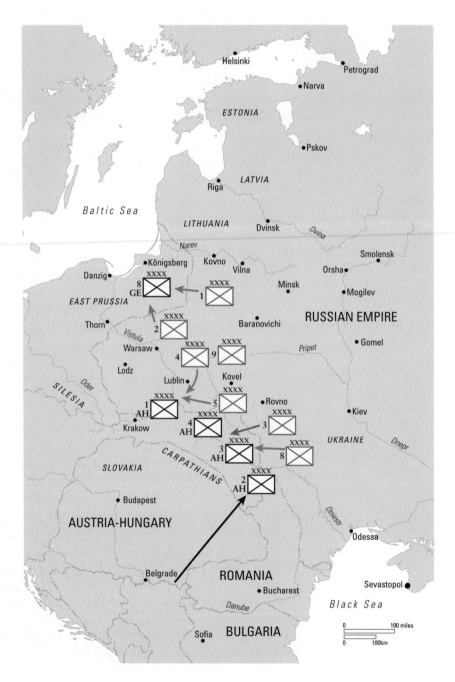

outmanoeuvred 8. Armee and were poised to win a famous victory. However, by 31 August, the Russians had suffered a strategic disaster in East Prussia: a reversal of fortunes in which the Germans snatched success from calamity and the Russians catastrophe from victory.

In a situation dominated by fearful uncertainty, on 24 August 1914 German intelligence intercepted Second Army's communications, broadcast *en clair*.[5] The Germans learned Second Army was moving north-west, not directly north, into the rear of 8. Armee. The Germans also discovered Second Army's logistics, communications, and supplies were in chaos. The Day 15 timetable meant Second Army had attacked before it was ready and was losing momentum, meaning that Samsonov's movements were not as threatening as the Germans had feared.[6]

In addition the North-Western Front was not a coherent operational force and its position in East Prussia had been established by accident not design. East Prussia's shape and First and Second armies' initial deployment appeared to dictate North-Western Front would attempt to encircle 8. Armee. However, on 14 August 1914, Zhilinskiy announced 8. Armee was to be driven out, not encircled. He never intended to carry out a double envelopment by the two armies, merely to push the Germans out of East Prussia.[7]

Therefore, while Second Army struck deep to trap 8. Armee, First Army tried to push it out of East Prussia, meaning, in effect, First and Second armies conducted separate operations. The chronic lack of operational synchronization was exposed by First Army's conduct after Gumbinnen on 20 August 1914. In combination with Second Army's advance, by drawing the Germans east, Gumbinnen created significant operational possibilities for the Russians. However, First Army, untroubled by Zhilinskiy, did not move until 23 August[8] this created a gap in time and space that 8. Armee seized on.

The German counterstroke

On 25 August 1914, further interceptions revealed First Army was not cooperating with Second Army. The German command gambled it could hold First Army with two divisions, while it committed eight divisions against Second Army. German troops disengaged from First Army concentrated against Second Army's right wing while more troops deployed against Second Army's left flank. The Russians had been out-thought and outmanoeuvred, but the oblivious Zhilinskiy hounded Second Army and ignored First Army's leisurely progress.

On 26 August, Second Army, driving north-west, was attacked on its left and right flanks. During 27 August, German troops advanced east towards

German troops coming from the north-east, and by the evening of 28 August, Second Army was encircled. Finally, Zhilinskiy ordered First Army to support Second Army but it was too late. During the night of 29/30 August, overwhelmed by Second Army's disaster, Samsonov committed suicide. By 31 August, 18,000 Russian troops were dead and 92,000 had been taken prisoner.

It was a calamitous defeat. The Second Army had been destroyed and after Tannenberg, in subsequent operations in the Masurian Lakes (7–17 September 1914), 8. Armee drove First Army east, inflicting heavy casualties, but failed to encircle it. By the end of September 1914, the Russians had withdrawn from East Prussia having suffered losses of 250,000 in six weeks.[9]

The Galician operation

In Galicia, the South-Western Front commanded by Ivanov had four armies, in two groups, northern and southern. The northern group of 337,000 men consisted of Saltsa's Fourth Army and Plehve's Fifth Army; the southern group of 354,000, Ruzskiy's Third Army and Brusilov's Eighth Army. Russian strategy envisaged the northern group moving south-west while the southern forces moved from eastern Galicia towards Lemberg. The Austro-Hungarians deployed three armies from north to south: Dankl's First Army, Auffenberg's Fourth Army, and Bruderman's Third Army which guarded Lemberg. The right flank was initially held by the Kovess Group because Second Army had been sent to Serbia. It did not return until 25 August 1914.

In August 1914, the Austro-Hungarians and Russians attempted to out-think, outmanoeuvre and out-fight each other, but initially the Galician operation was dominated by frontal collisions. In the north from 23 August to 3 September 1914, the Austro-Hungarian First and Fourth armies fought a series of encounters with the Russian Fourth and Fifth armies. The Austro-Hungarians inflicted heavy casualties on Fourth Army south-west of Lublin, and Ivanov ordered Fifth Army to help Fourth Army but in doing so exposed Fifth Army's left flank. Ivanov also ordered Third Army north-west to prevent Austro-Hungarian forces supporting the Austro-Hungarian Fourth Army against the Russian Fifth Army.

In a week of continuous fighting Fifth Army linked up with Fourth Army and fought a successful withdrawal operation against the Austro-Hungarian Fourth Army. By 3 September 1914, Fifth Army had established a solid defensive line on the Vistula, west of Lublin. The Russian northern group had survived but come off worse. Plehve's Fifth Army had suffered 30,000 casualties but saved the Russian northern group from a decisive defeat. Above all, it had drawn the Austro-Hungarians north: on 30 August 1914, Conrad had diverted the Austro-Hungarian Third Army's left wing north to reinforce the Austro-Hungarian Fourth Army's attempt to encircle Fifth Army. This created a significant Russian superiority in the south.

On 18 August 1914, the South-Western Front's southern group began its drive west. Its aim was to take Lemberg, cross the San, take Przemsyl, south-east of Krakow and drive the Austro-Hungarians out of Galicia through the Carpathians. The operation began slowly, but in contrast to Second Army in East Prussia, robust logistics created a sustained fighting power that contributed to decisive operational success. In a series of battles east of the city, the southern group advanced on Lemberg. First, on the Zolotaya Lipa (26–27 August) Russian firepower broke the Austro-Hungarian Third Army. Subsequently, Brusilov's Eighth Army prevailed on the Gnilaya Lipa (28–31 August) against the Austro-Hungarian Second Army. The Austro-Hungarian position east of Lemberg was broken, and on 3 September 1914, Third Army entered the city.

The Russian counteroffensive, 4–15 September 1914

It is ironic that just as Conrad's irrational optimism induced him to pursue the encirclement of Fifth Army, so Ivanov's unnecessarily pessimistic response to Fifth Army's plight persuaded him to divert Third Army north-west on 25 August 1914, a decision that would have significantly undermined the Russian assault on Lemberg. Ruzskiy, Third Army's commander, dazzled by Lemberg,[10] refused. He was right for all the wrong reasons and it was his insubordination as well as Eighth Army's victories that paved the way for the Russian success in Galicia. However, by early September 1914, when Third Army finally sent troops north, Conrad ordered part of the Austro-Hungarian Fourth Army to block the Russian Fifth Army. The rest of the Austro-Hungarian Fourth Army marched south to strike the Russian Third Army while Dankl's Austro-Hungarian First Army contained the Russian Fourth and Ninth armies in the Polish salient. This was delusional: the Austro-Hungarian Fourth Army, in action for ten days, was shattered, and as it turned south the Austro-Hungarians sacrificed their position in the north for little gain in the south.

On 4 September 1914, as the Austro-Hungarian Fourth Army moved south it was attacked by Fifth Army moving west. The phantom menace of Third Army was in Lemberg, and the Austro-Hungarian Fourth Army's southern diversion enabled the Russian Fourth and Ninth armies to drive the First Army west. Two Austro-Hungarian counter-attacks were repulsed, and in the central zone Fifth Army became pivotal to the Galician operation. First, on 9 September, it compelled the Austro-Hungarian First Army to withdraw over the San by manoeuvring round its southern flank. Second, by threatening to outmanoeuvre them from the north, Fifth Army forced the Austro-Hungarians in the south to withdraw west. On 11 September, the Austro-Hungarian withdrawal began but descended into a rout. By 15 September, the Russians were over the San but rain reduced Galicia's roads to a morass. As Russian logistics collapsed, the Austro-Hungarians stabilized their line west of Krakow, leaving 120,000 troops trapped in Prezemsyl.

The Russians lost 250,000 men in the Galician operation. However, the armies of Austria-Hungary suffered 300,000 casualties and lost Galicia. It was a significant defeat and from this point on the Austro-Hungarians would need German assistance in order to survive.[11]

Naturally, historical attention has focused on Lemberg but Plehve's Fifth Army also played a decisive strategic and operational role in Galicia. Its defensive operations stabilized the Russian northern group at a critical time while its role in the counter-offensive enabled the Russians to out-think, outmanoeuvre, and eventually out-fight the Austro-Hungarians.

The invasion of Germany and the Lodz operation

In early October 1914, *Stavka,* the Supreme High Command of the Russian Army, ordered an offensive on the Polish axis. The *Stavka*, nominally headed by Grand Duke Nicholas, uncle of Tsar Nicholas II, was supposed to oversee the strategic direction of the war, establish tactical priorities, and coordinate the Russian armies. The Polish axis appeared to offer an opportunity to grasp the strategic initiative on the Eastern Front, but it had to be reconciled with other operations on the Eastern Front. In short, operations in East Prussia and Galicia either had to be reduced or coordinated with Russian operations in Poland to prevent the Germans moving troops from dormant areas to the Polish sector.

During October 1914, 9. Armee barely contained extensive Russian operations in Poland but by early November 1914, nine Russian armies and 2 million troops were in the Polish salient. A strike force of Scheidemann's Second Army, Plehve's Fifth Army, Evert's Fourth Army and Ninth Army under Lechitskii was protected on its right by Rennenkampf's First Army and Pflug's Tenth Army. The South-Western Front would strike the Austro-Hungarians in Galicia while the main Russian blow struck north-west towards Posen and Berlin. The Germans' destruction of the road and rail network delayed the Russian offensive, but, more significantly, Russian communications were once again intercepted and enabled the Germans to outmanoeuvre the Russians. As a result of definite

Poland and Galicia, November–December 1914

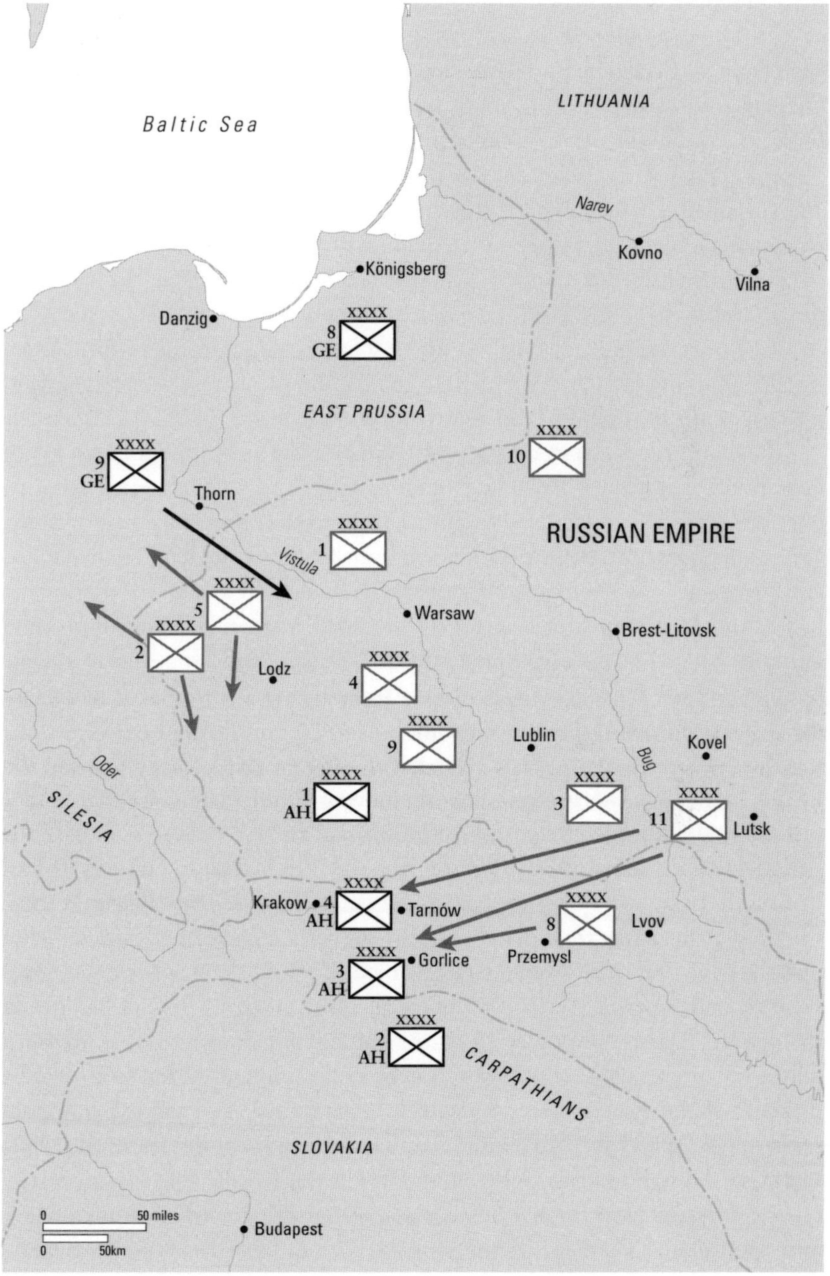

intelligence about Russian intentions, from 3 to 10 November 1914, 9. Armee was redeployed, by train, from central southern Poland, to Thorn on the northern flank of the Russian forces.[12]

On 11 November, as Second Army and Fifth Army advanced west, their right flank, neglected by First Army, was attacked by 9. Armee. By 14 November, German troops were moving south into the rear of Second and Fifth armies. However, in an epic feat of endurance and ghastly forced marches, Second Army and Fifth Army beat 9. Armee to Lodz, a major Russian supply centre. By 18 November 1914, 500,000 Russian troops were in the city. The Germans remained confident, but as they moved south-east of Lodz they were outmanoeuvred by the Russians, who trapped XXV Armee-Korps and fixed the Germans north and west of the city. However, in a remarkable feat, Scherer's XXV Armee-Korps not only escaped but took 16,000 Russian prisoners unmolested by the bumbling First Army which, in the darkness, mistook the prisoners for a Russian unit moving north to secure the encirclement.

Therefore, the Russian invasion of Germany was pre-empted by an act of operational impudence facilitated by appalling Russian operational security, but *Stavka* had also squandered a significant strategic opportunity. In November 1914, the German strategic position was fraught: the Schlieffen Plan had failed and Germany was simultaneously engaged on two fronts, the scenario that had haunted German strategists for two decades. A sustained Russian invasion in November 1914 would have presented the Germans with a strategic nightmare, but they escaped due to incompetent Russian strategic and operational command: an enduring theme of the war in the East.

The key to Russian success in November 1914 – indeed throughout the war in the East – was the strategic coordination of simultaneous, not successive, operations designed to stretch Austro-Hungarian and German resources. In the period October–December 1914, the Russians did launch operations in East Prussia, northern and central Poland, as well as Galicia, but although some occurred at the same time, they were not properly coordinated, simultaneous operations as part of an overall strategic plan. Logistic chaos, poor operational security, and superior German mobility all contributed to Russian failures in the period August–November 1914 and throughout the war, but operational failure was often a symptom of poor strategy and coordination. *Stavka* repeatedly diminished the Russian Army's strategic, operational, and tactical power in poorly coordinated successive, not simultaneous, operations. Therefore, while Germany did fight on two fronts, in the East it was usually able to concentrate on one operational sector at a time. *Stavka* was unable to fashion simultaneous and coordinated Russian offensives across the Eastern Front or to create a hierarchy of strategic and operational priorities that achieved successive operational victories as part of an overall military strategy. Ideally, *Stavka* should have done both successive and simultaneous operations; it did neither.

The Carpathians

In mid-November 1914, as Austro-Hungarian forces moved north to support 9. Armee, in typical fashion, successively not simultaneously, *Stavka* ordered South-Western Front to attack the Austro-Hungarian Third Army, south-east of Krakow. As Radko-Dmitiriev's Third Army fixed Austro-Hungarian forces in the north, to the south Brusilov's Eigth Army drove west into the Carpathians. However, in early December 1914 an Austro-German counter-attack struck Third Army and forced the diversion of two corps from Eighth Army. The Eighth Army's remaining corps was driven east by the Austro-Hungarian Third Army which recaptured the Carpathian passes. A ghastly pendulum of winter operations followed in which thousands of Austro-Hungarian and Russian troops were lost in the Carpathians. However, in a series of limited tactical bursts, Eighth Army drove the Austro-Hungarians west and Przemysl was taken on 22 March 1915 with 100,000 prisoners.

The Gorlice-Tarnów operation, 2–22 May 1915

In April 1915, Chief of the German General Staff Erich von Falkenhayn concluded Germany had to defeat or seriously damage Russia in the east to release German forces into the west.[13] He devised a strategy designed to inflict maximum attrition at the operational and tactical levels in order to achieve 'the crippling of her strength for an indefinite period of time'.[14] The German blow, delivered by Mackensen's 11. Armee, targeted Third Army, east of Krakow.

In April 1915, *Stavka* was preoccupied by incessant wrangling with North-Western Front about who should do what, where, when, how, and why in relation to East Prussia. In strategic terms eastern Galicia was dormant, a backwater which left South-Western Front isolated. The Third Army was established on the Dunajec between Tarnów and Gorlice, with Eighth Army on its left. Its position had three defensive lines, the first with troops in the line given depth by a second and third defensive zone. In reality, this system of defence was no system. The front line was a brittle perimeter of shallow entrenchments that lacked depth and density, while Third Army's lack of manpower meant the second and third defence lines were barely occupied by poorly trained, ill-equipped troops.[15] Indeed, Brusilov,

Eighth Army's commander, believed, 'The defeat of the Third Army was in the circumstances inevitable.'[16]

At 0600hrs on 2 May 1915, a four-hour bombardment by 700 guns reduced the Russian defences to rubble, and dazed Russian troops were overwhelmed by German infantry. In 72 hours Third Army was shattered and as German engineers frantically constructed roads to sustain the offensive, it acquired a relentless momentum. 11. Armee broke the entire defensive position and by 10 May 1915, Third Army was in full retreat, its units decimated. General Radko-Dmitriev told *Stavka* it had 'bled to death'.[17] Third Army's collapse exposed Eighth Army and induced the withdrawal of the entire South-Western Front. On 10 May 1915, South-Western Front's Chief of Staff wrote, 'The strategic position is quite hopeless. Our line is very extended. We cannot shuffle troops around it with the required speed, and the very weakness of our armies makes them less mobile; we are losing all capacity to fight.'[18]

In addition, for having the temerity to advise *Stavka* to prepare defensive positions on the San, the same Chief of Staff who had predicted the attack was sacked. On 15 May 1915, Radko-Dmitriev was removed but still, on 16 May 1915, 11. Armee crossed the San. By 22 June 1915, Lemberg was in German hands and the Russians had been driven out of Galicia.

The evacuation of Poland and the Great Retreat

The Russian casualties were staggering, with South-Western Front losing 412,000 killed, wounded, or captured in May 1915 alone.[19] The defeat in Galicia made Poland virtually indefensible and on 25 June 1915, the rational, but emotionally unthinkable, option of a coherent, deliberate strategic withdrawal from Poland was proposed.[20] It would shorten the line, create depth, and draw the Germans into an attritional struggle in the Russian heartland by contesting every metre. However, in late June, *Stavka* could not stomach the cold logic of a planned strategic, operational, and tactical withdrawal but in July, it was driven into a ghastly, improvised retreat.

Falkenhayn was acutely aware that 'the Russians can retreat into the vastness of their country, and we cannot go chasing them for ever and ever'[21] but planned further attritional offensives to bleed the Russians. 11. Armee would strike north from Galicia towards Lublin, while von Gallwitz's Narew Army advanced south from East Prussia. On 13 July 1915, 11. Armee attacked and made steady progress towards Lublin, which fell at the end of the month. In contrast, initially, the German northern attack advanced rapidly, driving Fifth Army east and moving south. The two wings of the

The Great Retreat, May–October 1915

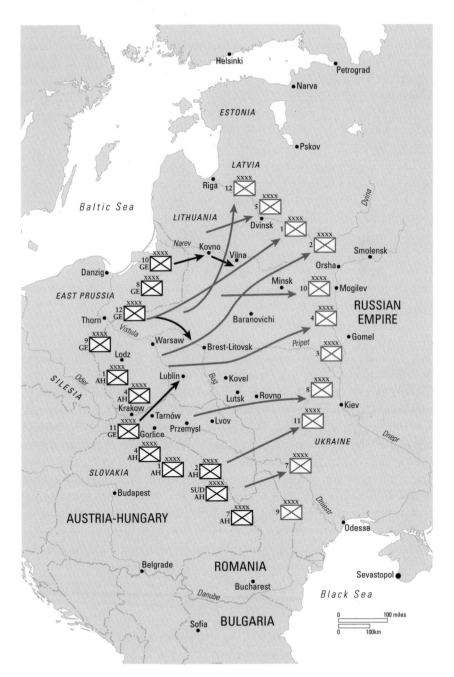

German offensive converged on the Polish salient and *Stavka*, pressed from the north, west, and south, ordered a strategic retreat.

Alexeyev, the North-Western Front's commander, sought an organized withdrawal but was undermined by public hysteria. On 5 August 1915, Warsaw fell; on 9 August the symbolic fortress of Novo Georgievsky, north of Warsaw, fell. In total, 90,000 troops, 1,600 guns, and 1 million shells were lost by an army short of manpower and shells. The fall of Kovno on 18 August ignited the public mood and forced more Russian troops to defend Vilna and Riga on the St Petersburg axis. In the febrile atmosphere of summer 1915, all losses were catastrophic: Riga fell, followed by Vilna on 18 September 1915, as reason gave way to panic.[22]

The strategic withdrawal of summer 1915 saved the Russian Army but also brought Russia to the edge of national defeat. It tested the relationship of the Russian government, army, and people to breaking point but in military terms the withdrawal made absolute strategic, operational, and tactical sense. The Russian Army survived, just, as an organized fighting force and earned the respect of the Germans. In contrast, for the Russian people, subject to the martial law of an ill-prepared *Stavka*, the withdrawal was apocalyptic. Towns were evacuated, crops destroyed, animals slaughtered, and desperate columns of people were driven east by their own army, pursued by the Germans. The mood was bitter, vindictive, and occasionally hysterical, and the Russian people blamed *Stavka*: on 12 August 1915 the Grand Duke was dismissed and replaced by Tsar Nicholas II even though 'Everyone knew that Nicholas II understood literally nothing about military matters.'[23]

By October 1915 the Russian Army of August 1914 was gone. It had suffered grievously against the Germans but inflicted serious damage on the Austro-Hungarians. The Great Retreat strained the army's chain of command and soldierly habits of obedience to the limit. The leadership of Russian officers often left much to be desired, and while Russian soldiers were tough and resilient, in terms of education, technical, and tactical competence they were often inferior to their British, French, and German – if not Austro-Hungarian – counterparts. In the Russian Army quantity did not automatically have a quality of its own. In addition, the Russian Army struggled to coordinate its tactical arms and weapons systems. The artillery was infamously reluctant to cooperate with the infantry, while the cavalry was no match for modern infantry weapons.

In addition, by 1915–16, the Russian Army was actually struggling for manpower. The horrendous losses of August 1914–October 1915 (1.2 million in August–December 1914,[24] 2 million alone in the Great Retreat)[25] the notorious exemptions system, and the inefficiency of the Russian state all contributed to the ineffectual mobilization of Russia. In truth, the government feared a sustained attempt to mobilize more of Russia's manpower would provoke domestic unrest. The Russian state was frightened of its people and feared they would not fight for the Romanovs. The relationship between the Russian government, Army, and people – apart from August 1914 – was distinctly fragile. This ensured that the Russian Army was never as powerful as it should have been, or its enemies feared it would be.

The Lake Narotch operation and the new Russian Army of 1916

In spring 1916, new Russian officers emerged – civilians in uniform – and in 1916–17, for better and for worse, the habits, inclinations, strengths, weaknesses, and grievances of Russian society slowly influenced the Russian Army. These new men, officers and soldiers, enabled an army on its knees in October 1915 to take the field in spring 1916, better equipped than ever before. However, before the new Russian Army (over 6.2 million strong) made its mark, the old Russian Army suffered a catastrophic defeat at Lake Narotch. It was 'an affair that summed up all that was wrong with the army'.[26]

In spring 1916, to help the French at Verdun, *Stavka* planned an operation against 10. Armee at Lake Narotch. The Northern Front's Fifth Army was to advance south-west to meet the Western Front's Second Army moving north-west and encircle XXI Armee-Korps. Northern Front's Twelfth Army and Western Front's First Army were to prevent German reserves intervening and in total, the Western Front, commanded by Evert, committed 400,000 men on a 40-mile front.

In his desire to make certain the uncertain business of a breakthrough, Evert, the Western Front commander, delayed the offensive to acquire more firepower. The protracted preparations simply warned the Germans, but, on 17 March 1916, despite a thaw that turned the region into a quagmire, the Western Front attacked on a 5-mile front. It was supported by a bombardment that fired 40,000 shells in eight hours but the Russians were slaughtered, their bodies piled on the wire.[27] On 20 March 1917, snow followed by a thaw flooded trenches, soaked troops, demolished roads, and created a swamp. On 2 March 1916, Fifth Army attacked and made small gains for heavy losses. The Lake Narotch operation continued until 7 April 1916, and in three weeks the Russians lost 100,000 men.[28] No German troops were diverted from Verdun.

Old thinking vs. new thinking

The commanders of the old army believed success was dependent on massive artillery fire concentrated on a narrow front to obliterate the obstacles to an advance. However, the narrow concentration of firepower and force required to guarantee a breakthrough ensured enemy formations untouched by the initial onslaught could devastate the attacker's flanks.[29] Furthermore, it was impossible to conceal such massive numbers of guns and troops. In short, the secret to success forfeited surprise and revealed the location, if not timing, of an attack.

A competent enemy commander invariably withdrew to create killing zones manned by troops with enormous firepower supported by the main body, deployed in depth, capable of intervening in the battle but not exposed to it. Yet, to attack on a broad front, to preserve troops from devastating flanking fire, denied an attacker the concentration of fighting power that was considered essential to a breakthrough. In summary, by spring 1916 most Russian commanders considered breadth of assault and concentration of firepower incompatible.

In April 1916, *Stavka* ordered further Russian offensives designed, yet again, to divert German troops from the Western Front. The main assault was to be conducted by Evert's Western Front and Kuropatkin's Northern Front. In the south, *Stavka* authorized limited Russian attacks towards Lutsk by Brusilov's South-Western Front. However, Brusilov, who replaced Ivanov in March 1916, was brewing a pot of operational and tactical innovation that transformed the Russian Army.

Brusilov believed breadth of assault and tactical concentration of force were not just compatible but essential in creating a breakthrough. He argued a broad-front deployment would spread the enemy, and, by forcing opponents to cover a wider operational frontage, diminish the density and depth of their defences. In contrast to Russian commanders who forfeited deception and surprise to gain firepower, Brusilov reduced the concentration of firepower in favour of a meticulous deception plan[30] to disguise breakthrough zones and achieve surprise. A simultaneous assault across the entire front would, in conjunction with deception, undermine the enemy's ability to identify 'where the main blow will be launched against him'.[31] Russian reserves, secretly deployed behind the breakthrough sectors, would ensure tactical success was rapidly exploited, denying the enemy time to deploy reserves.

The Brusilov Offensive and Kovel operation

On 4 June 1916, South-Western Front launched a simultaneous attack with four armies on a front of 350 miles. It was astonishingly successful. In the north, Kaledin's Eighth Army swept through the Austro-Hungarian Fourth Army, and in the south Lechitskiy's Ninth Army overran the Austro-Hungarian Seventh Army. In the centre Shcherbachev's Seventh Army struggled, and initially Sakharov's Eleventh Army made limited progress against the Austro-Hungarian Second Army.

The Brusilov Offensive, June–October 1916

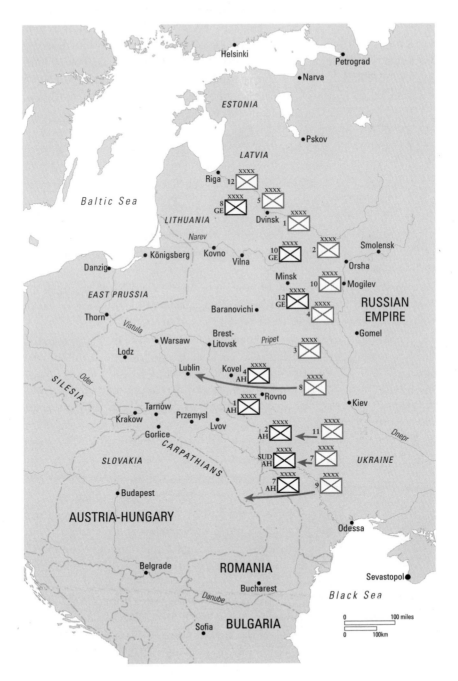

However, the simultaneous nature of the assault by Seventh Army and Eleventh Army fixed their opponents, and protecting Eighth and Ninth armies' inner flanks enabled them to smash the Austro-Hungarians. On 9 June 1916, Eighth Army took Lutsk from the Austro-Hungarian Fourth Army, which 'melted away into miserable fragments'.[32] By 11 June, the Russians had advanced 30–90 miles, and on 15 June, Eighth Army forced the River Stokhod and drove on Kovel. In the south, Ninth Army routed the Austro-Hungarian Seventh Army and crossed the Prut on 18 June.

The key was Kovel, a rail junction that facilitated operational mobility up and down the front. In mid-June 1916, Eighth Army beat off heavy German counter-attacks but unknown to Brusilov, 'exasperated beyond measure'[33] at Western Front's inactivity and concerned about his northern flank, the road to Kovel was virtually open. However, Brusilov missed his opportunity: Germans troops raced east and Eighth Army was halted on 8 July 1916, 25 miles short of Kovel.

The initial phase of the Brusilov Offensive was marked by meticulous preparations, deception, and innovation. The second stage, the Kovel operation of July 1916 – better resourced, indeed *Stavka's* main effort – was not. In the rush to take Kovel, Brusilov forgot the secrets of South-Western Front's earlier success. The assaults began on 23 July, led by Seventh and Ninth armies in the south, followed on 28 July further north by Eighth and Third armies taken from the inert Western Front and the elite Guard Army.

The Russians were repeatedly mown down due to strong German resistance, difficult terrain, and unimaginative command, not least by Brusilov, who appeared bereft of ideas. Ironically, Eleventh and Ninth armies achieved further success using the original, innovative methods, now forgotten by Brusilov. The Ninth Army drove the Austro-Hungarian Seventh Army west, and in August 1916 the Romanians entered the war only to be smashed in September by a German offensive. The Romanian collapse lengthened the Eastern Front and turned Ninth Army into a harassed defensive force trying to contain 9. Armee. In early October, Eighth Army was dispatched to the Romanian border, and on 10 October 1916, Tsar Nicholas II terminated the Brusilov Offensive.

In four weeks Brusilov destroyed the Austro-Hungarian Army as an effective fighting force and caused a major crisis for the Germans on the Eastern Front. He rehabilitated the Russian Army with intelligent and innovative command. Indeed, it has been argued that the Russians had succeeded in breaking the deadlock of trench warfare at the operational-tactical level.[34]

It was the most significant Russian victory of the war, a triumph of the art of command that enabled the Russians, albeit briefly, to out-think, outmanoeuvre, and out-fight their opponents on the Eastern Front. If Brusilov had curtailed the South-Western Front's operations in early July 1916 or conducted the second phase in a more imaginative manner, as in June 1916, his reputation as Russia's most able commander in World War I would be unblemished. However, he did neither, and by October 1916, the Russians had suffered 1.2 million casualties including 200,000 prisoners.

War and revolution

The army was not the catalyst of revolution in March 1917[35] and in general Russian soldiers remained loyal to Russia if not the Romanovs. In the bitter cold of February 1917 food prices rocketed, fuel shortages escalated, military casualties continued, and the transport system collapsed. The Russian people – starved, exhausted, and frozen – turned on the Romanovs. On 12 March 1917, the 170,000 Petrograd garrison mutinied, and on 15 March, threatened by the people and an army not willing to fight its own countrymen, Tsar Nicholas II abdicated. The trinity of government, army, and people remained intact, at least initially, because all three supported the continuation of the war. The provisional government was determined to fight on, bolstered by Britain and France as well as fear of Germany. The Russian Army did not actively support the revolution but acquiesced in the vain hope of galvanizing the Russian war effort by securing the commitment of the people. In March 1917, even the Bolsheviks accepted the Russian people would not countenance a craven peace.

However, the Russian Army's July 1917 offensive revealed a brittle army tired of war, worn down by three years on the Eastern Front. In July 1917, Russian attacks dissolved into mutinies, while entire units disintegrated when confronted by German counter-attacks. By August 1917, the Russian Army was in a state of collapse, its last resistance being Twelfth Army's futile defence of Riga in September 1917. The attempt by General Kornilov, in September 1917, to establish a military dictatorship broke the Russian Army as an organized fighting force. The soldiers wanted it to end; Kornilov wanted the war to continue. By October 1917, the Russian Army's soldiers did not need Lenin to tell them they wanted peace, bread, and if they were lucky, a bit of land. In October 1917, a *Stavka* report concluded, 'The army is simply a huge, weary, shabby and ill-fed mob of angry men, united by their common thirst for peace and common disappointment.'[36]

In the wake of the October Revolution, the Bolsheviks sued for peace. On 17 December 1917, the Germans agreed to an armistice. On 3 March 1918, the Peace of Brest-Litovsk, paid for by 1.7 million Russian dead, brought the war on the Eastern Front to an end.

CHAPTER 10

ANZACS AND THE ROCKY ROAD TO TACTICAL EFFECTIVENESS, 1916–17

Dr Andrew Macdonald

By mid-1918 there were few in the New Zealand Division who doubted that they were superior soldiers to their British counterparts. This belief had begun among New Zealand soldiers on the carrion escarpment of Gallipoli in 1915, was nurtured in the trenches of Flanders, and then flowered in the offensives of 1916 and early 1917 in France and Belgium.[1] The division's role in helping stem the Michael Offensive in March–April 1918 only served to consolidate the New Zealand rank and file's self-subscription to the superior-soldier myth, and there is plenty of evidence to show this theme was present within other Dominion formations on the Western Front.[2] This cult of the superior soldier was endorsed by the soldier-published magazine *Chronicles of the NZEF*, which was laden with the imagery of tough, independent, physically strong, and laconic New Zealand infantrymen who were successful in battle. It was this that Corporal Neil Ingram alluded to when he wrote of the New Zealand Division being 'rushed up [in March 1918 in response to the German breakthrough] to fill the breach and stem at all costs this invasion'.[3] In a considerably more emotive passage, Rifleman Vincent Jervis said the New Zealanders and Australians 'get shoved into all the hot spots. I'll bet it is because they don't run away.'[4] These sentiments were shared by numerous other New Zealand soldiers, in their personal diaries or letters home, and had obvious appeal to the communities in New Zealand from which they hailed. According to one Auckland newspaper, the New Zealand Division was 'known everywhere as one of the hardest-working and hardest-fighting'.[5] For all their pithy appeal, suggestion of a robust *esprit de corps*, and bias towards the cult of the superior soldier, these comments remain subjective assessments of the New Zealand Division and its testing path towards military effectiveness in the period 1916–17.

The New Zealand Division

The New Zealand Division was formed in the wake of the ill-fated Gallipoli campaign and sent to the Western Front in early 1916. It had one commander throughout the war, Major-General Sir Andrew Russell. Aside from its roles of holding the trenches in quieter parts of the front line and labouring work, the division participated in three of Field Marshal Sir Douglas Haig's offensives in the period 1916–17. These were the Somme in September–October 1916, Messines in June 1917, and Third Ypres in October 1917. Collectively, these provided the professional basis for the New Zealand Division's battle performance in 1918, first in helping to stop the German Army's Michael Offensive in March–April and then in the 'Hundred Days' Offensive leading to the armistice on 11 November 1918. Russell – a New Zealand-born officer who had been trained at the Royal Military Academy, Sandhurst, and had served as a regular soldier in India and Burma – had a bent to mould the New Zealand Division into one of the best on the Western Front. He sought to shrug off the division's amateur status and convert his civilian soldiers into highly skilled professionals. Russell demanded excellence and performance at all times and from every level of his formation, be it brigadier generals or privates. He leaned on the tools of military doctrine, law, and command, and supplemented these with cross-unit learning and on-going organizational introspection. By the time of its dissolution in 1919, the New Zealand Division had been on a three-year professional learning curve driven by Russell.

By early 1917, the division's participation in offensives was based around two doctrinal pamphlets, which were being used throughout the British Army. These were *SS135 Instructions for the Training of Divisions for Offensive Action* and *SS143 Instructions for the Training of Platoons for Offensive Action*. These pamphlets were based on the lessons taken from the Somme, and codified the practices already emerging in formations and units that had participated in that fighting. *SS135* set out the best practices for subjects such as issuing orders, setting battle objectives, the cooperation between artillery and infantry, deployment and manoeuvre on the battlefield, and communication. It provided the basis for training divisions ahead of offensive actions, and was designed to see them and their subordinate units repeatedly succeed on the battlefield. *SS135* recognized that generals could do little to control a battle once it had started, and as such provided them with tools to create the preconditions for success and allow their soldiers to get on with the job.[6] *SS143* was essentially a stormtrooper's handbook that set out the fire-and-movement tactics to be used by platoons in battle.[7] It also provided the basis for platoon-level training, whereby a platoon fire team comprising Lewis gunners and rifle grenadiers laid siege to any given German defensive obstacle, such as machine-gun posts, while the manoeuvre teams of riflemen and bombers outflanked and captured it. Ahead of participating in the offensives of 1917, the New Zealand Division was one of many in the British Army that actively embraced the contents of these two pamphlets in their training for future offensive actions.

Learning organization

This approach reflected Russell's ceaseless drive for excellence as he turned his division into a top-to-bottom learning organization. By late 1917, Russell was requiring all divisional training to be carried out in accordance with the principles of *SS135*. He espoused the need for pace and determination, which he described as the 'handmaidens of success in war'.[8] By 'pace', Russell was referring to the speed at which his soldiers could complete successive battlefield tasks.[9] 'You cannot do that unless you put your back into training,' he said.[10] Determination, and all that it implied, was instilled over time. 'If, in every single thing that you attempt, you endeavour to do your very best, paying attention to every trifling detail, you will be well on the road to the acquisition of this quality.'[11] Russell was emphasizing the importance of doctrine-based training, and the benefits of repeatedly practising tactics at platoon, company, battalion, and brigade levels so that those units were highly skilled, rather than merely proficient, in employing them on the battlefield. Specialist units embraced the training doctrine specific to their roles. 'Now, there are no such things as excuses in war. There are no half-way houses,' wrote Russell.[12] From his experiences on the Somme and Messines, and lessons learnt from the same, Russell knew his division's future battle performances would be influenced by the quality of its training regimen and he repeatedly emphasized this to his subordinate commanders and men.

Russell had identified the importance of this as early as 1916, and it became a hallmark of his preparations before each major action. This was true of the Somme, Messines, and also Third Ypres. Ahead of Third Ypres, for instance, he insisted his infantry practise section, platoon, and company drill, followed by battalion-level training and then exercises organized by his infantry brigadiers. This broadly mirrored the New Zealand Division's training sessions before the Somme and Messines. Beyond the requirements of *SS135*, Russell insisted his units undertook their training according to *SS143*, at the same time synthesizing tactical lessons from across the British Army, in particular from the highly experienced Canadian Corps, into his training programme. He circulated studies of the latest fighting and the lessons to be taken from it,[13] translations of captured German documents outlining their defensive doctrine, and drew on the knowledge base of more experienced formation commanders, whether Dominion or British. At Third Ypres in autumn 1917 the German Army was employing defence-in-depth tactics, with the carefully coordinated use of machine guns in concrete pillboxes, artillery fire, and pre-allocated counter-attack formations. A British attack would have to advance through increasingly well-defended German positions before arriving at the main defensive line, all the time suffering casualties and being open to counter-attack. Collectively the *SS*-series of doctrines provided the best practice, or standard operating procedure, for overcoming these German tactics and Russell left few stones unturned instilling this within his division.

Looking more widely at the British Army, the evidence shows that Russell was far from alone in recognizing the importance of this type of training. While serving in Lieutenant-General Sir Alexander Godley's II Anzac Corps, Russell's methods were replicated in Major-General Sir John Monash's 3rd Australian Division, which was part of the same formation. This was also true of the various divisions in Lieutenant-General Sir Arthur Currie's Canadian Corps,[14] and among the divisions in Lieutenant-General Sir William Birdwood's I Anzac Corps. Of the latter, the practices in Major-General Sir Harold Walker's 1st Australian Division mirrored those in Russell's and Monash's.[15] The evidence also shows that the divisional-level emphasis on doctrine-based training was not confined to Dominion formations. In September 1917, the 48th (South Midland) and 9th (Scottish) divisions used the same training programme as Russell's.[16] These examples were not isolated. The 4th, 7th, and 11th divisions also used *SS135* and *SS143*, proving these pamphlets provided the basis for training across the British Army at this time, and specifically in the Second and Fifth armies. As a company commander in the 1/5th Royal Warwickshire Regiment wrote, in the aftermath of the Somme the best divisions had worked out the value of the tactics that were later contained in the doctrine and the training programmes of 1917, and then built on this foundation.[17] This included the 4th, 7th, 9th (Scottish), 11th, and 48th (South Midland) divisions, all of which were battle experienced and just as capably embracing the same tactical lessons as Russell's New Zealanders.

The model of attack

For all its worth, training was only one element of the model of attack developed by the British Army by late 1917. In isolation it could not guarantee battlefield victory; all the elements of the model of attack, which had come of age by the dawn of 1918,[18] needed to be present. This model of attack was based on the crucial artillery-infantry-engineering relationship, the considered application of finite resources from each of these branches, and the use of limited objectives within an attack framework that was organized by army corps and implemented by divisions. In essence this meant that if an attack was to succeed, the artillery, infantry, and engineering units involved had several critical tasks to perform, both individually and collectively. The artillery had to be deployed on time, in sufficient numbers, and with enough ammunition to neutralize German defensive obstacles, and also cover the infantry with a creeping barrage – one that moves forwards in increments of, say, 100 yards every few minutes – as it advanced to engage the enemy. The infantry not only had to know the tactics of attack, but also have predefined roles and limited objectives – those it was to capture and not move beyond – to achieve with the support of the artillery before, during, and after the operation. The engineers were to facilitate this by building and maintaining a robust logistics and infrastructure network for bringing men and materiel such as artillery guns and supplies forward according to demand and an attack timetable. Given the difficulties involved in controlling a battle once it had been joined,[19] the model of attack's success was clearly conditional on the scale and quality of all preparations undertaken beforehand according to the artillery-infantry-engineering paradigm.

The importance of corps

Against this background the army corps emerges as a key element in the application of the tactical-level model of attack in the context of World War I. An army corps, such as II Anzac, was a formation subordinate to an army headquarters that held administrative responsibilities for the geographic area it was located in and the operations it undertook. Army corps were commanded by lieutenant-generals, such as Godley, had a permanent complement of staff officers, corps troops, and usually composed three or four infantry divisions. Each infantry division usually numbered about 18,000 soldiers, of whom about 12,000 were infantry and 4,000 were gunners. The role and responsibilities of corps evolved during the war so that by 1917 they had taken on a far greater importance in the conduct of operations, and particularly that of the artillery, via an increasing move towards decentralized command. By late 1917, corps comprised several departments that reflected the enlarged scope of its administrative role, and the managerial role it played for attached divisions. The General Staff (GS), Corps Artillery Headquarters (CAH), and Corps Heavy Artillery Headquarters (CHAH) branches were primarily focused on planning and preparing for operations that involved infantry and artillery, while the attached Corps Commander, Royal Engineers (CCRE) was responsible for the logistics and infrastructure. The Adjutant & Quartermaster General (A&QMG) branch managed stores and supply, while the Administrative Services and Departments branch oversaw signals, medical, ordnance, and postal services. By late 1917, the corps was the highest level of command concerned with the detail of tactical-level operations.

This structure was used in both Dominion and British corps, although there were some differences in how these were composed. British corps were generally tied to specific geographic locations, with many divisions being rotated through their commands over a period of time. By contrast, the Australian and Canadian corps normally had the same divisions permanently attached, which meant that these units were arguably better placed to synthesize the British Army's doctrines and learn from their experiences. Godley's II Anzac straddled both models by having two Dominion divisions on strength, while various British divisions were assigned to it at different times, such as at Messines and Third Ypres. Traditionally, the analysis of corps performance has been artificially divided along the lines of nationality.[20] Such an approach overlooks the fact that Dominion and British corps had much more in common – such as structure, doctrine, training, and military law – than not. At Vimy Ridge, for instance, the Canadians relied on British expertise in the form of commanders, tactical doctrine, logistical support and even infantry[21] The same was true of the two Anzac corps, and, indeed, of every British corps on the Western Front. Even then, with the exception of Currie, the vast majority of corps commanders and staff officers were products of the British army training system, including Godley and Birdwood. In reality, corps composition – whether Dominion or British – was a secondary factor in the attainment of tactical effectiveness, and battlefield performance had more to with the experience, ability, and character of individual corps commanders and their staffs.

Four of the branches that comprised a corps headquarters had a particular bearing on the attainment of tactical effectiveness in an attack. These were, because of their direct contributions to the artillery–infantry–engineering effort underpinning an operation, the GS, CAH, CHAH, and CCRE branches. These departments were responsible for planning and preparing for attacks in which the artillery, infantry, and engineering were supposed to have an organic relationship with one another. While overall artillery framework was devised at army level, corps produced the detailed fire scheme in consultation with its divisions. The CAH's General Officer Commanding, Royal Artillery (GOCRA), coordinated the activities of field and heavy artillery, as well as between the corps' infantry and artillery. He directly controlled the mix, quality, and application of artillery supporting an infantry attack, and the CHAH reported to him. In the GS branch, a Brigadier-General, General Staff (BGGS), and several other staff officers coordinated infantry attack plans within their own corps and with neighbouring ones, in consultation with GOCRA. The actual detail of the infantry element was decentralized to divisions. Meanwhile, the CCRE's job was to ensure the logistics and infrastructure networks supporting the artillery and infantry elements of an attack were present by overseeing the work of pioneering and engineering units, whether attached to corps headquarters or the divisions it comprised. It is apparent that a division's performance in battle was intrinsically linked to that of army corps and therefore the process of decentralized command.

Decentralized command

The process of decentralized command became increasingly important as the role of corps evolved with the expansion of the British Army. Early in the war, British Army Headquarters exerted a prescriptive influence on tactical-level operations, but this began to change towards the end of 1916. Gradually, corps commanders took on a greater importance in the conduct of battlefield operations, and so too did their subordinate divisional and brigade commanders.[22] This was the notion of decentralized command. At the time of Third Ypres, corps were taking an increasingly hands-on role in preparing and planning tactical-level operations. By September 1917, they had taken this further and were being issued with maps at an Army level with the respective corps being left to decide how to attain their various objectives.[23] Underpinning decentralization of command was the principle that — as prescribed in *Field Service Regulations* (FSR) — the 'man on the spot' knew best.[24] This meant the man in closest proximity to any event – be it an attack, worsening road conditions, and so on – was best placed to make qualitative assessments and decisions about it, subject to his experience, personality, and relationships with senior officers.[25] Thus, in 1917, corps commanders, as they filled the role of 'man on the spot' for army headquarters, began to exert a much greater influence over the level of tactical effectiveness achieved by their divisions.

There is ample evidence to suggest that corps' enlarged role in the model of attack worked very well. The opening day of the battle of Arras on 9 April 1917 saw Lieutenant-General Sir Julian Byng's Canadian Corps, Lieutenant-General Sir Charles Fergusson's XVII Corps and Lieutenant-General Sir Thomas D'Oyly Snow's VII's Corps all produce favourable results as part of General Sir Edmund Allenby's Third Army. However, the British Army could not convert the initial 'break-in' to a 'break-through', with the battle thereafter floundering and ultimately being closed down.[26] Using the set-piece model of attack in June 1917, Godley's II Anzac, Lieutenant-General Sir Alexander Hamilton-Gordon's IX Corps, and Lieutenant-General Sir Thomas Morland's X Corps captured the Messines Ridge in a meticulously planned and well-resourced 'bite-and-hold' operation by General Sir Herbert Plumer's Second Army. The 'planning and conduct of the battle of Messines was a model for modern warfare and the principal root from which the BEF [sic] grew in 1918.'[27] There were other success stories, too, such as at Menin Road on 20 September, Polygon Wood on 26 September and Broodseinde on 4 October, these battles variously involving II Anzac, I Anzac, IX Corps, Lieutenant-General Sir Edward Fanshawe's V Corps, Lieutenant-General the Earl of Cavan's XIV Corps, and Lieutenant-General Sir Ivor Maxse's XVIII Corps. In each case, whether in a British or Dominion corps, the successful 'bite-and-hold' attacks were characterized by generally realistic operational tempos, sufficient quantity and application of artillery resources,[28] and methodical planning and preparations within the artillery-infantry-engineering paradigm.

Comparable performance

Looking more closely at the corps-controlled model of attack, a number of striking similarities can be observed between British and Dominion divisions operating within it. At Broodseinde, as a representative example, Russell's New Zealand infantry advanced in artillery formation behind the II Anzac-organized creeping barrage that neutralized most of the German defensive obstacles. In keeping with the German defence-in-depth doctrine, the New Zealanders encountered increasingly stiff resistance in the form of machine guns in ferro-concrete pillboxes, and used fire-and-movement tactics they had trained in to successfully overcome them. By day's end the division had captured its interim and final limited objectives and was consolidating its just-won positions, again with artillery support. Looking across the Broodseinde battlefield, a strong correlation can be noted between the New Zealanders' performance and that of the 4th and 48th (South Midland) divisions in Fifth Army, and the 7th Division in Second Army. In 48th (South Midland) Division, each of its brigades was well supported by artillery, used a two-phase operation to capture their objectives, and modified their pattern of advance to suit broken or difficult ground and local obstacles. As one British officer noted, the 'battle-drill [training] had not been in vain'.[29] Again in keeping with Russell's New Zealanders, the three British divisions at times suffered from localized confusion, disruption from hostile shell- and small-arms fire, and casualties. The comparison holds true if the various Australian divisions of I Anzac and II Anzac are factored in.[30] The experiences of these three British divisions, several Australian divisions, and the New Zealand Division reveal a homogenous standard of tactical effectiveness among both British and Dominion divisions within a doctrinally based attack framework administered by corps.

This theme applies if the disasters of Poelcappelle and First Passchendaele are considered, using II Anzac as a looking glass to assess performance. The mud, the breakdown of the logistics and infrastructure networks, and the accelerating operational tempo agreed to by Godley after Broodseinde meant that on 9 October the corps-organized artillery supporting the 49th (West Riding) and 66th (East Lancashire) divisions'[31] attacks could not provide a reliable creeping barrage to cover the infantry. The patchy and weak creeping barrage failed to suppress the German defensive obstacles on Bellevue Spur, namely the barbed wire and multiple machine guns housed in pillboxes and strongpoints. Sodden ground conditions meant attacking British infantry in both divisions struggled to make even slow progress. Platoons were unable to get through the barbed wire or near the numerous German machine–gun posts behind it, and were quickly debilitated by heavy casualties. The situation rendered fire-and-movement tactics redundant. Three days later – on exactly the same piece of ground, with conditions having worsened – New Zealand infantry was shot to a standstill and had no hope of deploying fire-and-movement tactics to overcome German defensive obstacles. The experiences of II Anzac's divisions were again in keeping with those of their Australian and British counterparts in Second and Fifth armies, particularly in the case of the 11th and 48th (South Midland) divisions at Poelcappelle and the 9th (Scottish) Division at First Passchendaele. Further south, the Australian divisions of I Anzac found their advance difficult, and any hard-won gains were rendered untenable by II Anzac's failure. What emerges is

The Third Battle of Ypres, 1917

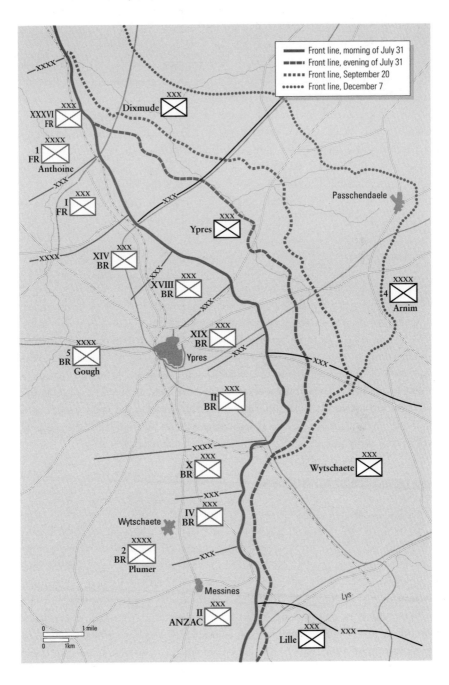

a picture of multiple Australian and British divisions that, like their New Zealand counterpart, were unable to show how tactically effective they could be because the II Anzac-organized attack frameworks for Poelcappelle and First Passchendaele, which neighbouring corps were compelled to follow, were flawed.

This claim holds true if the Canadian Corps' capture of Passchendaele in October–November is considered. Currie's attack plans show he understood the artillery-infantry-engineering paradigm, how this related to doctrine, and how both translated into robust planning and preparation for the drive up Passchendaele ridge. Currie realized the success of the coming battle largely depended on his 'men on the spot' and the role of his engineering and artillery units in facilitating an infantry attack.[32] Unlike Godley before him, who had missed the Somme, Currie knew from experience that the heat needed to be taken out of Haig's operational tempo, and he sought and won more time to plan and prepare. What followed was a successful multi-phase operation that saw the Canadian infantry force its way into the layered German defensive network and capture Passchendaele, always well supported by artillery and backed up by a solid engineering effort.[33] The Canadians took limited time between phases to reassess the situation and factor necessary changes into the attack scheme.[34] What emerges is a picture of a corps operating as one, with the professionalism and skill at corps headquarters matched by that at other levels of the hierarchy. The lessons of the Somme prepared Currie and his corps both tactically and intellectually for the challenge of Passchendaele Ridge.[35] These were the hallmarks of Currie's command style, are evident in his diary,[36] and prove Plumer's bite-and-hold tactics could work on a muddy battlefield and in atrocious weather and ground conditions. The inevitable conclusion is that Currie possessed a tactically mature and professional formation, valued his men, and knew exactly what steps were necessary to succeed against a well-prepared enemy.

No guarantees for success

Clearly, the model of attack could and often did work, but success on the battlefield was by no means guaranteed. Poelcappelle, First Passchendaele, and the Canadian advance up Passchendaele Ridge reveal corps to be the pivot point between tactical success and failure, even in atrocious environmental conditions. Godley had too readily agreed to Haig's desire for an accelerating operational tempo, but was unable to match this with robust preparations within the artillery-infantry-engineering paradigm. In real terms this meant that after Broodseinde, II Anzac's artillery was unable to deploy sufficient guns or ammunition on time, which was due to the corps-organized engineering effort failing because of the diminishing number of days between each attack and worsening weather. Both had negative implications for the infantry. Godley's command throughout could be characterized as hands-off rather than hands-on; he knew the conditions in the forward area and their impact on preparations at divisional level, but did nothing to intercede. He had got away with hands-off command at Messines and Broodseinde because of the generally fine weather and abilities of Russell and Monash. Godley's failure to call for a delay was a breach of his 'man on the spot' responsibility to army headquarters, and – irrespective of how good his subordinates were – condemned the New Zealand, Australian, and British divisions in II Anzac to failure. Because II Anzac formed Second Army's vanguard on 9 and 12 October, his acceptance of Haig's operational tempo also had a profound effect on the ability of neighbouring corps and divisions to produce tactically effective performances. As we have seen, Currie did everything Godley had not in preparing his corps for Passchendaele, and his success reflects that. The generally advanced and homogenous level of tactical skill present in Dominion and British divisions in late 1917 counted for little if not matched by corps in implementing the established model of attack.

The ratio of casualties to ground captured for II Anzac and the Canadian Corps on the Passchendaele battlefield reveals much about the differing styles of their commanders.[37] Attacking up the Bellevue Spur on 9 and 12 October, Godley's corps advanced about 700 yards at best for a cost of about 11,650 New Zealand, Australian, and British casualties. II Anzac's minor advance and failure to achieve anything close to its objectives worked out at about 16.6 casualties per yard. After attacking over more or less the same piece of ground in October–November, Currie's corps advanced to a total depth of about 2,500 yards, racking up about 16,041 casualties in the process, or 6.4 Canadian casualties for each yard gained. The difference between these two figures, 10.2 casualties a yard, was the premium for Godley's failure as a corps commander. It represents a tragic waste of lives, and, in contrast with Currie, the litany of mistakes he made in planning, preparing, and executing the attacks of Poelcappelle and First Passchendaele.

The superior-soldier myth

Taken as whole, this evidence undermines the belief held by many New Zealand soldiers that they were superior to their British peers. In both victory and defeat the above examples show the New Zealanders' performance was comparable to that of other Dominion and British formations. The conventional view that portrays a 'charmed circle' of innovators during World War I is generally incorrect as tactical innovation is to be found everywhere[38] This is most obviously found in the evolving relationship that would continue into 1918 between the tools of battle – namely weapons, doctrine and technology – and those using them.[39] The Canadian soldiers were not sheep led to slaughter, but constantly updated their methods and tactics in the face of a well-trained and well-motivated enemy.[40] By 1918, the Canadian Corps had moved away from the concept of the citizen soldier, to an army of technicians, which, even in infantry battalions, specialized in particular aspects of fighting battles.[41] These assertions were also true of numerous other divisions, whether British, New Zealand, or Australian. They can be seen in the British 18th (Eastern) Division in the period 1914–18.[42] It was what the 9th (Scottish) Division's historian meant when he commented that by late 1917 there were 'few novices in the Ninth in the art of mounting an attack'.[43] It is not surprising to find Dominion and British divisions fighting similarly to one another in 1917 and producing similar outcomes in both battlefield success and failure; this merely reflects the widespread tactical evolution underway, the common usage of doctrine in training and battle preparations,[44] and the key role of corps in the attainment of tactical effectiveness on the battlefield.

Not all divisional commanders were advancing along the tactical learning curve at an equal rate. The best Dominion and British divisional commanders evaluated the Somme experience and profited from it.[45] This was true of Russell, whose command at Messines and then Third Ypres confirms the Somme taught him the importance of the artillery-infantry-engineering relationship in planning and preparing for tactical-level operations. More specifically, the Somme gave Russell a tangible insight into the value of training, the importance of artillery, building functional infrastructure and logistics networks, communication, the use of limited and interim objectives, flank support, structuring an attack according to both the ground and German defensive obstacles, and meaningfully engaging with his corps and army commanders. He was not alone. Divisional commanders in the Canadian Corps had begun a similar experience-based course as early as 1915, and they were followed by those in I Anzac and then II Anzac from 1916. The same, for instance, can be seen in the 18th (Eastern) Division, with Maxse – who became a corps commander in 1917 – warning subordinates not to assume that it would be 'all right on the night'.[46] The commanders of British and Australian divisions at Menin Road used doctrine to plan and prepare for battle, so that they could commit their troops with confidence.[47] This can be seen at both the planning and preparation stages, and was a hallmark of the staff work issued by these formations.[48] The year 1917 saw numerous divisional commanders engage with a model of attack that gave the wider British Army a critical mass of professional expertise going into 1918.

The 'Hundred Days' Offensive

This critical mass of professional expertise is borne out by the statistics of Dominion and British divisions in the 'Hundred Days' Offensive, which concluded on 11 November 1918. In 221 individual attacking operations, a sample of Dominion divisions produced a success rate of 68.8 per cent in opposed attacks.[49] By contrast, a survey of 966 individual operations by British divisions yielded a 58.81 per cent success rate in opposed attacks.[50] The success rate of the nine British divisions that served in Fourth Army during the 'Hundred Days' was 70.7 per cent, while for the 17 British divisions in Third Army the rate was 64.38 per cent.[51] On a division-by-division basis, the statistics show a comparable success rate between British and Dominion divisions in opposed attacks, although there were outliers representing over- and under-performance. In this period, the Australian and Canadian Corps retained their static composition of divisions, while British corps continued to have divisions (including Russell's New Zealanders) revolved through their command. Thus it emerges that the real keys to success in the 'Hundred Days' were the weapons system, the manner in which those weapons were being employed, and the model of attack, much of which dated back to the process of tactical maturation in the period 1916–17. In the three months leading to the armistice, British divisions were generally as successful as their Dominion counterparts, suggesting that the attainment of tactical effectiveness and superior-soldiery were not limited to Dominion formations.[52]

This claim is further supported by an evaluation of corps' role in the 'Hundred Days'. By 1918, a much greater role in the management of operations was delegated to divisions than in 1916–17.[53] In other words, in the 'Hundred Days' army corps generally took a more hands–off approach to planning, preparing, and conducting operations than in 1917. If viewed in this light, the comparable performances of many British and Dominion divisions in the 'Hundred Days' can be seen as evidence of how far their commanders had advanced along the tactical learning curve of 1916–17, and the extent to which they continued to embrace doctrinal evolution moving into 1918. The comparable level of battle effectiveness demonstrated by many divisions in 1918 – and then with corps taking a less hands–on role – strongly suggests the cult of the superior soldier was not the exclusive domain of Dominion formations, but in fact had a much wider and considerably less vocal subscription across the wider British field army.

A pronounced confidence

Nevertheless, the growing confidence in tactical ability remains most pronounced in the diaries and correspondence of Dominion soldiers. As we have seen, the New Zealanders were far from alone in plotting their course along the tactical learning curve; there were other British and Dominion formations at a similar stage of this process, and equally there were those that were either ahead of or behind them. The difficulty with Dominion soldier self-assessments lies in their inability or reluctance to divorce the issues of culture and identity from those relating to the acquisition of a professional skillset over a prolonged period of time. It is nonetheless reasonable to note that many Dominion soldiers saw themselves as different from British soldiers, and the first point of contrast was usually accent of speech, followed by differences in uniform items such as badges and headwear. While such differences helped create unique identities and fostered robust *esprit de corps*, they cannot be shown to have any direct link to the attainment of tactical effectiveness. Something more than the presence of distinctive national traits accounts for success in battle.[54] The partisan views expressed about British troops by the New Zealand Division and other Dominion formations should be seen for what they are: fitful expressions of their growing competence and confidence that amount to incomplete comparatives.

Conclusion

There can be little doubt that soldiers of the New Zealand Division self-subscribed to the superior-soldier myth, but in truth they were far from unique in terms of their ability to turn in tactically effective battlefield performances. This tendency can also be seen in other Dominion formations throughout the war, and probably found its origins in those civilian soldiers contrasting their differing national identities and cultures with those of the more numerous 'Tommies'. But, the Anzac, Canadian, South African, and Newfoundland soldiers were again far from alone in negotiating the tactical learning curve of the Somme, Messines, and Passchendaele; the evidence shows there were plenty of British divisions advancing at a similar rate, and perhaps even faster, as data relating to their relative battle performances in 1918 has revealed. Much of this had to do with the tactical-level advances across the British Army over the period 1916–17, where doctrine and weapons systems were seamlessly integrated into a model of attack that could and often did work. Against this backcloth divisional commanders – such as Russell, among others – emerge as key drivers in Haig's push to build an army capable of producing the victories of 1918 and ultimately helping to force the armistice. At the grassroots level it was the experience, skill, and drive of individual divisional commanders and their subordinates that decided how quickly their formations embraced the prevailing doctrine, training, weapons system, and the artillery-infantry-engineering paradigm underpinning the model of attack. The same was true of army corps – whether Dominion or British in composition – and this level of the military hierarchy emerges from the battles of late 1917 as a key pivot point between tactical-level success and failure. Finally, there is ample evidence to show the Anzacs were among a vanguard of British and Dominion formations that were together treading the often difficult path towards tactical maturation that culminated in the attainment of a British army-wide critical mass of expertise and ultimately the victory of 1918.

CHAPTER 11

A SIDESHOW OF A SIDESHOW?

The Arab Revolt (1916–18) and the Development of Modern Desert Warfare

Dr David Murphy

During the 1920s, T. E. Lawrence referred to the Arabian Desert campaign of World War I as 'a sideshow of a sideshow'.[1] It was a campaign in which he had played a significant part and he would later do much to form public perceptions of the Arab Revolt through his own writings. In both *Revolt in the Desert* (1927) and *The Seven Pillars of Wisdom* (first public edition, 1935) T. E. Lawrence outlined a campaign that was largely conducted by tribal forces and through raids of various sizes. As Lawrence's writings have since influenced historians of the campaign, not to mention his own biographers, this perception has remained in vogue.[2] David Lean's movie *Lawrence of Arabia* (1962) reintroduced Lawrence to a modern audience and reconfirmed the perception that the Arab Revolt was waged through a campaign of dashing desert raids and adventures and that this campaign was primarily fought by tribal forces. While a fascinating and romantic depiction of the revolt, it also encouraged detractors of the whole campaign to dismiss it quite simply as 'a sideshow of a sideshow'.

Modern scholarship has forced a major revision of these perceptions while the archaeological work of the Great Arab Revolt Project is gradually uncovering the physical evidence of a major desert campaign.[3] While Lawrence played a significant role in the desert campaign, the vision he presents through his writings is actually quite limited. By 1918 the Arab Revolt represented a large and impressive operation that included the use of Arab regular forces, light armour, truck-mounted artillery, an increasingly sophisticated use of artillery and support weapons, and also the integration of air assets. Furthermore, the campaigns of the Arab Northern Army in particular would greatly assist the offensives carried out by the Egyptian Expeditionary Force (EEF) commanded by General Allenby in 1917 and 1918. Alongside other desert campaigns of World War I, it would serve as a model for desert operations during World War II.

The Arab Revolt had its origins in pre-war contacts between the Sharif of Mecca, Emir Hussein ibn Ali, and British authorities in Cairo. While the Hejaz region of Arabia (in modern-day Saudi Arabia) had been under Ottoman control since the 16th century, Hussein recognized that the Young Turk government was dedicated to strengthening its grasp throughout the Ottoman provinces. A pre-war crackdown on dissenters in Syria further forced his hand and the Emir made overtures to GHQ in Cairo in order to gauge possible British support for a future revolt.[4] After the outbreak of war in 1914, a steady supply of small arms and money was ferried across the Red Sea by the Royal Navy and landed on the Arabian coast. By 1916, the Emir felt that his position was strong enough to begin a revolt and, with his sons (the Emirs Ali, Abdullah, Feisal, and Zeid) he rallied tribesmen to his banners during the summer months. On 5 June 1916, Emirs Ali and Feisal informed the Turkish commander at Medina, General Fakhri Pasha, of the Arabs' intention to withdraw from the Ottoman Empire. An attack on Medina was repulsed by Ottoman forces and thereafter attacks began on the strategically crucial Hejaz Railway. On 10 June, Emir Abdullah proclaimed the revolt in Mecca and further attacks occurred on Ottoman garrisons at Ta'if and Jiddah. The Arab Revolt had begun.[5]

In Cairo, General Sir Archibald Murray was now forced to factor a new front in Arabia into his plans. He had begun an advance through Sinai – an advance that brought considerable logistical challenges. It soon became apparent that without Allied assistance, the Arab Revolt would soon be in serious difficulties as Turkish forces advanced out of Medina with the intention of crushing this insurrection.[6] In June and July, the Royal Navy's Red Sea Patrol ferried Egyptian troops and artillery, under British officers, to the Hejaz. These additional forces led to the surrender of further Turkish garrisons and also opposed Turkish advances on the Arab-held coastal towns such as Jiddah,

Rabegh, and Yenbo. The Royal Navy provided crucial fire-support in the defence of these towns while seaplanes launched from the carrier HMS *Ben-My-Chree* attacked Turkish columns. By December 1916, the Turkish countermoves against the revolt had been stopped and Arab and Allied leaders began to plan the future of the Arab Revolt.

It should be remembered that this was indeed an 'Allied' effort. The French also had interests in Arabia and they would eventually form a 'Military Mission to Egypt' based as Port Said, numbering just over 1,100 men. In fact, the French had a significant advantage over the British in being able to deploy Muslim officers and men, drawn from the regiments raised in their North African colonies.[7]

The British mission to the Hejaz was code-named Operation *Hedgehog* and by 1917 would number over 40 officers acting in an advisory capacity. Lawrence was just one of these and he would not arrive in Arabia until October 1916. By 1918, *Hedgehog* had expanded to include machine-gun and mortar teams, an armoured car battery, artillery teams of various types, air and logistics elements. These elements would include teams from the Indian Army and also later Imperial Camel Corps troops. During the course of the campaign, therefore, the Arab armies developed quite dramatically, and the efforts to increase the potential of this force would suggest that this operation was viewed by Allied commanders as much more than a mere sideshow. This is indicated in the order of battle below, which outlines the development of the Arab armies between 1916 and 1918.

1916

9,000 tribesmen under Emir Ali, located south of Medina
8,000 tribesmen under Emir Feisal, encamped near Yanbu
1,500 Egyptian troops and irregulars sent by the British

The Arab Northern Army, 1917–18

Commander: The Emir Faisal ibn Hussein
Deputy Commander: The Emir Zeid ibn Hussein

The Regular Sharifian Army (around 2,000 men)

Commander: Jafar Pasha al-Askari
Chief of Staff: Nuri as-Sa'id
1st Division (Aqaba). Hashemite Infantry Brigade (two battalions of around 400 men each). In April 1918, commanded by Brigaier-General Amin al-Asil.
2nd Division (Quwayra) Hashemite Infantry Brigade (800). In April 1918, commanded by Lieutenant-Colonel Majid Hasun.

An artillery contingent of eight guns crewed by 150 men and commanded by Rasim Sardast.

A machine gun detachment, commanded by Abdullah Al-Dulaimi.

A battalion of the Hejaz Camel Corps, commanded by Khalid Sa'id.

Mule-mounted infantry originally commanded by Mawlud Mukhlis.

Associated logistical and medical units.

The Irregular Army/Tribal Forces

Around 6,000 tribesmen from various tribes including the Howeitat, the Bani 'Ali, the Bali, the Juhaynah, and the Utaybah, among others.

Commanded by their own tribal chiefs including Auda abu Tayi, Sharif Nasir ibn Ali, Sharif Ali ibn Arayd, and Sharif Mastur, among others.

Operation *Hedgehog*: the British military mission to the Arab Northern Army

Colonel P. C. Joyce commanding until March 1918.

From March 1918, Colonel Alan Dawnay.

This force included Stokes mortar and machine-gun crews attached from the British and Indian armies. There were also Egyptian troops, Gurkhas, and a labour corps. In 1918 a company of over 300 men of the Imperial Camel Corps was also attached. The force also contained:

The Hejaz Armoured Car Company, consisting of Rolls Royce Armoured Cars;

The Hejaz Talbot Car Battery, consisting of Talbot cars, some of which were mounted with 10-pounder guns;

Assorted transport vehicles including Rolls Royce tenders, Crossley tenders, and Ford cars.

Air Support

X Flight, 14 Squadron RFC (later RAF).

Elements of 1 Squadron Australian Flying Corps.

These of BE2 aircraft, Martinsydes, RE8s, and later Bristol F2 Fighters.

The Arab Southern Army, 1916–18

Based at Rabegh and commanded by the Emir Ali ibn Hussein, this force opposed the Turkish forces at Medina. It consisted of:

2 x infantry battalions;

1 x battalion mule-mounted infantry;

1 x battalion of camel-mounted infantry;

4 x artillery batteries;

1 x engineer company;

a contingent of tribal forces.

The Arab Eastern Army, 1916–18

This army was commanded by the Emir Abdullah ibn Hussein and it was based to the east of Mecca, operating against the pro-Ottoman Shammar tribe. It consisted of:

2 x battalions of camel-mounted infantry;

1 x cavalry squadron;

1 x battery of mountain artillery;

a contingent of Hashemite volunteers;

a contingent of tribal irregular forces.[8]

The initial focus of Allied advisors was to establish and train units of the Arab Regular Army, a force often overlooked by Western historians. By late 1916, the cadres of three Arab armies had developed. These would later be designated as the Arab Northern, Southern, and Eastern armies. They were commanded by former Ottoman officers who been previously taken prisoner and now had defected to the Allied side. Prominent among these were Jafar Pasha al-Askari, Nuri as'Said, and Aziz Ali al'Mazri, all of whom were Iraqi former officers of the Ottoman army with nationalist leanings.[9] Each of these armies would later number around 3,000 men, the majority of them Arab soldiers of the Ottoman army who were recruited from POW camps.

Each of the Arab armies had associated tribal forces, led by their own tribal chiefs. While the Eastern and Southern Armies remained in the vicinity of Medina and Mecca, the Arab Northern Army under Emir Feisal was to have a more active war that would see it operate in conjunction with the forces of the EEF during the final campaigns in the Middle East. This army was also to be the focus of the main effort of the British *Hedgehog* mission, while Lawrence operated with its associated tribal forces. During the course of the remainder of the war, it was largely this force that established some of the main principles of modern desert warfare.

The Hejaz Railway campaign

From the outbreak of the revolt, the Hejaz Railway had been identified as a potential target, and indeed, tribal elements had been sporadically attacking the railway even before 1914. This single-line railway was crucial to the survival of the Turkish garrison at Medina and also at other locations along the line. From 1917 attacks of increasing size and ferocity were aimed against it until large numbers of Turkish troops were tied down in its defence. These attacks established one of the main principles of this desert campaign. Lawrence would later write: 'We were to contain the enemy by the silent threat of a vast unknown desert, not disclosing ourselves till we attacked. The attack would be nominal, directed not against him but against his stuff, so we would not seek either his strength or his weakness, but his most accessible material.'[10]

The Hejaz Railway represented the single most important lifeline for the transport of all Turkish *matériel* and its vulnerability placed their forces in an precarious position. By 1918, stoppages along the line were becoming more frequent. The Turkish commander at Medina, General Fakhri Pasha, found his capacity for offensive action reduced while it also made a secure evacuation of all of his forces impossible if that became necessary. Indeed, as early as March 1917, he had been ordered to evacuate Medina, an order that he had sensibly refused to carry out. A campaign against the railway had been considered by Arab and Allied leaders since the outbreak of the revolt but this idea was greatly facilitated by the Arab Northern Army moving to Wejh in January 1917. In early 1917 French and British officers began to take small demolition parties out into the desert to mount attacks on the railway. These officers included Capitaine Raho of the French Army, British officers such as Lieutenant-Colonel Stewart Newcombe and lieutenants Hornby and Garland, and Arab officers such as Aziz al-Mazri. The initial attacks were modest in their scale and usually just succeeded in breaking the line. In February, Lieutenant Garland became the first officer to derail a moving train using a mine of his own design, later referred to as a 'Garland Mine'.[11]

In March 1917, T. E. Lawrence carried out his first raid on the line, breaking the line in two places and also placing a mine that later derailed a train. It was the first of his many raids on the railway and he was later credited with having derailed over 70 trains. The scale of these operations is suggested by an equipment request submitted by Lawrence in 1918:

> I want about 2,000 yards of insulated cable; if possible 1,000 yards of it twin, and 1,000 yards single. As light as possible. Also please electric 200 detonators or as many of them as you can spare. Also 3 pounds of adhesive tape. Also an electric exploder. Twenty boxes (1,000lbs) of blasting gelatine. Up to 5,000lbs (depending on camels) of guncotton. 100 yards of insulated fuse, 80 fathoms of safety fuse, 100 ordinary detonators, 300 guncotton primers, two clasp knives, ten wire cutters, tenon [?] saw. The Indian MG detachment want two months rations, two Lewis guns.[12]

Following the relocation of the Arab Northern Army to Aqaba in July 1917, and its reinforcement with armoured cars and further artillery assets, the railway raids became increasingly ambitious. Colonel P. C. Joyce, who commanded

The strategic situation in the Hejaz

Jurf ad Darawish

Bair

Wadi Sirhan

Petra • Ma'an • Jefer

Guweira • Ghadir el Haj

Shedia

SINAI

Shahm

Arab Northern Army (Main base)

Aqaba

Mudawwarah

Hallat Ammar

Wadi Fejr

Fejr

THE GREAT NEFUDH

AL-HOUL

Dira'a

Hejaz Railway

El Kurr • Al'Ula

ARABIA

Wejh

Um Lejj

Aba el Na'am

Medina

Fakhri Pasha

Nakhl Mubarak

Yanbu

Hamra

Red Sea

Bir ash-Sheikh

Masturah

Rabegh

Arab Southern Army

Emir Ali

EGYPT

Arab Eastern Army

Emir Abdullah

Jiddah • Mecca

Ta'if

→ Route of Aqaba raid

✚ RFC Airfields

✚ Turkish airfields

0   100 miles
0   100km

the *Hedgehog* mission, worked out procedures with British and Arab officers for large-scale attacks on the line. By 1918, they realized that they could approach quite large Turkish garrisons and while these were kept under suppressing fire from the armoured cars, machine-gun teams or mountain-guns, the demolition parties could work on the line. In a series of raids in July 1917, over 800 charges were laid along the line to the north and south of al 'Ula by parties led by Joyce and Newcombe. This major raid was also assisted by RFC planes that arrived to bomb and strafe the garrison at al 'Ula itself. Lawrence would later refine his own operations and sometimes use just a single machine-gun and Stokes-mortar team to contain Turkish troops while he carried out his demolitions. The effective use of firepower would increasingly become a hallmark of the Arab Revolt.

Such raids played a major part in this desert campaign, tying down Fakhri Pasha's garrison in Medina and reducing its overall effectiveness. Furthermore, they necessitated the maintenance of Turkish garrisons and reaction forces along the length of the line while further manpower was required to provide repair parties. At crucial junctures of the Middle East campaign, such as during General Allenby's Third Gaza Offensive in October 1917, further raids were organized to ensure that large formations of Turkish troops were not redeployed from the Hejaz to fight in the campaign in Palestine. These skills of railway demolition were passed on to Arab troops and tribesmen by the British officers and it is interesting to note that during the Iraq Rebellion of 1920, the railway was targeted. This limited the movement of British troops and it is known that former officers of the Arab or 'Sharifian' Army were involved in this later rebellion against the British.[13]

Long-range raiding

Both the Arab and Allied officers of the revolt very quickly recognized the Arabian theatre offered the potential for carrying out long-range raids into Turkish rear areas. Indeed, in the context of this campaign, the leaders of the revolt very quickly proved to the Turkish commanders that there were no safe rear areas. The vastness and the openness of the desert theatre offered multiple possible lines of advance to targets, and these could not all be adequately patrolled or defended by Turkish forces. The success of the raids against the Hejaz Railway throughout 1917 and 1918 served as adequate proof of this. The use of tribal forces, with their local knowledge and ability to travel long distances by camel, would also facilitate long-range operations.

On a strategic level, it was recognized in May 1917 that the capture of Aqaba on the Red Sea coast would bring a number of advantages to the Arab Northern Army. Firstly, it would deny the Turks their last remaining port on the Red Sea. Secondly, the capture of this port town would provide the Arab Northern Army with a new base from which to threaten both Ma'an and Mudawwarah. Finally, it would allow the Arab Northern Army to operate in Sinai and also in a north-eastern orientation towards Palestine, Lebanon, and Syria in conjunction with future planned operations. A further, and not insubstantial, benefit of the Aqaba plan was that it would facilitate the supply and support of the army by the Royal Navy.

Lawrence would emerge as the main protagonist in the Aqaba scheme and on 9 May 1917 he left Wejh with a small contingent including Sharif Nasir, Auda abu Tayi, and other tribal leaders. During the course of May and June, this small party covered over 600 miles of the worst and most inhospitable desert in the world in what must surely be one of the most difficult 'advances to contact' ever carried out. Having recruited further Howeitat tribesmen in the vicinity of Aqaba, the Arab force overran outlying Turkish garrisons before finally taking the town on 6 July 1917. Their plan was assisted in no small part by a Royal Navy gunboat that had recently shelled the town. Nevertheless, it was a significant success and was based on the ability of the Arab forces to carry out a long sweeping approach to the target and then emerge unexpected from the desert.[14]

This tactic would be used again throughout the revolt. Lawrence himself tried to repeat this success in October 1917 in order to carry out a major diversionary attack on the railway bridges in the Yarmuk Valley in Ottoman Syria. Again, this entailed an approach over several weeks and his small party included tribesmen and also Indian Army machine-gun and mortar parties. It was hoped that a well-timed attack on the line in the Yarmuk Valley would aid Allenby's Third Gaza Offensive by cutting the line and preventing reinforcements and supplies reaching the front, while also diverting troops from the front to protect the line. Ultimately, the attack on the night of 7–8 November was a failure, descending into near farce. On their final approach, a farmer fired on the raiding party before poor noise discipline alerted Turkish sentries. Having beaten a hasty retreat, Lawrence then found that his tribesmen had dropped much of the explosives in their haste to get away. Despite this, Allenby later stated that he was pleased with the raid as it had diverted Turkish troops from the front, facilitating the success of his troops in breaching the Gaza–Beersheba line.[15]

In November 1917 the Arab Northern Army was reinforced by the allocation of a squadron of Rolls Royce armoured cars and also the addition of Ford and Talbot cars. Some of the latter mounted 10-pounder guns. British armoured cars had operated in conjunction with Arab forces earlier in the revolt but these new elements were to remain attached to the army until the end of the war. This increased the army's potential in terms of both mobility and firepower. Previous long-range operations had, of course, been reliant on camels and these necessitated the careful choosing of fit animals for such operations. Consideration also had to be given to finding fodder and water once the operation began. The use of various types of cars came with its own difficulties. On some occasions, it would seem that they were handled rather inexpertly. In April 1917, Lieutenant-Colonel Joyce wrote, rather irritably, to one of *Hedgehog*'s drivers, 'I hear that you are stuck in the sand. Please send me, and exactly, what is required to get you back here.'[16] The later drivers of the Rolls Royce and Talbot car units would seem to have been more expert.

By early 1918, the evidence would suggest that Joyce, Lawrence, and the other officers of *Hedgehog* had fully grasped the potential of these cars and had begun exploring the area to the north-east of Aqaba in order to find the best possible routes towards the railway and also beyond. Increasingly the focus moved to the possibility of moving a mixed mobile column north-eastwards towards a route running to the west of the Dead Sea. The main Arab Northern Army would continue attacks along the railway and on Mudawwarah and later Ma'an, while a mobile column pushed north-eastwards using the ancient 'King's Highway' route, operating between the Dead Sea and the railway line. This would require careful preparation and the gradual laying in of depots and supplies throughout early 1918. Also, in the early months of 1918 towns such as Shawbek, Tafilah, and Kerak became the focus of *Hedgehog*'s efforts. Some of these towns had ancient Crusader castles, indicating their former strategic importance along the King's Highway route.[17]

In 1918, therefore, we see a shift in the focus of operations. Mobility and the ability to cross the desert were still key factors, but the emphasis was on integrating armoured car and other mechanized elements. While tribal forces and a mountain-gun battery often formed the advance party on operations, these were backed up with further mechanized elements in support. This combination could be used for operations on the railway, what Lawrence later referred to as 'fighting de luxe', as the armoured cars could operate with impunity to small-arms fire. Of equal importance, however, was the role that such assets played in 1918 while operating in even closer association with the British main effort in Palestine and Syria.

Airpower

The important role played by airpower during the Arab Revolt has been largely overlooked. From its very inception in 1916, aviation played a key role in ensuring the future of the revolt. Shorts floatplanes flying from HMS *Ben-My-Chree* provided crucial support for the Arab armies in the vicinity of

Yenbo and Rabegh, as two Turkish brigades moved out from Medina against them in December 1916. While not designed to operate in this role, these Shorts floatplanes bombed and strafed the Turkish columns with some effect. The effectiveness of these attacks played no small part in Fakhri Pasha's eventual decision to call off this Turkish countermove in January 1917. This was the first of many occasions in which airpower played a timely role in the Arab Revolt.[18]

From November 1916, the X Flight of 14 Squadron, Royal Flying Corps (RFC), was attached to the Arab forces and aircraft from this squadron also played a role in these initial actions. X Flight would later move to Wejh and then Aqaba with the Arab Northern Army. It would remain associated with that army until the end of the war. From 1917, it would also operate in cooperation with aircraft from 1 Squadron, Australian Flying Corps (AFC). In the early phases of this air war, X Flight operated BE2c and Martinsyde aircraft. They would later operate RE8s while 1 Squadron AFC used Bristol F2b fighter-bombers.[19]

The British and Australian pilots performed a wide range of duties, the primary ones being reconnaissance, bombing of Turkish garrisons, and also bombing and strafing of Turkish troops. A surviving report of 25 January 1918 by Lieutenant A. Murphy of X Flight records a typical sortie which started at the field at Abu Sawana and ended at Aqaba. Flying a Martinsyde, his activities included bombing, reconnaissance and also the strafing of ground targets:

> Left with 10 x 20lb bombs. Bombed Ma'an. On lines, 24 open trucks, 30 closed trucks. Two engines steamed away on approach of aeroplane. Two AA guns firing. 50 bell tents. 8 large huts. East of Ma'an station – Large Turkish hospital. 3 hangers. 1 canvas. 1 new matting. 1 mud walls with dummy machine. 12 tents, bell, to the south-east. Plenty of activity and movement of men. Detachment of about 200 mounted troops encountered on the road and machine-gunned them. On approach they opened fire with mountain gun. Landed.[20]

Some sorties confined themselves to bombing and the most frequent target was Ma'an. It was not uncommon by 1918 to have multiple plane raids on targets such as Ma'an and Mudawwarah. Planes also cooperated with the raiding parties, dropping messages to indicate targets and sometimes machine-gunning Turkish troops to keep their heads down while operations were carried out. Trains were considered prime targets and pilots had orders to 'bomb and machine gun where possible'.[21]

Apart from the main base at Aqaba, other outlying airfields were used. These would seem to have been very basic, just holding supplies of petrol, oil, and water. Some fields were prepared just for emergency landings out in the desert and local tribesmen were paid to light smoke signals every morning and evening. Sometimes these outlying fields would seem to have been more substantial with larger petrol supplies and also spare parts, ammunition, and bombs. On one occasion in 1917, Lawrence travelled to Sinai using motor transport and laid out a field, leaving fuel and bombs for planes transiting towards Aqaba and also further east.

There was also air activity on the Turkish side, and air raids on Aqaba were carried out by Turkish, German, and Austro-Hungarian pilots on an almost daily basis from July 1917. In September 1917, Lieutenant-Colonel Joyce wrote from Aqaba, 'Fritz comes over most mornings but is a damn bad shot so far, thank God! The Arabs now streak off into the desert at early dawn and stroll back again after the eggs have been laid.'[22] Throughout this period, Fakhri Pasha tried to maintain between two and four serviceable aircraft at Medina. To the north the main base was at Ma'an and, not surprisingly, these airbases were of extreme interest to the pilots of X Flight. A report of February 1918 noted that there were three Rumpler two-seaters at Ma'an, while intelligence reports suggested that a Halberstadt and an Albatros scout were expected. The latter was to be piloted by a 'crack Austro-Hungarian sergeant pilot'. At the same time at Amman, there were seven machines (2 x Albatros, 2 x Halberstadt, 2 x AEG and 1 x Fokker). While the Fokker pilot was Turkish, all the remainder were German.[23] By late 1917, the Turks were also placing single aircraft at temporary airfields as part of their wider efforts against the revolt. It would seem that these aircraft were tasked with reconnaissance and also attacking Arab columns and they acted in association with Turkish mobile columns. The British pilots referred to these locations as 'nests' and considered them priority targets. A report of January 1918 recorded repeated attacks by four X Flight planes on Mudawwarah station, one of the targets being a single Turkish aircraft that was based there.[24]

Despite this considerable amount of air activity, air-to-air combat as described by Lawrence in *Seven Pillars of Wisdom* would seem to have been reasonably rare. Planes were occasionally forced down or came down due to engine trouble and it would seem that both sides tried to salvage crashed planes. In February 1918 a Turkish plane was brought down by Arab ground fire and its pilot, named as Ismail Zaki, was captured. On arrival at the crash site, however, the RFC team found that the wings and engine were missing. Both the British and the Turks would seem, therefore, to have had competition with respect to cannibalizing downed aircraft as the Arabs saw these as a source of potential wealth.

On occasion, the RFC and AFC planes were used to carry supplies. This could take the form of ferrying boxes of ammunition or explosives to demolition parties in the field in the various two-seater types that were being used. On arrival, the aircraft could also assist the ground party by carrying out reconnaissance, bombing, and/or strafing. In the later phases of the desert campaign such supply operations became more ambitious. In August 1918 a Handley Page bomber was attached to X Flight and used to ferry larger quantities of supplies to the Arab Northern Army, which was then massing to the south-east of Deraa. As part of this scheme an 'advanced landing ground' was laid out near Azraq to accommodate the Handley Page, which also carried some spares and supplies for two other RFC planes based there. On the onset of the final offensive, these air elements operated extremely effectively against Turkish ground units while also seeking out the 'nests' of Turkish and German aircraft.[25]

In many ways the use of airpower in the Arab Revolt was extremely advanced and mirrored tactical developments taking place on the Western Front. They played an increasingly important role during 1918 while acting in the tactical air support role. During an assault on the strategically important station at Mudawwarah on 8 August 1918, a signaller of the Imperial Camel Corps directed attacks by RFC planes by using a series of ground signals. This allowed the RFC to direct their attacks at a Turkish redoubt north of the station that was still holding out and thus impeding the attack. When this redoubt was bombed into submission, the final assault carried the position. This level of cooperation would continue until the end of the war in the Middle East. Between 1916 and 1918, the use of airpower in the desert had moved from being a rather ad hoc, amateurish, affair and had developed into an integrated and sophisticated instrument of desert warfare.

Ottoman counterinsurgency

In recent years much attention has been paid to the Arab Revolt in light of modern counterinsurgency, or COIN, campaigns in Iraq and Afghanistan. Such an approach requires caution. World War I Arabia holds few contextual similarities to modern Iraq or Afghanistan. Also, the literature of the revolt focuses on the actions of the insurgent rather than the counter-insurgent. Nowhere is this more so than in Lawrence's own writings, which have enjoyed much recent attention. In Chapter XXXIII of *Seven Pillars of Wisdom*, Lawrence outlined his philosophy of guerrilla warfare and it has much to offer the modern student of asymmetric warfare.[26] He shed little light, however, on Turkish countermoves or, what we would term today, COIN strategies.

The Turkish campaign in Arabia has been the focus of some recent scholarly attention and it is now possible to build a picture of the strategies they employed to counter the Arab Revolt.[27] All Turkish forces in the Hejaz were part of the Ottoman Fourth Army. With its HQ in Damascus, this army defended the Ottoman territories of the Middle East and as such was the focus of the offensives of the British EEF. Arabia also fell within Fourth Army's area of operations and its garrisons in the Hejaz were the first to respond to the Arab Revolt. After the initial countermoves of December 1916 to January 1917, it would appear that Turkish policy was to reinforce their garrisons along the Hejaz Railway while also organizing columns to act as rapid reaction forces. The Turks had traditionally made much use of their camel corps (*Hecins Var*), and an increased use was made of such mobile patrols and also of volunteer Arab cavalry. There is also evidence to suggest that they were building ad hoc armour defences onto the actual trains running on the Hejaz line by 1918.

By late 1916, two new Turkish formations had been organized to react to the developing situation in the Hejaz. In future operations, the emphasis was on desert mobility. The 1st Kuvve-i Mürettebe, under the command of General Cemal Pasha (Küçük), was based at Ma'an and was tasked with railway protection. Its formation was composed of infantry, field artillery, gendarmerie, and cavalry units and also various support units. Apart from providing the garrisons along the Hejaz Railway, it also deployed mixed mobile columns into the desert. These searched for Arab raiding parties and also were used as reaction forces to respond to reports of attacks. Another key Turkish formation was the Hicaz Kuvve-i Seferiyesi ('the expeditionary force of the Hejaz') that had been dispatched to Medina in the summer of 1916 as tensions grew and rebellion seemed likely. This fell under the command of General Fakhri Pasha and its units included cavalry, camel corps, infantry, field artillery, and associated support units. For the duration of the war, it would continue to send mobile columns into the field to defend the southern sections of the Hejaz Railway, while also seeking out and attacking forces from the Arab Southern and Eastern armies.[28]

The continued excavations of the Great Arab Revolt Project in Jordan have also shown that the defences at locations such as Ma'an and Mudawwarah were quite extensive. It had been assumed that Ottoman defences were actually quite simple – perhaps even just blockhouses surrounded by barbed wire. Excavations have revealed the remains of well-positioned and entrenched field fortifications, including machine-gun and support lines.[29] This would suggest that Ottoman doctrine regarding position warfare had also developed during 1916–18. What emerges is the suggestion of an increasingly sophisticated defence of the Hejaz that incorporated strongly defended field positions, the use of mobile reaction forces, and also the use of air assets.

1st Kuvvei Murettebe,
Railway protection group based at Ma'an
Command by General Mehmed Cemal Pasha (Küçük or Üçüncü).
138th Infantry Regiment
161st Infantry Regiment
1/79th Infantry Battalion
One battery from the 6th Field Artillery Battalion
3 x cavalry squadrons

Ma'an Gendarmerie Battalion
2 x infantry companies (from 31st Infantry Regiment and 130th Infantry Regiment)
2 x railway companies
Circassian Volunteer Cavalry Regiment
Logistical and medical support elements

Hicaz Kuvvei Seferiyesi ('Expeditionary force of the Hejaz')
HQ at Medina. Commanded by General Fakhreddin ("Fakhri") Pasha.
Hecins Var Regiment (camel corps)
1st Aknc Regiment (volunteer Arab cavalry)
3 x field artillery batteries
2 x signal companies
Medical and logistical support elements

Medina Fortress Command
Commanded by General Basri Pasha
2nd Aknc Regiment
4/131st Infantry Battalion
2/129th Infantry Battalion
Gendarmerie Battalion
1 x railway battalion
2 x artillery batteries

As the war progressed, the Ottoman forces in the Hejaz found it increasingly difficult due to the gradual erosion of the Fourth Army by the continued offensives of the EEF further north. Equally, the depredations of Arab raiders gradually undermined their logistical systems in the Hejaz and reduced their military capabilities. Nevertheless, the garrison at Medina held out until after the war's end, when around 10,000 effectives under Fakhri Pasha finally surrendered in January 1919.[30]

While Lawrence gives little insight into the wider Turkish campaign against the Arab Revolt in *Seven Pillars of Wisdom*, he was more forthcoming in later letters. In a letter of 1923 to Colonel (later Field Marshal) Archibald Wavell, he suggested that it was a lack of imagination, and the inability of the Turks to use cars in the desert, that resulted in their failure to counter the Arab campaign. Lawrence wrote:

> If the Turks had put MGs on three or four of their towing cars & driven them on a weekly patrol over the admirable going of the desert east of Amman and Ma'an, they would have put an absolute stop to our camel parties & so to our rebellion. It wouldn't have cost them 20 men or £20,000 … <u>rightly applied.</u> They scraped up cavalry & armoured trains & camel corps & block houses against us: because they didn't think hard enough.[31]

The final campaigns of 1918

Despite the considerable Ottoman forces ranged against them, the Arab Northern Army continued to evolve and throughout late 1917 grew increasingly confident and aggressive in its operations. In October 1917, soldiers of the regular contingent of the Arab Northern Army halted a Turkish column at Wadi Musa near Petra. By the end of 1917, the army had been reinforced by the armoured car and mobile artillery of Operation *Hedgehog*, and, with these new capabilities, preparations began for a new phase of operations in early 1918. Long-range reconnaissance began in earnest using the Rolls Royce armoured cars and other vehicles.

Furthermore, Lawrence assembled a large tribal force to serve as the vanguard of the army as it began its move north-east towards Amman. On 25 January 1918, he enjoyed a significant victory when his party of around 600 tribesmen met and defeated a Turkish column of around 1,000 men at Tafila, a small but strategically important town to the south-east of the Dead Sea. The efficient use of firepower was a key element to this victory and Lawrence was later awarded a DSO for his part in the action. The Arab Northern Army had truly come of age.[32]

In the months that followed, important towns along the King's Highway route were seized and held. In April 1918 Arab regular forces began a series of attacks on Ma'an. Following a major assault on 17 April, the railway line to the south of the town was cut and remained closed for the rest of the war. Ma'an ultimately did not fall and remained besieged until its evacuation by Turkish forces on 23 September 1918. Interestingly, the commander of the Arab regular troops, Jafar Pasha al-Askari, suggested the use of gas to break this siege.[33]

In the build-up to General Allenby's decisive Megiddo Offensive, raids on the railway line increased and the capture of Mudawwarah by the Imperial Camel Corps played an important part in these preparatory operations. By the opening of the Megiddo Offensive on 19 September 1918, a contingent of around 1,000 men of the Arab Northern Army under Sharif Feisal had assembled to the south-east of Deraa. Of these, around 450 were Arab regulars and they were supported by Indian and Gurkha machine-gun and mortar teams, the armoured car and mobile artillery detachment, and also some aircraft of X Flight.

In the weeks that followed this force constantly harried the left wing of the Ottoman Fourth Army, accelerating that army's disintegration as Allenby's forces exploited the initial successes of the Megiddo operations. Allenby's main line of advance saw his army follow a coastal route through Acre, Tyre, Beirut, and on towards Tripoli, while his cavalry forces ranged further inland. Also further inland, the Arab Army advanced north of Deraa, operating in conjunction with Major-General Barrow's 4th Cavalry Division. By 1 October, Arab forces had entered Damascus and they had reached Aleppo by 26 October. Military operations in the Middle East theatre ceased on 29 October with the capture of the crucial railway junction at Muslimiya. This junction controlled the branch line to Mesopotamia and it was taken by British cavalry and regular troops of the Arab Northern Army. The Ottoman government was granted an armistice two days later on 31 October 1918.[34]

Conclusion

The Arab Revolt of 1916–18 was not just a mere sideshow of World War I. In the immediate context of the Middle East campaign, it played a valuable role in harassing and tying down large numbers of Turkish troops in Arabia. Furthermore, the Arab Northern Army proved itself to be a highly effective military force, contributing to the final collapse of the Ottoman Fourth Army, and its associated German and Austro-Hungarian support, during the final months of the Middle East campaign in 1918.

Between 1916 and 1918, the forces of the revolt had evolved dramatically and had gone from being a force of irregular tribesmen to becoming a small but well-equipped mobile army that incorporated both regular and irregular elements while also including air assets, artillery, and light armour. While the Arab Revolt had encountered many setbacks during the course of the war and had, in fact, stalled on some occasions, by 1918 Arab forces could engage Ottoman formations with some confidence.

The experiences of this force also suggested how future desert campaigns would be fought. The revolt had demonstrated that the desert could, in modern warfare, be used to great advantage if one's forces had the proper survival and navigational skills and the also the equipment necessary to cross it. If the desert could be tamed as an operational environment, then attacks could be mounted on enemy rear areas, bases, and lines of communication. As raiding parties were by necessity small, it also became increasingly obvious that they should carry as much firepower as possible. Good communications and logistics were vital and cooperating with air assets was desirable. These lessons had also been learned by the British forces that campaigned against Senussi tribesmen in the Western Desert between 1915 and 1917. This was particularly true with respect to Brigadier-General H. W. Hodgson's mobile force, which took part in the 'Band of Oases' phase of the Senussi campaign.[35]

The lessons learned from these desert campaigns of World War I were not incorporated in inter-war British doctrine. Methods of desert travel continued to develop, however, during the 1920s and 1930s through a series of civilian expeditions to the Libyan and Egyptian deserts, many of which were associated with the Royal Geographical Society. Some of those involved in such expeditions, in particular Ralph Bagnold, would later serve in World War II. Bagnold, who admitted that he had been fascinated by Lawrence's wartime exploits, was the prime agent in the establishment of the Long Range Patrol in 1940, and this unit would subsequently evolve into the Long Range Desert Group (LRDG).[36] In many ways, the operational methods of the LRDG mirrored those adopted by the Arab forces in World War I, and they placed an emphasis on desert mobility, long range penetration, and concentration of firepower. The desert campaigns of the LRDG and later the SAS in the North African theatre during World War II were directly informed, therefore, by World War I experience.

The Arab Revolt has been regarded by some as a romantic or an eccentric episode of World War I. Yet the methods employed during this campaign had long-term effects and contributed to the development of the operational methods employed in modern desert warfare. Future desert campaigns would mirror the developments that took place between 1916 and 1918, and during World War II we can see the same emphasis on desert navigation and logistics, while the development of survival skills adequate to the challenge of desert conditions became a key priority. Just as in World War I, the units deployed by the LRDG and SAS were small but efforts would be made throughout the North African campaign to increase their firepower, while at the same time cooperation with air elements became increasingly important. It could also be argued that Lawrence's tactic of carrying out long-range raids was re-adopted by desert units during World War II and that it inspired some of the more dramatic and long-range raids of that war. Far from being a 'sideshow', the Arab Revolt of 1916–18 established many of the methods in the modern desert warfare playbook.

CHAPTER 12

THE RELUCTANT PUPIL

The American Army on the Western Front, 1917–18

Professor Andrew Wiest

By October 1918 the tide of the Great War on the Western Front had truly turned. While German forces still fought tenaciously and were capable of making the Allies pay a steep blood cost for every step towards victory, the initiative had slipped to the British, French, and Americans. Allied forces, utilizing a series of interlocked offensives coordinated by Supreme Allied Commander Marshal Ferdinand Foch, steadily pressed the Germans back and even crashed through the vaunted Hindenburg Line. The end was at hand. Amid the general optimism over a war that had finally turned in their favour, though, the British and French were concerned with the faltering performance of their American allies.

While British and French forces made historic gains on other parts of the Western Front, the American Expeditionary Force (AEF) was bogged down in the difficult terrain of the Argonne. Tactically incompetent, and with his AEF suffering from a near total logistic breakdown, Pershing became the subject of merciless criticism from British and French commanders who were concerned that American ineptitude might squander a priceless opportunity to achieve victory on the Western Front after nearly five long years of war. The situation became so strained that French Prime Minister Georges Clemenceau wrote to Foch urging that he relieve Pershing of command:

You have watched at close range the development of General Pershing's extractions. Unfortunately, thanks to his invincible obstinacy he has won against you as well as your immediate subordinates. The French Army and the British Army, without a moment's respite, have been daily fighting for the past three months ... but our worthy American allies, who thirst to get into action and who are unanimously acknowledged to be great soldiers, have been marking time ever since their forward jump on the first day, and in spite of heavy loses, they have failed to conquer the ground assigned to them as their objective. No one can maintain that these troops are unusable; they are merely unused... If General Pershing finally resigns himself to obedience, if he accepts the advice of capable generals, whose presence at his side he has until now permitted only that he might reject their councils, I shall be wholly delighted.[1]

While the tide of Allied victory quickly muted criticism of the AEF and saved Pershing's career, the question remains: why had American forces comparatively fared so poorly on the Western Front? The shortcomings of the AEF seem all the more difficult to understand in light of the fact that Pershing and his command cohort had failed to take advantage of an opportunity almost unparalleled in the history of warfare. While the British and French had to learn the bitter realities of World War I in the crucible of battle, the Americans theoretically had the luxury of watching the war from afar for over three years, while receiving accurate reports from the battlefronts on the revolutionary developments taking place in both technology and tactics. After the American declaration of war in April 1917, the military leadership of the AEF had a second chance to learn from the experience of the British and French, because no American units saw significant fighting on the Continent for the next 13 months. Stubbornly, though, in both cases the AEF failed to adapt its outdated, pre-war doctrine of reliance on open warfare,[2] dooming the American soldiers to face their own version of the Somme.

The American way of fighting

Since the close of the War of 1812 the United States had been secure behind its ocean walls and had focused on its manifest destiny. Certainly there were moments in which the outside world loomed large, usually when Americans worried that Europeans might violate their hemisphere. Those moments, though, were fleeting, leaving the American military with a remarkably inwardly focused and self-aggrandized view of its role in the world. Building on a largely mythologized past, the American tradition of arms glorified the ideal of an army of citizen soldiers, rugged frontiersmen with their Kentucky long rifles in hand, and envisioned a professional military as somehow un-American.[3]

Americans at the turn of the 20th century lauded a culture of armed democracy and held that the rough and resourceful American frontiersman was superior to the overly trained automatons of the old world. This uniquely American martial culture led to a US tendency to ignore the European experience of World War I. It was, indeed, in the minds of many the 'European-ness' of the militaries involved that had led to the stagnation of the Great War in 1915 and the perceived disasters of Verdun and the Somme. During the first three years of World War I, then, while American military observers followed the ebb and flow of the distant conflict with great interest, they believed that the fighting harboured no lessons for the American military except negative ones. If anything, the US military believed that, rather than learning from the difficult experience of the Allies on the Western Front, that it should instruct the Europeans in the nature of modern, democratic war.

When the US Congress passed the declaration of war, the United States Army numbered roughly 139,000 men, populating units that needed months of training before they would be ready to see action on the Western Front. President Woodrow Wilson appointed General John 'Black Jack' Pershing to command what would become the American Expeditionary Force, and Pershing left for a whirlwind tour of the war zone to discern how best the United States could ready and employ its fighting men. Pershing returned with disturbing news: the United States would need to raise a military force of over 3 million men in order to be able to play a decisive role in the conflict. With their new ally facing the daunting, and tedious, task of mobilizing for war, France and Britain were concerned that American forces would not be able to arrive in time to help defend against an expected tidal wave of German offensives in 1918. Fearing the worst, British and French liaisons pressured Pershing and Wilson to abandon the notion of an independent AEF and instead urged them to send individual soldiers to Europe to make good the losses of existing British and French units, a proposal dubbed amalgamation. Chief of the Imperial General Staff, Field Marshal Sir William Robertson, made his fears clear to Pershing, stating, 'The Germans had been able to cripple one or other of the Allies each year. Russia in 1915, France in 1916, Italy in 1917. In 1918 it might be the British if America could not help in the way suggested [amalgamation].'[4]

There were several reasons why the United States resisted amalgamation, including President Woodrow Wilson's desire to have an independent AEF on the Western Front in an effort to strengthen his hand in eventual peace talks.

However, Pershing also had tactical reasons to stand against amalgamation, believing that the presence on the Western Front of an independent AEF, with its democratic frontier traditions, was a needed corrective to the 'European-ness' that so plagued the war. If divided piecemeal into the Allied armies, the AEF would lose its curative potential. On 16 April 1918 Pershing made the cultural connection clear when he addressed the officers of the American 1st Division as they readied to enter the lines near Cantigny, stating, 'You have behind you your own national traditions that should make you the finest soldiers in Europe to-day. We come from a young and aggressive nation.' America stood for democracy and liberty; 'we now return to Europe, the home of our ancestors, to help defend the same principles upon European soil.'[5]

Because of cultural inflexibility and strategic hubris, the United States had chosen to 'go it alone', and, as a result, the AEF faced a crisis of preparedness in 1917 that was most closely analogous to the situation that Britain had faced in 1914. From a standing start, the United States had to prepare for total war. What is sometimes forgotten is that, in strategic terms, the United States' effort was a resounding, even miraculous, success. Upon the American declaration of war in April 1917, the Regular Army numbered only 133,000 men and 5,800 officers, while the National Guard consisted of 67,000 men and 3,200 officers. By the end of the war, the enlisted strengths of the Regular Army and the National Guard had swelled to 527,000 and 382,000 respectively, all while the US also constructed a new National Army of 3 million men – an astounding feat accomplished in just 19 months.[6]

On the tactical level, though, American inexperience and inflexibility would have disastrous consequences. The task of translating American democratic visions of warfare into battlefield reality fell to the small and relatively inexperienced US officer corps. Many of the officers who eventually became senior leaders in the AEF had seen action in the Philippines or in the hunt through northern Mexico for Pancho Villa, but those open, sweeping campaigns had limited relevance to the reality of warfare on the Western Front.[7] Making matters worse, thousands of officers who eventually saw significant combat in World War I had, until very recently, been civilians, and received only rudimentary training before assuming their command duties.[8] Having suffered through a difficult wartime expansion of their own military, British military liaisons were especially sensitive observers of the American officer corps, with one representative reporting to Whitehall, 'The American commanders and staffs are almost wholly untrained, and without military experience.'[9] While visiting a training camp in New York another British representative commented that while the training of individual soldiers was excellent, that of officers was severely lacking:

There are no non-commissioned officers of any value, and that while the sub-alterns from the reserve officers schools show keenness and enthusiasm, the company and battalion commanders are entirely inexperienced and badly in need of acquiring the habit of command. The staffs consist of intelligent and energetic officers, who are, however, as yet ignorant of the conditions of modern war.[10]

Lessons unlearned: expectations for the war in Europe

Preparing to lead an inexperienced and only partly trained military into the inferno that was the Western Front, Pershing and his officer corps had to fall back on the lessons provided by a system of military training and education that was designed to produce a pure tactical expression of the American frontier spirit – a spirit that would leave the American military the last worshiper at the Great War altar of the cult of the offensive. The lessons of the war, as filtered through the frontier military ethos, resulted in the Command and General Staff College at Fort Leavenworth and other officer training schools of the US Army downplaying the use of firepower as the method by which to overcome enemy entrenchments in favour of the tactics of open warfare, and the dominance of morale, the rifle, and the bayonet.[11]

The process of de-emphasizing European tactical developments began in late 1914, when, in the face of contrary evidence from a stagnating Western Front, an editorial in the *Infantry Journal* contended that the lessons of World War I meant that in modern combat American infantry could expect to:

> leap up, come together and form a long line which is lit up [with fire] from end to end. A last volley from the troops, a last rush pellmell of the men in a crowd, a rapid making ready of the bayonet for its thrusts, a simultaneous roar from the artillery … a dash of the cavalry from cover emitting the wild yell of victory – and the assault is delivered. The brave men spared by the shot and shell will plant their tattered flag on the ground covered with the corpses of the defeated enemy. Such is the part played by infantry on the field of battle today.[12]

Perhaps one can forgive an American rendition of the anthem in praise of the cult of the offensive so early in the conflict. However, for the next three years the editorial department of the *Infantry Journal* continued to emphasize the moral element of war and the offensive and reject the dominance of firepower. In 1915, the editors approvingly quoted a French colonel who stated, 'It is the infantry which we have to proclaim today. It is vain to speak of ballistics and pyrotechnics. The soul stands very much above them. And in battle it is the most resisting soul that triumphs.' For the next year, articles and letters in the journal continued to stress the offensive and even openly denied that World War I had become an 'artillery war,' which correspondingly diminished the 'human element' of combat.[13]

The official doctrine of the American military, as expressed by US Army's *Infantry Drill Regulations* (IDR) of 1917, best demonstrates the American failure to come to grips with the reality of the Western Front in the window of time before the nation's entry into the war. According to the IDR, even in 1917, after the horrors of the Somme and Verdun, bravery and the infantry charge over open ground remained the key to success in battle. Artillery fire would, 'aid … the infantry in gaining fire superiority', but 'In the advance by rushes, sufficient rifles must be kept constantly in action to keep down the enemy's fire.' After the infantry charge had routed the enemy position, the IDR contended that formed bodies of troops following the assaulting force would engage in a 'vigorous' pursuit in order to 'reap the full benefits of victory'.

Perhaps most ominously, the IDR also patently failed to understand the defensive dominance of the machine gun, stating that 'machine guns must be considered as weapons of emergency … of great value at critical, though infrequent, periods of an engagement'. Most surprisingly, though, the IDR downplayed the killing power of machine guns as part of defensive systems, and contended that infantry employing concentrated rifle fire could overcome the entrenched machine guns of a defending enemy force.[14] Tens of thousands of dead, whose bodies still littered no man's land of the Western Front, were grim testament to the power wielded by the machine gun over exposed infantry formations. It was a lesson that the Americans chose to ignore.

Deciding doctrine: bayonets versus artillery

Upon American entry into the conflict, Pershing and the high command of the AEF journeyed to the Western Front, where it became even more clear, after visiting the trenches, that the problem with the war was 'European-ness' rather than a technological imbalance. Pershing remarked:

> The armies on the Western Front in the recent battles that I had witnessed had all but given up the use of the rifle. Machine guns, grenades, Stokes mortars, and one-pounders had become the main reliance of the average Allied soldier. These were all valuable weapons for specific purposes but they could not replace the combination of an efficient soldier and his rifle.[15]

Pershing followed his visit with a flurry of messages to Washington regarding mobile warfare and the preeminent value of the rifle and bayonet. He insisted that all soldiers be taught that 'the rifle and the bayonet remain the supreme weapons of the infantry soldier', and that 'the ultimate success of the army depends on their proper use in open warfare'.[16]

But there remained a fly in the American open warfare ointment. The War Department had ordered a special fact-finding team, known as the Baker Mission, to visit French and British commands on the Western Front, to learn all it could about Allied methods of war and to report its findings to both Pershing and the War Department. Colonel Charles Summerall, future commander of the 1st Division and future United States Army Chief of Staff, served as the senior artillery officer with the Baker Mission, and was blunt in his report to Pershing and his staff at AEF headquarters. In July 1917, Summerall warned that the American reliance on infantry manoeuvre and open warfare was misguided, and that the AEF needed to increase its artillery support in plans for battle, 'without which the experience of the present war shows positively that it is impossible for the infantry to advance'. Nonplussed by the tactical heresy, members of Pershing's staff attacked Summerall as 'arrogant' and rejected his artillery heavy form of warfare.

Just a month later, Lieutenant-Colonel John Parker, an expert in the use of the machine gun, conducted a tour of a French automatic weapons training centre. In a report submitted to Pershing's staff after the visit, Parker concluded that 'the day of the rifleman is done. He was a good horse while he lasted, but his day is over... The rifleman is passing out and the bayonet is fast becoming as obsolete as the crossbow.' Like Summerall before him, Parker did not get a warm reception at AEF headquarters. Lieutenant-Colonel Paul Malone, then heading the AEF training section, wrote on his copy of Parker's report, 'Speak for yourself, John!'[17]

Internal debate concerning American tactics had ceased, but Pershing and the AEF command structure fretted that there was another means by which heretical ideas could contaminate the frontier spirit of the American military. Short on officer cadre on all levels, the fledgling AEF had to rely on experienced British and French officers for much of its training. The dangerous situation involved Allied units performing demonstrations and manoeuvres for AEF units once they arrived in France, while British and French officers served as instructors and advisers to American commanders and taught courses at the AEF staff school at Langres.[18]

Colonel Harold Fiske, who later became head of the AEF training section summed up the danger posed by Allied training of American units:

> The offensive spirit of the French and British Armies has largely disappeared as a result of their severe losses… Our young officers and men are prone to take the tone and tactics of those with whom they are associated, and whatever they are now learning that is false or unsuited for us will be hard to eradicate later. In many respects, the tactics and technique of our Allies are not suited to American characteristics or the American mission in this war. The French do not like the rifle, do not know how to use it, and their infantry is consequently too entirely dependent upon a powerful artillery support. Their infantry lacks aggressiveness and discipline. The British infantry lacks initiative and resource.[19]

Concurring with Fiske's conclusion that 'Berlin cannot be taken by the French or the British… It can only be taken by a thoroughly trained, entirely homogeneous American Army', Pershing made it very clear to his subordinates that they were to reject British and French training methods in favour of concentration on musketry and techniques of open warfare.[20] Believing, then, in the word of one of his senior staff officers, that 'An American army cannot be made by Frenchmen or Englishmen',[21] Pershing and the AEF yet again rejected the valuable military experience of their European allies. Since, in his mind, British and French cultural weakness, over-reliance on firepower, and tactical fixation on the defensive were the root causes of the stagnation of the war, only a truly American force, full of native frontier spirit and ready to fight in the open, could put the war to right again.

Aided by the obstinacy of its commander-in-chief, but abetted by very nearly the entirety of its command structure, the AEF had quashed internal doctrinal debate and had rejected the advice and training of its British and French mentors, the sum total of Allied tactical knowledge gained in over three years of grinding battle from Mons to Passchendaele. In a war in which their European allies had learned that gains could be made only through the utilization of devastating levels of firepower, the Americans courted disaster by preparing for open warfare. America had remained true to its frontier soul, scoring a victory over 'European-ness' that caused General Robert Alexander proudly to claim:

> in all instruction one dominating principle was insisted upon – that training for the open was of primary value and of that training the utilization of the rifle as a firearm was indispensable to success… Instruction was of course also given in the use of the bayonet, hand and rifle grenades, the automatic rifle … and other auxiliaries, but that they

were merely auxiliaries and could never replace the ability to maneuver, which in turn must be accompanied by the ability to use the firepower of the rifle, was always insisted upon.[22]

Many British and French military observers were dismayed by the Pershing's out-of-hand rejection of Allied military methods and feared that the US commander was doomed to face his own battle of the Somme. All they could do, though, was worry and write reports; they were powerless to alter Pershing's chosen course. In a report to his superiors in Whitehall, Deputy Chief of the Imperial General Staff, General W. Kirke, reported:

> The Americans ... [believe] that their untrained troops have more fighting value than veteran French divisions, and they have formed the opinion that their staff arrangements also are as good, if not better, than those of their mentors... It is no more use our trying to keep them back ... than it would be trying to prevent a young man of independent means from getting married when he has made up his mind to do so... It is quite possible that a little later on the Americans may find that they want some help from us again in training, but the request must come from them.[23]

As American training proceeded apace, in March 1918 a thundering series of German offensives on the Western Front forced Pershing's hand. Overcoming his aversion to amalgamation Pershing put his own national desires to the side and informed Foch, 'I have come to tell you that the American people would consider it a great honor for our troops to be engaged in the present battle... At this moment there are no other questions than fighting. Infantry, artillery, aviation, all that we have are yours; use them as you wish.'[24] Pershing's decision meant that American forces would enter the line in dribs and drabs and initially be engaged in small battles, including Cantigny and Belleau Wood, under the command of Allied forces, instead of as a part of an independent American force.

The American units, of up to divisional size, that served under the command of the French Army or the BEF generally acquitted themselves well. The claim of the 1st and 2nd divisions to making the greatest Allied advance during the Second Battle of the Marne stands as an example of the exemplary record of American units brigaded to Allied formations. However, as part of Allied forces, under Allied command and utilizing Allied tactics and firepower, the experience of such brigaded divisions did not stand as a true test of American training or doctrine.

The first test: the offensive at St Mihiel

After the delay imposed by the German spring offensives, in August 1918 Pershing achieved the first of his goals with the activation of the American First Army, which took over a sector of the Allied front lines in Lorraine near St Mihiel. Confident in the ability of his untested forces and staff, Pershing pressed Allied Supreme Commander Ferdinand Foch for permission to launch an offensive against vulnerable German positions within the St Mihiel salient. After a testy set of exchanges, Foch reluctantly complied, setting the stage for the largest American military operation since the Civil War.

Beset by a series of interlocking Allied offensives further to the north, and fearing an imminent attack in the area, on 8 September the German High Command ordered the evacuation of the St Mihiel salient. The process was not yet complete when, on 12 September 1918, 16 divisions of the American First Army moved forward into the assault on the flanks of the salient, while French forces held the centre. Although some Germans resisted the advance with tenacity from long-prepared positions, many simply attempted to complete their withdrawal before being cut off by the advancing Americans. By 16 September it was all over, and the American First Army had scored what seemed to be a remarkable victory, reducing the St Mihiel salient and capturing 15,000 German prisoners and 450 artillery pieces at the cost of only 7,000 US casualties.

To Pershing the results of the offensive served to vindicate the American emphasis on the power of the offensive and open warfare, commenting:

> No form of propaganda could overcome the depressing effect on the morale of the enemy of this demonstration of our ability to organize a large American force and drive it successfully through his defenses. For the first time wire entanglements ceased to be regarded as impassable barriers and open warfare training, which had been so urgently insisted upon, proved to be the correct doctrine.[25]

While Pershing saw St Mihiel as a validation of American training and dogma, others within the Allied camp viewed the situation differently. General Robert Lee Bullard, eventually promoted to command the American Second Army, remarked:

> St. Mihiel was given an importance which posterity will not concede it. Germany had begun to withdraw. She had her weaker divisions, young men and old and Austro-Hungarians. The operation fell short of expectations.[26]

In a blistering appraisal of the American performance at St Mihiel, British liaison officer Lieutenant-General J. P. Du Cane reported to the British Chief of the Imperial General Staff that the American attack had succeeded only because of the German withdrawal, remarking that the US artillery 'bombardment did not cut the wire and the Americans had to stamp it down or cut it by hand', which could have resulted in a death-trap for American troops. He continued, 'Fortunately there was practically no resistance.' Du Cane went on to report that US staff work had been so lacking that it had resulted in two American units fighting each other instead of their German adversaries:

> The American attack from the South reached the neighbourhood of Vigneulles just about the same time as the Northern [American] attack was approaching it, and the two appear to have engaged each other, both reporting that they could not get on on account of intense machine-gun fire [coming from their sister units]… The Germans appear to have got clear away, owing to the great confusion existing in the American lines.

Du Cane, speaking for many British and French observers, worried that the easy victory at St Mihiel would only serve to convince Pershing that he had nothing left to learn concerning the nature of warfare on the Western Front:

> The most unfortunate part of an otherwise successful operation was that it confirmed the American High Command in an exaggerated estimate of the efficiency of the American military machine – and of their ability to control it.[27]

A different story altogether: the offensive in the Meuse-Argonne sector

At the end of September 1918, the Allies unleashed a series of four coordinated attacks meant to dislodge the Germans from the powerful defensive network dubbed the Hindenburg Line. To Pershing's forces, augmented by the French Fourth Army, fell the task of advancing in the Meuse-Argonne sector towards the distant goal of Sedan. Instead of facing German troops bent on retreat, the Americans were now tasked with attacking in difficult terrain on one of the most sensitive areas of the volatile front – an area critical to the overall cohesiveness of the German defensive network and one that the Germans chose to defend to the last. What was to become known as the Meuse-Argonne Offensive, then, formed the first true test of Pershing's belief in American military exceptionalism and his reliance on the tactics of open warfare.

The Meuse-Argonne Offensive, 1918

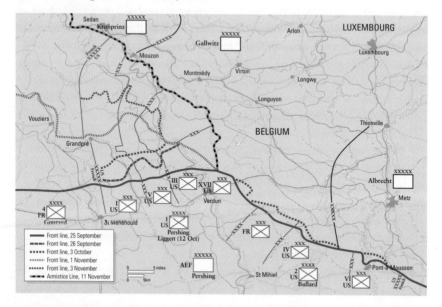

The American and French forces[28] under Pershing's command moved forward into the attack on 26 September, advancing up to 7 miles against stunned German defenders and even seizing the critical heights of Montfaucon. Reeling from the collective blow of the coordinated series of Allied offensives on the Western Front, the German High Command quickly decided to send six additional divisions to stabilize the situation in the Meuse-Argonne. Long before the German reinforcements could arrive, however, the American forward momentum had collapsed under the weight of its own success.

Already under incredible strain from the sheer effort of transferring more than 400,000 men, 90,000 horses and mules, 3,900 guns, and 900,000 tons of ammunition from the St Mihiel sector to the new attack frontage in only ten days, the shock of battle in the Meuse-Argonne caused American staff, logistical, and command efforts to collapse completely after only two days of battle. Instead of sturdy American infantrymen pressing their hard-won advantage and advancing over open ground to victory, traffic jams behind the American lines, some lasting over 12 hours, resulted in front-line soldiers not receiving food or ammunition. Some American divisions had no idea where they were, or where they should be going, and the roads were full of scattered groups of American soldiers attempting to discern their orders.

The result of the disorder was a logistical coma that lasted for several days, which brought the advance in the Meuse-Argonne to a standstill and afforded the Germans time to reinforce and prepare their defences anew. In a diary entry on 1 October 1918, Field Marshal Sir Douglas Haig, the commander-in-chief of the British Expeditionary Force, commented:

> Reports from Americans (west of Meuse) … state that their roads and communications are so blocked that the offensive has had to stop and cannot be recommenced for four or five days. What very valuable days are being lost! All this is the result of inexperience and ignorance on the part of … [the American staff] of the needs of a modern attacking force.[29]

For his part British Chief of the Imperial General Staff, Field Marshal Sir Henry Wilson, made his feelings clear regarding American failings by writing in a diary entry, 'The state of chaos the fool [Pershing] has got his troops into down in the Argonne is indescribable.' In a later entry, Wilson even went so far as to call Pershing a 'vain, ignorant, weak ASS.'[30]

Amid the logistical turmoil and command confusion, the American units that were able to continue the attack paid a high price. A German officer of V Reserve-Korps, commenting on American losses, wrote:

> American infantry is very unskillful in attack. It attacks with closed ranks in numerous and deep waves, at the head of which come the tanks. Such forms of attack form excellent targets for the activity of our artillery, if only the infantry does not get scared on account of the advancing masses and loses its nerve.[31]

The failure of the continued American offensive operations, which were the centrepiece of Foch's overall plan to rupture the German lines, came as little surprise to many British and French observers, who just months earlier had seen their advice and training rejected. Commenting on the stalled offensive, Du Cane wrote:

> The net result of all of this [logistical and command difficulty] was that from the 27th of September to the 18th of October the [American] Army only gained another 5 kilometers, whilst wastage from wounds, sickness and straggling was very severe… From the 26th September to the 18th October, 17 American divisions were employed, equivalent

in strength to over 30 of the French, British or German divisions [due to American divisions being established at 25,000 men rather than the European standard of 15,000 men]. These 17 divisions engaged 23 weak and tired enemy divisions and at the cost of heavy losses effected very little.[32]

Since the American divisions that were still fighting as part of the French Army and the BEF had 'done splendidly', Du Cane did not fault the bravery or ability of the American soldier, but rather problems in the American command structure, commenting:

The general impression is that, in spite of the gallantry and spirit of the individual, and owing to inexperience, particularly at the higher ranks, American divisions employed in large blocks under their own command, suffer wastage out of all proportion to results achieved, and generally do not pull more than a fraction of their weight.

It is felt that in insisting on the premature formation of large American Armies, General Pershing has not interpreted the altruistic wishes of the American Nation, and that he has incurred a grave responsibility both as regards unnecessary loss of life among his troops, and in the failure of the operations.[33]

The fighting during the remainder of October was difficult for Pershing and the AEF, which was beset by continued logistic and command difficulties and faced the strength of the German Kreimhilde Line defences. As a result, American troops only inched forward and were often found in considerable state of disarray. Matters became so strained that Foch, irritated that the Meuse-Argonne Offensive had fallen behind the other Allied advances on the Western Front, very nearly relieved Pershing of command. In a heated encounter between the two leaders Pershing complained that his forces faced stiff German resistance in difficult terrain. Foch responded that he only judged his commanders by the results they achieved. Pershing survived the encounter and went on to reorganize the AEF, helping to overcome many of its worst staff and logistical shortcomings. But, even as US forces remained involved in an attritional struggle that more closely resembled the Somme than the successful Allied operations of 1918, Pershing remained adamant that open warfare and infantry rifle-power remained the key to success. The problem, in Pershing's mind, was not that American tactical theory was flawed, but that it was not being implemented thoroughly enough – a viewpoint that Pershing had made clear in his 'Combat Instructions' of September 1918, which stated, 'The principles [of open warfare doctrine previously] enunciated ... are not yet receiving due application.'[34]

As the war lurched toward its conclusion, American forces – reorganized, resupplied, and rejuvenated – on 1 November launched a final offensive, one that broke German resistance along the Kriemhilde Line, leading to a pursuit of a defeated enemy. With even the British admitting that the Americans had learned from past mistakes,[35] US units swept towards Sedan. In part the newfound American success was due to the combined effect of the comprehensive defeat of German forces that was underway on the Western Front. Additionally, American officers on the tactical level had become more proficient in their craft, while units had gained invaluable on-the-job training. These successes, however, came in spite of the lack of any doctrinal shift at the upper echelons of US command. Indeed, Pershing remained convinced that his belief in open warfare had been correct all along and had, in the end, carried the day, claiming in his memoirs, 'Ultimately, we had the satisfaction of hearing the French admit that we were right, both in emphasizing training for open warfare and insisting upon proficiency in the use of the rifle.'[36]

Although Pershing, and the other purists of the American military ethos on his staff, continued to espouse the efficacy of open warfare long into the inter-war period, their insistence on the primacy of the rifle and morale in combat during World War I had led the United States into a tactical dead end and had resulted in needless losses and inefficiencies on the part of the AEF. Rejection of the collective military wisdom of its Allies resulted in an over-reliance in the AEF upon anachronistic military ideas, while fruitless attempts to fight in the open merely served to exaggerate the weakness of the unevenly trained American units. The result was that US commanders often ordered their untested units into battle without enough artillery covering fire, a tendency initially obscured by the ease of the American victory at St Mihiel. At the Meuse-Argonne, though, the combined weaknesses of American doctrine and training crashed together. Fired by the belief in American exceptionalism, and buoyed by his first significant victory, Pershing planned for his untested and tactically unsound units to achieve a breakthrough victory – a goal that neither the force nor the plan employed could ever hope to attain.[37] Like their Allies before them, the Americans went to battle unprepared, but for the AEF the result was perhaps even more tragic, because instead of learning from the mistakes of their Allies, they stubbornly preferred to learn from experience.

CHAPTER 13

THE GERMAN OCCUPATION OF THE UKRAINE, 1918

Blitzkrieg and Insurgencies

Dr Peter Lieb

All was quiet on the Eastern Front. At the turn of the year 1917/18 military activity was limited to patrolling, and sometimes German, Russian, and Austro-Hungarian soldiers even used the truce for scenes of fraternization. At the same time diplomats of the Central Powers and Bolshevik Russia negotiated at Brest-Litovsk the terms for post-war Eastern Europe. Hopes were high to conclude the first peace treaty after all the painful losses the war had brought to their people. But by early February 1918 the talks came to a standstill, as both sides did not want to give up their initial stance. Thus, the telegram the German Supreme Commander East (Oberost) sent on 16 February 1918 did not really come as a surprise. He announced to his troops the start of Operation *Faustschlag* ('Punch') for 18 February; it meant the reopening of the hostilities in the East. His order ended with the following words:

> The resumption of the military operations does not aim at the Russian people, but the Bolsheviks, the enemies of all state order, who prevent peace and declared war on the Ukraine which had concluded peace. The purpose of the operation is to topple the Bolshevik government and hence to bring us peace with Russia.[1]

German, and around ten days later Austro-Hungarian, troops crossed the ceasefire line in the East between the Baltic Sea and the Black Sea and penetrated deep into Russian territory. The Baltic provinces and Belorussia came exclusively under German control in the following weeks. The Ukraine was shared between the two Central Powers. In summer 1918 the size of the German sphere of influence in the East was almost comparable in size to the area under German rule some 24 years later during World War II.

Political background

Over the course of the Great War Germany's war aims became increasingly ambitious in the East; at least parts of the Baltic provinces and Poland should be annexed.[2] In contrast, neither politicians nor military commanders initially paid a lot of attention to the Ukraine. By the outbreak of the war the Central Powers briefly contemplated stirring up Ukrainian nationalists in a revolt against the Russian tsar, but this idea was soon discarded. A proper Ukrainian nationalism did not exist to give an insurgency an ideological foundation. In the following months and years some pressure groups from German heavy industry and particularly exiled Ukrainians in Berlin and Vienna still tried to convince the German and Austo-Hungarian governments of the importance of the country and its potential to destabilize the Russian giant. But all these attempts were to no avail, as Vienna and even more so Berlin did not display any interest in the country.

This altered during 1917 when fundamental domestic changes emerged in the Russian Empire which also impacted on the Ukraine. In March 1917 the Ukrainian *Rada* (Council) was established as the new government of the country and claimed national autonomy. On 20 November 1917 the *Rada* finally declared even national independence from Russia. The *Rada* was a heterogeneous, but leftist-dominated, mix of various political fractions. The Bolsheviks were not part of this new government, but deemed enemies.

This new situation in the East shifted the focus of German policy, particularly when the peace talks stalled at Brest-Litovsk. Germany had demanded from Bolshevik Russia to cede considerable parts of its territory, particularly the Baltic provinces and Poland. The Russians categorically refuted this plan and instead insisted on a 'peace without annexations and reparations'. To break the diplomatic deadlock, Hindenburg ordered to start negotiations with the Ukrainian representatives the *Rada* had sent to Brest-Litovsk some weeks before. The Ukraine was now the lever to enforce the German aims on the negotiation table.

Despite the Ukrainian delegation at Brest, the *Rada*'s domestic situation was extremely fragile. It could only exercise limited power, as the Bolsheviks contested its authority in large parts of the country. Finally, they overthrew the *Rada* on 8 February 1918 and established a regime of terror. The toppled *Rada* quickly turned towards Germany and desperately asked for military assistance in exchange for extensive food deliveries. In the same night, from 8 to 9 February, both countries signed head over heels a peace treaty at Brest-Litovsk, the first peace treaty of World War I. Only a few days later the *Rada* lodged an official request for help which gave the German Empire the legal basis for a military intervention that it could thus justify at home and on the international stage. Austria-Hungary remained hesitant; it never signed the peace treaty and joined the military operation only later.

What were the Central Powers' and in particular Germany's intentions behind this military and political adventure in the East? The desperate food supply was certainly the key factor for famine-struck Austria-Hungary to intervene. Even though the food situation in Germany was also fairly tense in early 1918, too, its motives for the invasion were not this one-dimensional. Expansion of the German influence in Eastern Europe certainly played a role. However, the main reason for the German intervention in the Ukraine was certainly to force Bolshevik Russia to sign eventually the Brest-Litovsk treaty. The High Command of the German Army, the OHL, desperately needed as many troops as possible from the East for the big Spring Offensive in the West. Time was critical. This offensive should commence sooner rather than later, before the US military potential could be fully realized.

From this point of view the German intervention in the Ukraine was a success: shortly after the start of the German campaign the Russian Bolsheviks returned to the negotiation table at Brest-Litovsk. They had to bite the bullet and lost Finland, the Baltic provinces, Belorussia, and the Ukraine. The peace treaty signed on 3 March 1918 was a humiliation for the new Bolshevik regime in Moscow and guaranteed Germany an uncontested hegemony in the East. But the architects of this 'diktat peace', the chief of the OHL, Generalfeldmarschall Paul von Hindenburg and particularly his Generalquartiermeister Erich Ludendorff, overlooked one key consequence for the German policy in the East: Germany was now directly involved in the political quagmire of former Tsarist Russia and was no longer able to pull the strings externally by using different rivalling groups and new emerging states. The Ukraine turned out to become Pandora's Box. Anarchy reigned in large parts of the country, social tensions between big landowners and impoverished peasants were impossible to solve, and politically the country was split between Bolsheviks, supporters of the *Rada* (later the Directory), Anarchists, and old Tsarist elites. Furthermore, the economy suffered from the consequences of three years of war.

The railway campaign, February–May 1918

Initially, however, things looked positive: German troops occupied the Ukraine in a Blitzkrieg-style campaign, although the quality of the army in the East was rather poor. Most of the younger ranks and the best officers had been transferred to units on the Western Front. The cavalry units suffered from a lack of horses, and finally some soldiers sympathized with the new communist ideology or at least with some of the socialist ideas. Furthermore, the snowy conditions in February rendered all advance along the roads difficult.

Ludendorff and his OHL could not offer a proper operational plan; the only objective given was the liberation of Kiev from the Bolsheviks to lift the *Rada* back into power. The forces initially designated for this mission were relatively small in numbers: only six infantry and *Landwehr* divisions as well as one cavalry brigade. Yet, the campaign quickly gained momentum due to various unforeseen factors.

The Germans soon realized that they had to rely on speed and surprise in order to achieve their mission. Hence, only two days after the start of the campaign they decided to advance not on roads, but largely on railway lines instead. Even though Ukrainian public life lay in a state of anarchy, the railways remained functional and the personnel supported the Germans. They hoped the liberation of the country from Bolshevik rule would end all misery. Instead of advancing on a broad front the Germans concentrated on key terrain, mostly communication centres. German troops advanced on trains to the next major station, took Bolsheviks or Red Guards prisoner, jumped onto the trains again, and moved further east. The operation in the Ukraine became the 'railway campaign'.

The Korps Knoerzer, which served as the spearhead in the campaign, noted: 'Taking into account the strength of our own forces it is not possible to occupy the whole Ukraine. It is about to take quickly the provincial capitals and economic centres.'[3] Similar to the 'Blitzkrieg campaign' against the Soviet Union in 1941 this approach, however, had the long-term disadvantage that the control of the country remained superficial owing to the relatively low number of friendly forces; off the main axis of communication irregulars emerged. In this sense General Wilhelm Groener, in March/April 1918 Commander of I Armee-Korps, wrote to Ludendorff on 22 March, 'We urgently need more troops for the vast areas; otherwise we will lose our authority.'[4]

On 3 March the first German troops arrived in Kiev and drove the Bolsheviks out of the city. This meant they needed only two weeks to cross 340 miles from Kovel on the armistice line to the Ukrainian capital. The speed of advance in this 'railway campaign' surpassed all comparable military campaigns in history, even those in recent years. For example, in 2003 the US Army needed about three weeks

The German and Austro-Hungarian occupation of the Ukraine, 1918

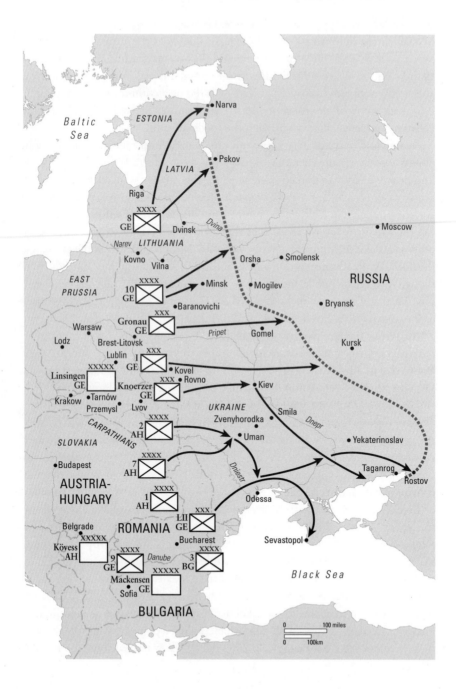

to cover the same distance from the Saudi–Iraqi border to Baghdad despite having the most modern equipment available. From early March 1918 on, however, the campaign slowed down, as the Bolsheviks started to destroy parts of the infrastructure during their retreat, in particular railways and bridges, and put up some armed resistance to the German and Austro-Hungarian troops. Yet, the onslaught to Rostov for another 560 miles did not take longer than another two months.

Initially the Germans intended to occupy only the western part of the Ukraine, but things worked out different. Military success could be easily gained against an often disorganized and poorly equipped Bolshevik enemy who was no real match for the German troops. By exploiting the enemy's military weakness junior officers often advanced further on their own initiative. This caused confusion and astonishment amongst the enemy and the local population. There was everywhere 'an almost magical fear' of the 'approaching "Germanski"'. The maintenance of this moral prestige seems to be the foundations for future success', as the liaison officer from the Foreign Office reported. [5]

After the capture of Kiev the Bolsheviks retreated to the east and the Germans quickly realised the *Rada*'s lack of power over the country. Hence they decided to pursue the Bolsheviks and take control of the industrial and coal centres such as Charkiv and Yekaterinoslav. All this needed more troops than initially planned. Finally, in early March the German Generalkommando zbV 52 (LII Armee-Korps) joined the campaign with three divisions from occupied Romania. Their objective was the Crimean peninsula and the harbour of Sevastopol where the Russian Black Sea fleet anchored. Furthermore, on 28 February Austro-Hungarian troops had also started their own advance into southern Ukraine, as the Habsburg monarchy wanted to get hold of the fertile Podolia province. But both Central Powers could not agree on a joint high command and as a result fought their own separate campaigns and pursued their own occupation policies.

At the start of the campaign German forces encountered only unorganized and ill-disciplined Bolshevik troops which – according to German and Austro-Hungarian military reports – terrorized and looted civilians. They only rarely wore uniforms and commonly blended in with the general population. The commander of Generalkommando zbV 52, General Robert Kosch, summarized the situation in a letter to his wife with the following words: 'A war against the civilian population is always a nasty business, because it is unpredictable and exposed to 1,000 different sorts of eventualities.'[6]

Like in Belgium and northern France in 1914 the nightmare of a *francs-tireurs* war haunted the minds of German troops in the Ukraine in 1918. An order of 9. Armee even made explicit reference to these events at the outbreak of the war. Yet, civil resistance was not a figment of imagination, but a reality in the Ukraine.

In contrast to 1914, however, there are no records suggesting the Germans shot hostages and innocent people in collective reprisals. German troops did not seem to have derailed from Heeresgruppe (Army Group) Linsingen's guidelines issued prior to the start of the campaign: 'The reopening of the military operations does not aim at the Russian people, but the Bolsheviks, the enemies of all national order.'[7] Armee-Abteilung (Army Detachment) Gronau in northern Ukraine had expressed it in even more moderate words: 'Most considerate treatment of the population is pointed out again. We must quickly succeed in winning over the trust of the Ukrainian population.'[8]

Indeed, German troops were often greeted as liberators from Bolshevism or at least received a warm reception. But the first positive contacts soon cooled off. German units often looted or imposed unfair food requisitions which caused bitterness amongst the local population. Officially, they had to live off the land. This policy, however, became increasingly problematic and counter-productive. Many counter-orders showed the higher command's willingness to remedy the abuses, but finally to no real avail.[9]

Terror was, however, only applied against armed Bolsheviks. The Germans initially took armed enemies prisoner, but this policy was soon to change. They had learnt of atrocities the Bolsheviks had committed during their previous short-lived reign over the country, such as the execution of around 1,000 former Tsarist officers in Kiev alone. Consequently, the Germans changed their orders: 'Organized Bolsheviks … are our enemies and thus are to be treated according to martial law.'[10] In other words: 'Captured Bolsheviks were to be shot'. A report of 1. Bayerische Kavalleriebrigade justified this ruthless no-quarter policy: it scared the Bolsheviks and they did not dare to offer any further organized resistance. Evidence of a similar policy can be found in the records of other – though not all – German units.[11]

As the Bolsheviks also shot the few German prisoners they took, it is impossible to determine which side started first with these executions. Yet, the Germans certainly shot more Bolshevik prisoners than vice versa, if just for the simple reason that they took a much larger number of them. Bolshevik violence seemed to have been directed more against their country fellows and less against the Germans. The civilian population was simply an easier target.

The no-quarter policy culminated in the bloody events at Taganrog on the Black Sea coast between 10 and 14 June 1918 – after the end of the actual campaign. Despite a local ceasefire several thousand Bolshevik troops landed in an amphibious assault at the mouth of the Mius River near Taganrog in the back of the German front. An ad hoc force of about 2,000 men under the command of Oberst Arthur Bopp defeated the Bolshevik expeditionary force within only two days. Some of the surviving Bolsheviks could flee onto their boats again; the rest surrendered. German losses totalled 39 killed and 169 wounded.

Already during the battle the Germans had taken no prisoners. But whilst these killings happened in the heat of the battle with often confusing close combat, the roughly 2,000 Bolshevik survivors were murdered in cold blood. Bopp gave a written order to execute them all with the exception of ten men for interrogation.[12] The events at Taganrog had a political sequel, when a Socialist member of the German parliament learnt about this crime. The highest military authority, Heeresgruppe Eichhorn-Kiew, was forced to launch an official investigation about this mass execution. Oberst Bopp justified his actions by pointing out that the enemy had not been uniformed and represented 'nothing else than just murderer types'.[13] The Army Group's Chief of Staff, Generalleutnant Groener, did not endorse Bopp's execution order, but failed to draw any consequences from this affair. A few days before the end of the war Bopp was even promoted to *Generalmajor*.

The events at Taganrog and the no-quarter policy on both sides showed that the campaign in the Ukraine had developed into an ideological war. This is one strong line of continuity between the battlefields of the Eastern Front in both world wars. Ironically, Imperial Germany had lifted the Bolsheviks into power in Moscow in 1917 and had signed an official peace treaty with them at Brest-Litovsk shortly after. In the Ukraine, however, the Bolsheviks were considered mortal enemies. Military and political considerations led to a Janus-faced German policy in the East.

Overview of the occupation, April–November 1918

When the city of Rostov was captured in early May, the campaign finally came to an end. One month later Kaiser Wilhelm II officially ordered not to advance any further into Russian territory, even though Ludendorff started another political military adventure in August by deploying more than 10,000 men to Georgia. They were to secure potential oil sources and German influence in the Caucasus region. At this time the German occupation in the Ukraine was already well established.

Strictly speaking the term 'German occupation' is wrong in a factual and a legal sense. Factually, because roughly between one-quarter to one-third of the country was occupied by Germany's ally Austria-Hungary; after some tedious negotiations both Central Powers agreed to cede the fertile southern provinces to Austria-Hungary, whereas the rest and hence the majority of the Ukraine plus the Crimean peninsula should fall into the German zone of influence.

During the entire period of German and Austro-Hungarian presence in the Ukraine, Germany always remained the dominating power, even though Austria-Hungary often tried to pursue its own economic policy. The term 'occupation' is also wrong from a legal point of view. Though in many respects soon a *de facto* occupation, the Central Powers had officially not entered a hostile, but a friendly, country after having followed a request for help by the Ukrainian government. This did not only impact on the entire occupation strategy, but also on the relationship between German troops and the Ukrainian administration, as will be seen later.

The highest German military authority over the country was initially Heeresgruppe Linsingen, named after its commander Generaloberst Alexander von Linsingen. Since Linsingen was seen by many as too inflexible for this primarily political job, he was replaced in late March by Generalfeldmarschall Hermann von Eichhorn, a venerable officer of 70 years. The army group was renamed after Eichhorn-Kiew. In late July Eichhorn was assassinated by a Ukrainian social revolutionary. Under his successor, Generaloberst Günther von Kirchbach, the name of the army group changed again, this time to Heeresgruppe Kiew. The 'strong man' throughout the months of occupation was however the Heeresgruppe's Chief of Staff, Generalleutnant Wilhelm Groener. Stemming from the lower-middle class, Groener had achieved a stunning career in the army; his character combined eloquence, social skills, pragmatism, organizational talent, and diligence.

In summer 1918 Heeresgruppe Eichhorn-Kiew consisted of six army corps with around 20 divisions. The number of German occupation troops in the Ukraine totalled just over 300,000 men before dropping to around 250,000 in autumn 1918, organized in 16 divisions. Besides the Ukraine, the Germans had another seven divisions in the Baltic provinces and Belarus in autumn 1918.[14] Hence, the overall number of German troops in the east amounted to about 500,000 men in summer 1918. This was much more than the Germans had originally planned, even though the occupation troops were mostly second or third class.

Besides the military, the *Auswärtiges Amt* (Foreign Office) had also sent its envoy to Kiev, Philipp Alfons Baron Mumm von Schwarzentstein. As the Ukraine was officially an independent country, the *Auswärtiges Amt* internally claimed the dominant role for the German policy towards the Ukraine. But the diplomats soon had to face the reality of an occupation regime based on German military might. Despite the dominance of the army over the Ukrainian policy, the situation resembled an inadvertent system of checks and balances in which generals and diplomats were often forced to find political compromises. The *Reichswirtschaftsamt* (Imperial Economy Office) also sought to expand its influence in the East, but under its representative, Otto von Wiedfeldt, it remained the least important player of the three institutions.

Very soon the Germans were confronted with almost insurmountable problems. Despite being able to expel the Bolsheviks very quickly not only from the capital Kiev but also from the rest of the country, the *Rada* remained powerless and was unable to gain any substantial backing in their own country. A Ukrainian national identity did not exist and the *Rada*'s politicians were inexperienced; Groener put it in disdainful and nonchalant words when he called the *Rada* a 'convent of immature students and other youthful dreamers and unpleasant elements'.[15] Moreover, the Ukrainian economy lay in shambles as a consequence of the war and did not show any signs of recovery. The overarching problem, however, was the pending question of land distribution for which the small peasants had so hoped, but the *Rada* remained inactive and instead adhered to socialist dispossession ideas. Under these circumstances the *Rada* could not and was not willing to meet its contractual liabilities with the Central Powers on grain deliveries.

Anti-Bolshevism was the bond that kept the strange marriage between Imperial Germany and the socialist *Rada* alive for a while, but by late April the tensions between both parties reached an irreconcilable stage. Groener initiated the overthrow of the *Rada*, and on 29 April 1918 the former Tsarist general Pavlo Skoropadskiy was declared the new Hetman of the Ukraine. Under his authoritarian regime the young Ukrainian state finally stabilized, at least superficially. The Hetman's most important measure was the re-establishment of the administration which consisted mostly of the old Tsarist elites. The economy slowly started to recover, a new Ukrainian educational policy began to emerge, and the Central Powers felt they had a reliable partner in the Hetman, particularly when compared to the former *Rada*. Yet the Hetman could not meet the food delivery agreements, either. Popular support in his country stayed modest, as his enemies – the Bolsheviks and the followers of the old *Rada* (now reformed under the name 'Directorate') – blamed him for being the occupiers' puppet and a representative of the old hated elites. In essence, the Hetman could not form a stable Ukrainian state; his power rested on feet of clay. But he not only struggled with the lack of domestic support; the Germans and the Austro-Hungarians also did not want to concede him too much power. For example, they did not allow the Hetman to build up his own Ukrainian army. This policy altered only when the military situation deteriorated for the Germans on the Western Front in late summer 1918. Now the Germans started to rethink their politics towards the Ukraine. If they wanted to keep the country as a partner in Eastern Europe after the war, they would need a stable Ukrainian state with its own army. Thus,

'Ukrainization' combined with a process of democratization was the official policy for the last phase of the occupation. But it was too late. With the Central Powers' withdrawal in autumn/winter of 1918, the Hetman regime quickly collapsed and a brutal civil war commenced between Bolsheviks and the Directorate under Sijmon Petljura. This war was to last until 1921.

For the Central Powers the entire Ukrainian adventure ended in dreadful disaster. One of the key problems had always been the inability to agree on a common policy. Whilst Austria-Hungary was only interested in short-term exploitation due to the critical food situation at home, the German occupation authorities remained undecided. On the one hand the army leaders often favoured the Austro-Hungarian model, but on the other hand the remaining key players from the Foreign Office and particularly the Imperial Economic Office had sincere intentions to build up long-term commercial and political relations between Germany and a stable Ukraine – an idea we would call 'nation building' today. In the end both approaches failed; despite a series of treaties the Central Powers could only get 130,000 tons of grain out of the country until autumn 1918 – only 13 per cent of the contractually agreed 1 million tons.[16] With other agricultural goods like fodder or cattle the situation did not differ substantially. The entire economic policy had finally turned into a huge loss. Trade between the Ukraine and the Central Powers just did not want to kick off, and so the state-building efforts lacked any substantial economic foundations. Despite all its flaws and failures, in at least one field the state-building efforts displayed a tangible success: the suppression of the insurgencies and the stabilization of the country's internal security, although the starting point for this mission was anything but favourable.

Rebellions and pacification in rural Ukraine, summer 1918

After the official end of the campaign in May 1918 the country was far from pacified despite the presence of German and Austro-Hungarian troops. In the Ukrainian countryside the central government had always exercised only limited powers, even during Tsarist times. A culture of violence had been rife for decades and the consequences of World War I exacerbated this state. Armed bandits, mostly consisting of demobilized former Tsarist soldiers, wandered around, robbed farmers, and terrorized the population. The most prominent gang was the 'Revolutionary Insurrection Army' under the leadership of the infamous anarchist Nestor Makhno in the rural south-eastern Ukraine. The social question was another powder-keg, as neither the *Rada* nor later the Hetman dared to tackle the difficult landowner question. The result was a dissatisfied and impoverished rural population of small or landless peasants who were susceptible to Bolshevik promises or just criminal activity. However, it was overall only a minority of them who had a taste for subversive political and military activities. Heeresgruppe Eichhorn-Kiew estimated this group to form only 10 to 12 per cent of the entire rural population.[17]

The most troubled region lay south of Kiev, in the area of Uman, Smila and Zvenyhorodka, where 15. Königlich Bayerische Reserve Infanteriebrigade was deployed. This brigade alone had to secure the vast rural area of the Čerkasy Oblast with 8,000 square miles – the equivalent in size to modern Wales. It reported to XXVII Reserve Corps in Kiev under the command of General Bernhard von Watzdorf. Upon his arrival in the country Watzdorf hoped to 'create order and to win over the trust of the population for us',[18] as he wrote in his personal diary; soon after he issued an order to his units along these lines.

Before the rebellion broke out German troops had tried to disarm the population by sending out numerous patrols to the villages. Watzdorf wanted to convince the locals to hand over their weapons peacefully and forbade his own troops from executing reprisals or burning down houses. He even supported the raising of local self-defence forces so that the villagers were able to protect themselves against bandit raids. All German military actions had to be closely coordinated with Ukrainian authorities; locals served as guides and translators. Mistakes in selecting supposed culprits or suspects should be avoided by all means. The use of firearms was only allowed for breaking enemy resistance and self-defence.

This relatively moderate German approach was soon put to the test. On 4 June a larger insurgency broke out in the area around Zvenyhorodka, where several hundred rebels attacked isolated German garrisons. The insurgents consisted mainly of former soldiers, Bolsheviks, and sailors of the Black Sea fleet and were armed with machine guns and even field guns. In the local vicinities they drafted and armed villagers, sometimes by force. German units, such as elements of the poorly trained *Landsturm* Infantry Battalion Gotha, surrendered to the rebels. Other smaller German units in Lysjanka and Vil'šana followed this example. The insurgency seemed to turn into a regional threat.

Heeresgruppe Eichhorn-Kiew's worst fears turned into reality. A month before the outbreak of the rebellion instructions had been given to apply 'most severe measures ... in order to nip insurgency movements in the bud'[19]. Now with the revolt in full swing there were orders to court martial and to shoot all people who had taken up arms against the Germans or who had only committed acts of sabotage. Even the hitherto moderate General Watzdorf shared this view and emphasized that 'ruthless measures' against the rebelling villages would certainly have a 'cooling off effect'.[20] In exceptional cases, to set an example, he even allowed the burning down of 'particularly rebellious villages deserted of their inhabitants [sic!]'.[21]

Yet, in the coming weeks the Germans seemed to have burned down only two villages: Lisianka and Jasenivka. Other orders tried to avoid arbitrary measures and collective punishment against innocent civilians. For instance, the taking of hostages was forbidden as was the shelling of villages to simply disarm a village; collective punishments, such as the seizure of grain or cattle, could only be imposed if the *entire* population of a village had joined the rebellion. In sum, the Germans clearly tried to distinguish between insurgents – armed civilians and their supporters – on the one hand and the majority of the civilian population on the other hand.

Planned and executed in an amateurish way, the insurgency very quickly collapsed. Already after one week, on 12 June, the Germans retook Zvenyhorodka and also relieved other isolated garrisons. The rebels dispersed and fled to the north where the Germans had to execute some tedious combing out operations in vast forests over the following weeks. Other elements tried to fight their way through towards the Russian border. Although the partly inaccessible terrain and the sheer size of the area prevented the Germans from completely destroying all rebel groups, the insurgency had nevertheless ended. By July the Zvenyhorodka region was reported to be quiet and by late August the entire country was seen as pacified. In autumn Groener could write to his wife: 'It is currently so peaceful and quiet in the Ukraine, that one could have an easy time here, if the uncertainties from other theatres of war and from Berlin did not cast their shadows here.'[22] Yet, the assassination of Generalfeldmarschall Eichhorn in the capital on 31 July by a leftist revolutionary showed that the Ukraine was not a completely safe place to be. But this spectacular coup remained an isolated case.

Why were the Germans able to pacify the Ukraine in such a remarkably short period of time given the generally protracted nature of insurgencies? Certainly, the Soviet idea of revolutionary wars carried by the masses had finally turned into an illusion; these uprisings in the Ukraine in the summer 1918 were the 'last flickers'.[23] As a consequence, Moscow ordered the Ukrainian Bolsheviks to stop all open confrontation for the time being. Resistance against the Central Powers and the Hetman regime seemed to be futile.

It must, however, also be emphasized that the Central Powers (and particularly the Germans) had laid the foundations for a sustained pacification; this was not based on confrontation, but on cooperation with the Ukrainian authorities. Heeresgruppe Eichhorn-Kiew ordered ruthless action against bandits and other agitators, but the rest of the population should remain unharmed. 'Foolish measures, such as mistreatment of civilians or the burning down of houses, damage the respect for the Germans',[24] the army group concluded. It seemed the senior military commanders understood that the sheer use of brutal force alone, as it had been partly applied before, was futile. There was a noticeable 'learning curve' in the German Army.

Cooperation with the host nation was seen as paramount to the pacification of the country. Prior to any anti-partisan operation Ukrainian authorities were to prepare the ground by delivering a coherent intelligence picture. 'Mutual misunderstandings' should be redressed, since they had 'often led to collective punishment like the burning down of villages'[25] before. Admittedly, the cooperation with the Ukrainian authorities was still far from being perfect in German eyes, but Heeresgruppe Eichhorn-Kiew entrusted a certain degree of self-responsibility to the locals. It stated in July: 'If we succeed in giving the entire population the feeling of being themselves in charge of law and order in their area, we will have achieved a lot.'[26] A modern day counterinsurgency strategy would not use fundamentally different words.

Everywhere in the country the security situation improved. A monthly report of 15. Königlich Bayerische Reserve Infanteriebrigade from September 1918 revealed the reasons for this success and drew an insightful picture of how things had altered in this once seriously troubled area around Uman. The brigade's units became static which allowed them to interact with Ukrainian authorities. The consequence was 'a standardised orderly and meticulous disarmament and arrest procedure based upon a systematically built up agent network in close contact with the population, the governmental administration and the militia'.[27] An amnesty program for 'bandits' commenced to bear fruits, too. Furthermore, not the killing of hostages, but courts martial was one of the main means in the pacification process. General allegations were deemed useless and 15. Königlich Bayerische Reserve Infanteriebrigade stated clearly in a central leaflet: 'A German court cannot sentence anyone whose guilt had not been proven in court.'[28] However, not all German troops endorsed this strict legal policy and some of them advocated a harsher approach – eventually to no avail.

Things had indeed not turned out as well as expected with local security forces; many of them were not deemed reliable and the Ukrainian militia turned out to be a double-edged sword: on the one hand they often effectively supported German troops in disarming villages; on the other hand, however, they generally applied brutal measures which 'did not help to win the population over for the new government and for us' as 15. Königlich Bayerische Reserve Infanteriebrigade criticized.[29] The largely negative attitude of the rural population towards the occupier did not fundamentally shift, either. German troops were seen as the executing authorities of the unpopular Hetman regime and as the embodiment of the old social order. Furthermore, German (and even much more so Austro-Hungarian) units still carried out excessive food requisitions and looted local farmers. All this shows the contradictions of the German pacification policy. The moderate approach often met its limits in the harsh reality.

Nevertheless, compared to the chaotic period in late 1917/early 1918 and particularly during the civil war between late 1918 and 1921 the Ukraine enjoyed a 'relatively calm hiatus imposed by the German occupation'.[30] Nothing may prove this fact better than the number of pogroms locals committed against the Jewish population. Between September 1917 and December 1921 1,289 pogroms were officially recorded in the Ukraine. Only 46 of them fell into the year 1918. There are even accounts of German troops protecting Jews against the local mob. In the light of the Holocaust some 23 years later, these facts are even more remarkable, although anti-Semitic tones were rife in many German military records.

Conclusion

German policy in the East in 1918 resulted in a massive failure – a consequence of the far-reaching, ambitious, and excessive expansionist aims of the top commanders in the OHL, in particular General Ludendorff. This general was certainly a brilliant tactician who also mastered the operational level of war. But as a strategist he was utterly inept and as such a reflection of German military art in the early 20th century. In March 1918 Ludendorff expressed the objectives for the big spring offensives in the West with the remarkable words: 'We just punch a hole and the rest will fall into place.' The same attitude determined his strategy in the East: the collapse of the Tsarist empire left a gigantic power vacuum where it was easy to expand the German sphere of influence. Tactical considerations determined the strategy, as campaigns were military walkovers and therefore nobody in the OHL had contemplated the political consequences. The adventure in the Ukraine was to become the prime example for this flawed policy.

The German hopes to receive grain and other goods from the Ukraine never truly materialized. Instead of the expected 1 million tons the Ukrainian government had promised at Brest-Litovsk in early 1918, the Central Powers could export only 130,000 tons to their home countries. Even though the Germans interfered in Ukrainian domestic politics and helped to replace the socialist *Rada* in late 1918 with the submissive authoritarian Hetman regime, the chaotic situation improved only slowly in the country. But all state-building efforts were in vain and cost the Germans large sums of money. Furthermore, the occupation policy strained the alliance with Austria-Hungary; at no point could the two

Central Powers agree on a common strategy. Whilst Germany was interested in a long-term stable Ukrainian state under its influence, Austria-Hungary pursued a policy of short-term exploitation. The food shortage in Austria made them believe this was to be the only viable option.

The Germans and the Austro-Hungarians did at least pacify the country after the rural revolts during summer 1918, and they granted the Ukraine a short, albeit fragile, respite before the ensuing bloody civil war. After a 'trial-and-error' phase the Germans were able to conceive a relatively modern and moderate approach to defeat the insurgents. It was based on a heavy hand against the rebels themselves, but at the same time on moderation towards the civilian population. Key to all this was a close cooperation with Ukrainian authorities. Indiscriminate brutality against civilians was certainly not inherent to German military culture, as some historians have claimed for the Imperial Army.

In the inter-war years the Germans failed to remember the many positive lessons from the pacification of the Ukraine in 1918. The opposite happened: Hitler himself considered the occupation policy from the Great War a failure; indirect rule was something he did not believe in. The German military did not reconsider the experiences from the swift railway campaign, either, as the circumstances seemed to be too unique. With the benefit of hindsight, however, this campaign in the Ukraine in 1918 displayed many classical features of the later Blitzkrieg campaigns such as surprise, speed, initiative on the lower tactical levels, and a concentration on capturing only key operational objectives such as railway stations and major cities. It is debatable whether there was another characteristic of this campaign which should repeat itself some 23 years later: using terror against the enemy to shatter his cohesion and will to fight. The often merciless treatment of captured armed Bolsheviks was already a precursor of things to come in Operation *Barbarossa*.

ENDNOTES

Chapter 1: Commanding Through Armageddon

1. Quoted in George Aston, *The Biography of the Late Marshal Foch* (New York: Macmillan, 1932), p. 117.

2. The British Army's leadership, including Henry Wilson, came largely from Anglo-Irish, Protestant, backgrounds. Wilson and others sympathized with the Curragh officers and warned the British government that any attempt to use the army against Protestants in Ireland might split it in two and/or cause a civil war.

3. Quoted in Robert Doughty, *Pyrrhic Victory* (Cambridge, MA: The Belknap Press of Harvard University Press, 2008), p. 180.

4. Quoted in Robert Asprey, *The First Battle of the Marne* (Philadelphia: Lippincourt, 1962), p. 42.

5. Barbara Tuchman, *The Guns of August* (New York: Random House, 1962), p. 516.

6. Tuchman, *The Guns of August*, p. 516.

7. Although often overlooked, the French did send naval assets and the Corps Expéditionnaire d'Orient to participate in the operations at Gallipoli. The French landed on the Asian side near Kum Kale. Joffre, however, insisted that these operations were distractions to the main theatre of war in France itself.

8. Gary Sheffield, *The Chief: Douglas Haig and the British Army* (London: Aurum Press, 2012), chapter five.

9. Some scholars take German General Erich von Falkenhayn at his word when he said that one of the goals was to knock 'England's best sword [France]' out of her hands. Whether or not England was the strategic goal of Verdun, and this point is highly debatable, it remains true that it was France, not England, that Falkenhayn wanted to 'bleed white'. This is a tricky one. The Christmas Memorandum, in which Falkenhayn allegedly states this does not exist and he mentions it for the first time in his memoirs published after the war. Quotations from Robert Foley, *German Strategy and the Path to Verdun: Erich von Falkenhayn and the Development of Attrition, 1870–1916* (Cambridge: Cambridge University Press, 2005), pp. 187 and 263.

10. William Philpott, *Bloody Victory: The Sacrifice on the Somme and the Making of the Twentieth Century* (London: Little, Brown, 2009), p. 83.

11. Philpott, *Bloody Victory*, pp. 121–127.

12. To be fair, no one in either the British or the French Army really believed that the Somme could provide such conditions. The extent to which the fighting at the Somme improved the odds for both the French at Verdun and the Russians in the east remains a point of historical debate.

13. Elizabeth Greenhalgh, *Foch in Command: The Forging of a First World War General* (Cambridge: Cambridge University Press, 2011), pp. 187 and 175.

14. Jonathan Schneer, *The Balfour Declaration: The Origins of the Arab-Israeli Conflict* (New York: Random House, 2010), p. 36. However limited Kitchener's strategic

vision turned out to be at times, it was no worse than that of British politicians. In fact, it was Kitchener who first saw the need to raise a large land army for a long war.

15. Philip Langer and Robert Pois, *Command Failure in War: Psychology and Leadership* (Bloomington: Indiana University Press, 2004), p. 127.

16. A description of the conference is in David French, *The Strategy of the Lloyd George Coalition* (Oxford: Clarendon Press, 1995), pp. 57–59.

17. Haig diary entry for Monday 26 February [1917] in Gary Sheffield and John Bourne, eds., *Douglas Haig: War Diaries and Letters, 1914–1918* (London: Weidenfeld & Nicolson, 2005), pp. 269–270.

18. Space forbids a full discussion of the Nivelle offensive debacle. See Doughty, *Pyrrhic Victory*, chapter seven.

19. Haig diary entry for Wednesday 18 April in Sheffield and Bourne, eds., *Douglas Haig*, p. 285.

20. Eliot A. Cohen, *Supreme Command: Soldiers and Statesmen in Wartime* (New York: Free Press, 2002), p. 54.

21. See David Zabecki, *The German 1918 Offensives: A Case Study in the Operational Level of War* (London: Routledge, 2006).

Chapter 2: German Operational Thinking in World War I

1. For a basic summary of the state of research see Gerhard P. Groß, *Mythos und Wirklichkeit: Geschichte des operativen Denkens im deutschen Heer von Moltke d.Ä. bis Heusinger*, Zeitalter der Weltkriege, 9 (Paderborn: Verlag Ferdinand Schöningh, 2012). For an overview see Gerhard P. Groß, 'Development of Operational Thinking in the German Army in the World War Era', in *Journal of Military and Strategic Studies* (JMSS), vol. 13, no. 4 (2011). Article can be viewed online at: <http://www.jmss.org/jmss/index.php/jmss/article/view/419/425>. See also Dennis E. Showalter, 'German Grand Strategy: A Contradiction in Terms?' in *Militärgeschichtliche Mitteilungen* (MGM), vol. 48 (1990), pp. 65–102. I wish to thank Gerhard Groß, Agilolf Kesselring, and Lars Zacharias for their constructive perusal of the manuscript.

2. For an overview of Frederician military history see Eberhard Birk, Thorsten Loch, and Peter A. Popp (eds.), *Wie Friedrich "der Große" wurde: Eine kleine Geschichte des Siebenjährigen Krieges,* published in association with the Military History Research Office, Potsdam, and the Bundeswehr Military History Museum, Dresden (Freiburg: Rombach Verlag, 2012).

3. Sven Lange, *Hans Delbrück und der Strategiestreit: Kriegführung und Kriegsgeschichte in der Kontroverse 1879–1914,* Einzelschriften zur Militärgeschichte, 40 (Freiburg: Rombach Verlag, 1995); Martin Raschke, *Der politisierende Generalstab: Die friderizianischen Kriege in der amtlichen deutschen Militärgeschichtsschreibung 1890– 1914*, Einzelschriften zur Militärgeschichte, 36 (Freiburg: Rombach Verlag, 1993).

4. See Stig Förster, 'Der deutsche Generalstab und die Illusion des kurzen Krieges, 1871–1914: Metakritik eines Mythos', in *Militärgeschichtliche Mitteilungen*, vol. 54 (1995), p. 61.

5. Johannes Lepsius, Albrecht Mendelssohn-Bartholdy, and Friedrich Thimme (eds.), *Die Große Politik der Europäischen Kabinette 1871–1914: Sammlung der*

Diplomatischen Akten des Auswärtigen Amtes, vol. 2, *Der Berliner Kongress und seine Vorgeschichte*, 4th edition, (Berlin, 1927), p. 154.

6. This idea can also be found in Clausewitz, *Vom Kriege* (Berlin: Ullstein Taschenbuch, 1998), p. 1012.

7. Of these four battles, only Königgrätz was really a decisive battle in a political sense. Leuthen and Sedan brought no breakthrough and the victor of Cannae finally lost the war.

8. For details on the history of military conscription see Roland G. Foerster (ed.), *Die Wehrpflicht: Entstehung, Erscheinungsformen und politisch-militärische Wirkung*, Beiträge zur Militärgeschichte, 43 (München: Oldenbourg Verlag, 1994).

9. Groß, *Mythos*, p. 94.

10. 'Erste Beratung des Gesetzesentwurfs betreffend die Friedenspräsenzstärke des deutschen Heeres, Reichstagssitzung vom 14.05.1890', in *Reden des Generalfeldmarschalls Grafen Helmuth von Moltke, Gesammelte Schriften und Denkwürdigkeiten des Generalfeldmarschalls Grafen Helmuth von Moltke*, vol. 7 (Berlin: Ernst Siegfried und Sohn, 1892), p. 139.

11. Groß, *Mythos*, pp. 72ff. For stimulating thoughts see Hew Strachan, 'Die Ostfront: Geopolitik, Geographie und Operationen' in Gerhard P. Groß (ed.), *Die vergessene Front: Der Osten 1914–15. Ereignis, Wirkung, Nachwirkung*, Zeitalter der Weltkriege, 1 (Paderborn: Verlag Ferdinand, 2006), pp. 11–26.

12. For the following, see Groß, *Mythos*, pp. 75–89.

13. The following is characteristic: Königgrätz was a politically decisive battle, whereas Sedan was a militarily decisive battle.

14. Groß, *Mythos*, p. 311.

15. See Gerhard P. Groß, 'There was a Schlieffen Plan: Neue Quellen', in Hans Ehlert, Michael Epkenhans, and Gerhard P. Groß (eds.), *Der Schlieffenplan: Analysen und Dokumente*, Zeitalter der Weltkriege, 2 (Paderborn: Verlag Ferdinand Schöningh, 2006), pp. 117–160. See also Groß, *Mythos*, pp. 90–97.

16. Groß, *Mythos*, p. 90.

17. Ibid.

18. Ibid., pp. 102ff.

19. Annika Mombauer, 'Der Moltkeplan: Modifikation des Schlieffenplans bei gleichen Zielen?', in *Der Schlieffenplan*, pp. 79–99.

20. For an overview of German warfare at the political, strategical, and operative levels see Wilhelm Deist, 'Die Kriegführung der Mittelmächte', in Gerhard Hirschfeld, Gerd Krumeich, and Irina Renz (eds.), *Enzyklopädie Erster Weltkrieg*, aktualisierte und erweiterte Studienausgabe (Paderborn: Verlag Ferdinand Schöningh, 2009), pp. 249–271.

21. Holger H. Herwig, *The Marne, 1914: The Opening of World War I and the Battle that changed the World* (New York: Random House, 2009).

22. Groß, *Die vergessene Front*.

23. Gerhard P. Groß, 'Im Schatten des Westens: Die deutsche Kriegführung an der Ostfront bis Ende 1915', in *Die vergessene Front*, pp. 49–64.

24. Gerhard P. Groß, 'Das Dogma der Beweglichkeit: Überlegungen zur Genese der deutschen Heerestaktik im Zeitalter der Weltkriege', in Bruno Thoß und Hans-Erich Volkmann (eds.), *Erster Weltkrieg Zweiter Weltkrieg: Ein Vergleich. Krieg, Kriegserlebnis,*

Kriegserfahrung in Deutschland (Paderborn: Verlag Ferdinand Schöningh, 2002), p. 150.

25. Hans Linnenkohl, *Vom Einzelschuss zur Feuerwalze. Der Wettlauf zwischen Technik und Taktik im Ersten Weltkrieg* (Koblenz: Bernard & Graefe, 1990).

26. Holger Afflerbach, *Falkenhayn: Politisches Denken und Handeln im Kaiserreich*, Beiträge zur Militärgeschichte, 42 (2nd edition, München: Oldenbourg, 1996).

27. Groß, *Das Dogma der Beweglichkeit*, p. 148.

28. Christian Stachelbeck, *Militärische Effektivität im Ersten Weltkrieg: Die 11. Bayerische Infanteriedivision 1915 bis 1918*, Zeitalter der Weltkriege, 6 (Paderborn: Verlag Ferdinand Schöningh, 2010), pp. 161–195.

29. Gerhard P. Groß, 'Ein Nebenkriegsschauplatz: Die deutschen Operationen gegen Rumänien 1916', in Jürgen Angelow (ed.), *Der Erste Weltkrieg auf dem Balkan: Perspektiven der Forschung* (Berlin: be.bra wissenschaft, 2011), pp. 143–158.

30. Deist, *Kriegführung*, p. 263.

31. Stephan Leistenschneider, *Auftragstaktik im preußisch-deutschen Heer 1871 bis 1914* (Hamburg: Mittler und Sohn, 2002).

32. On the change in land war tactics, see Ralf Raths, *Vom Massensturm zur Stoßtrupptaktik: Die deutsche Landkriegtaktik im Spiegel von Dienstvorschriften und Publizistik 1906 bis 1918*, Einzelschriften zur Militärgeschichte, 44 (Freiburg: Rombach Verlag, 2009).

33. Gerhard P. Groß, 'Unternehmen "Albion": Eine Studie zur Zusammenarbeit von Armee und Marine während des Ersten Weltkrigs', in Wolfgang Elz and Sönke Neitzel (eds.), *Internationale Beziehungen im 19. und 20. Jahrhundert. Festschrift für Winfried Baumgart zum 65. Geburtstag* (Paderborn: Verlag Ferdinand Schöningh, 2003), pp. 171–186.

34. That was the official German term. As for the German advances on the Western Front in 1918 see Dieter Storz, 'Aber was hätte anders geschehen sollen?' in Jörg Duppler and Gerhard P. Groß (eds.), *Kriegsende 1918: Ereignis, Wirkung, Nachwirkung*, Beiträge zur Militärgeschichte, 53 (München: Oldenbourg, 1999) pp. 51–95.

35. Deist, *Kriegführung*, p. 267.

36. Storz, 'Aber was hätte geschehen sollen?', p. 95.

37. Wilhelm Meier-Dörnberg, '*Die große deutsche Frühjahrsoffensive 1918 zwischen Strategie und Taktik*', in *Operatives Denken und Handeln in deutschen Streitkräften im 19.und 20. Jahrhundert*, Vorträge zur Militärgeschichte, 9 (Herford, 1988) pp. 73–95.

38. Storz, 'Aber was hätte geschehen sollen?', p. 65.

39. An overview of the different offensives is given by David T. Zabecki, *The German 1918 Offensives: A Case Study in the Operational Level of War* (London: Routledge, 2006).

40. Eugen von Frauenholz (ed.), *Kronprinz Rupprecht: Mein Kriegstagebuch* (Berlin, 1929), vol. 2, p. 364.

41. Storz, 'Aber was hätte geschehen sollen?', p. 73.

42. Agilolf Kesselring, 'Moltkes strategisches Denken', in Thorsten Loch, Lars Zacharias (eds.), *Eine kleine Geschichte der Reichseinigungskriege 1864–1871: Wie die Siegessäule nach Berlin kam* (Freiburg, 2011), pp. 102–107.

43. Groß, *Mythos*, pp. 128–140.

44. Ibid., p. 311.

45. For inspiring ideas on the era of the world wars see Bruno Thoß, 'Die Zeit der Weltkriege – Epoche als Erfahrungseinheit?', in *Erster Weltkrieg Zweiter Weltkrieg*, pp. 7–30.

46. Groß, *Mythos*, p. 313.

Chapter 3: The Expansion of the British Army During World War I

1. On 1 August 1914, the British Army was a force of some 733,000 officers and men. On 1 March 1918, when it was as big as it would ever be, its strength was somewhere in the vicinity of 3,910,000. Great Britain, War Office, *Statistics of the Military Effort of the British Empire During the Great War, 1914–1920* (hereafter War Office, *Statistics*) (London: HMSO, 1924), pp. 30, 78.

2. Not to be confused with the formations known as 'army corps', a 'corps' of the British Army was an administrative organization that might be as large as the Mounted Branch of the Royal Regiment of Artillery or as small as the Royal Veterinary Corps. On 1 October 1913, the former, which encompassed the Royal Field Artillery and the Royal Horse Artillery, had more than 28,134 officers and men on active service. On the same day, the latter had but 216. The most common form of corps, however, was an infantry regiment, the average strength of which was a little short of 2,000 officers and men. Great Britain, War Office, Army Council, *The General Annual Report of the British Army, 1913* (London: HMSO, 1914), p. 31.

3. For descriptions of the recruiting infrastructure of the Regular Army, see William Howley Goodenough and James Cecil Dalton, *The Army Book for the British Empire*, (London: HMSO, 1893), pp. 322–325; 'A Lieutenant Colonel in the British Army', *The British Army* (London: Sampson, Low, Marston and Company, 1899), pp. 18–20; and Stephen Thomas Banning and Reginald Francis Legge, *Administration, Organization, and Equipment Made Easy*, (London: Gale and Polden, 1907), pp. 100–104.

4. For a great deal of information on the various training units of the peacetime Regular Army, see *Report of the Committee on War Establishments (Home), 1912*, The National Archives, Kew (hereafter TNA), WO 33/612.

5. The full text of the Territorial and Reserve Forces Act of 1907 can be found in the *Public General Statutes Affecting Scotland* (Edinburgh: William Blackwood and Sons, 1907), pp. 17–45.

6. For an example of the use of the phrase 'miniature War Office', see *Hansard*, House of Lords, 13 February 1908, Vol. 184, columns 158–166. For a detailed description of the work of County Associations, see K.W. Mitchison, *England's Last Hope, the Territorial Force, 1908–1914* (Basingstoke: Palgrave Macmillan, 2008), pp. 7–52.

7. John Headlam, *The History of the Royal Artillery, Volume II*, (Woolwich: Royal Artillery Association, 1937), pp. 144-146.

8. *The General Annual Report of the British Army, 1913*, p. 108.

9. The majority of Special Reservists of the Cavalry of the Line were members of the two 'regiments of Irish horse'. The remainder belonged to King Edward's Horse, a regiment that had been transferred from the Territorial Force. E. A. James, *British Regiments*,

1914–1918 (Dallington: Naval and Military Press, 1998), p. 15. The Special Reserve units of the Royal Garrison Artillery were coast artillery companies stationed in the port cities of Ireland. K.W. Maurice-Jones, *The History of Coast Defence Artillery in the British Army* (Woolwich: Royal Artillery Institution, 1959), p. 188.

10. *Report of the Committee on War Establishments (Home), 1912*, TNA, WO 33/612.

11. *The General Annual Report of the British Army, 1913*, pp. 31, 102, and 108.

12. The figures for men of the Royal Field Artillery serving 'with the colours' and in the Army Reserve include both members of the Royal Field Artillery and the Royal Horse Artillery. However, as the Royal Horse Artillery had no men in the Special Reserve, the figures for the Special Reserve refer exclusively to men of the Royal Field Artillery. *Annual Report of the British Army*, pp. 31, 102, and 108.

13. *Minutes of the Military Members of the Army Council*, TNA, WO 163/44, 9 August 1914.

14. A. F. Becke, *Order of Battle of Divisions, Part I: The Regular Army Divisions* (London: HMSO, 1935), p. 84 and Christopher T. Atkinson, *The Seventh Division, 1914–1918* (London: John Murray, 1927), pp. 1–3.

15. Bruce Gudmundsson, *The British Expeditionary Force, 1914–1915* (Oxford: Osprey, 2005), p. 26.

16. Figures for all three types of batteries are taken from Headlam, *The History of the Royal Artillery, Volume II*, Appendix E.

17. Gudmundsson, *The British Expeditionary Force*, p. 46

18. Charles M. Watson, *History of the Corps of Royal Engineers, Volume III* (Chatham: The Royal Engineers Institute, 1915), p. 50.

19. For an overview of the structure of the Territorial Force, see, among others, *The Annual Return of the Territorial Force for the Year 1912* (London: HMSO, 1913).

20. 'Doubling' was not unknown to the Regular Army. The plan for providing siege artillery to the Expeditionary Force called for the three siege companies of the peacetime Regular Army to be doubled upon mobilization, thereby creating six siege batteries. Gudmundsson, *The British Expeditionary Force*, p. 38.

21. In the course of 1906, Haldane reduced the size of the Territorial Force he was planning to create from 14 army corps and 14 mounted brigades (some 450,000 men) to 14 infantry divisions and 14 mounted brigades (about 300,000 men). For details of the early evolution of Haldane's scheme for the Territorial Force, see *Memoranda Bearing on Army Organization Prepared by the Secretary of State for War Between 1st January, 1906 and 1st May, 1906*, British Library, BP2/9 (4).

22. For a description of a speech that dealt with the possibility of a 'nation-in-arms' of 'seven, eight, or even nine hundred thousand men', see 'Mr. Haldane and the Army', *The Times*, 15 September 1906. For a broader view of Haldane's views on the expansion of the Territorial Force after mobilization, see Edward M. Spiers, *Haldane: An Army Reformer* (Edinburgh: University Press, 1980), pp. 98–103.

23. More than two years after Haldane had ceased to mention his idea of a 'nation-in-arms', his friend and colleague Gilbert McMicking felt obliged to write a long letter to *The Times* to refute the widespread notion that Haldane wished to create a peacetime Territorial Force with a strength of 900,000 men. 'Mr. Haldane and the 900,000 Men', *The Times*, 24 November 1908.

24. The only references to a wartime force of 900,000 wartime volunteers to be found in the records of the relevant parliamentary debates took the form of hostile questions posed by members who were opposed to the creation of the Territorial Force. For details, see *Hansard*, House of Lords, 21 March 1907, Vol. 171, columns 1212–1258 and House of Lords, 17 July 1907, Vol. 178, columns 651–658.

25. Edmonds, *Military Operations, France and Belgium, 1914*, vol. 1, p. 8.

26. Haldane's idea to use the Territorial Force as the basis for a much larger 'nation-in-arms' finds no mention in either his memoir of his tenure at the War Office or those parts of his general autobiography that deal with that period in his life. R.B. Haldane, *Before the War* (London: Cassell, 1920) and *Richard Burdon Haldane: An Autobiography* (London: Hodder and Stoughton, 1929).

27. 'The Army Estimates: Memorandum of Lord Haldane', *The Times*, 28 February 1912. This article is a verbatim copy of a paper that Haldane submitted to Parliament.

28. *Richard Burdon Haldane: An Autobiography*, pp. 296–298.

29. See, among others, *The Times*, 7 August 1914.

30. *Minutes of the Military Members of the Army Council*, TNA, WO 163/44, meetings held between 9 and 13 August 1914 and *Addendum to the Volume of Proceedings of the Army Council for 1914*, 11 August 1914, TNA, WO 163/21.

31. In August 1914, the Territorial Force fielded 28 engineer field companies, 151 field batteries, and 165 Yeomanry (cavalry) squadrons. (This figure does not count the depot squadrons formed on embodiment.) The divisions of the New Army, which were to be formed on the same pattern as the divisions of the original Expeditionary Force, needed 12 engineer field companies, 72 field batteries and six cavalry squadrons.

32. On 1 October 1913, the authorized strength of the Territorial Force was 312,400 officers and men. As the actual strength on that day was 245,779, the organization as a whole thus was 66,621 officers and men below establishment. *Annual Report of the British Army*, p. 122.

33. 'Growth of the Army', *The Times*, 13 August 1914, p. 4.

34. For an account of how the officers of one Territorial Force battalion reacted to its impending deployment to India, see A. J. Smithers, *The Fighting Nation, Lord Kitchener and his Armies* (London: Leo Cooper, 1994), p. 93. For an overview of the composition of the last three of the five divisions formed from pre-war Regular Army units drawn from Imperial garrisons and India (the 27th, 28th and 29th Divisions), see A. F. Becke, *Order of Battle of Divisions, Part I: The Regular Army Divisions*, pp. 100, 109 and 120. For details, see R. M. Johnson, *29th Divisional Artillery, War Record and Honours Book, 1915–1918* (Woolwich: Royal Artillery Institution, 1921).

35. The field batteries of the Regular Army were armed with field pieces that were far more modern, and thus superior in range, rate-of-fire and terminal effect, than those of the Territorial Force. For a cursory comparison of the two sets of weapons, see Gudmundsson, *The British Expeditionary Force*, pp. 74–78. For a list of the weapons sent out from India, see *Minutes of the Military Members of the Army Council*, TNA, WO 163/44, 5 October 1914.

36. Mitchison, *England's Last Hope*, p. 210.

37. K. W. Mitchinson, *Defending Albion: Britain's Home Army, 1908–1919* (Basingstoke: Palgrave Macmillan, 2005), p. 163.

38. Gudmundsson, *The British Expeditionary Force*, p. 28.

39. War Office, *Statistics*, pp. 30 and 139.

40. *Minutes of the Military Members of the Army Council*, TNA, WO 163/44, 12, 13, and 14 August 1914.

41. The advertisement that announced both the call for an additional 100,000 men and the relaxed standards of enlistment first appeared in the pages of *The Times* on 28 August 1914.

42. For a discussion of the problem of congestion in depots and reserve units, see *Hansard*, House of Commons, 10 September 1914, Vol. 66, columns 663–76. For a detailed description of the situation at the Royal Engineers recruit depot at Chatham, see W. Baker Brown and others, *History of the Corps of Royal Engineers, Volume V,* (Chatham: The Institution of Royal Engineers, 1952), pp. 133–137.

43. For an overview, see Ray Westlake, *Kitchener's Army*, pp. 139–145. For an investigation into the role played by the Ulster Volunteer Force in the appointment of officers for the division it raised, see Timothy Bowman, 'Officering Kitchener's Armies: A Case Study of the 36th (Ulster) Division', *War in History*, April 2009.

44. The project to create the 'Welsh Army Corps' failed to raise two complete infantry divisions. It did, however, raise one complete infantry division and a spare infantry brigade. For details, see *Welsh Army Corps, 1914–1919, Report of the Executive Committee* (Cardiff: Western Mail Limited, 1921).

45. For brief discussions of the involvement of County Associations in the raising of the New Armies, see Mitchison, *England's Last Hope*, pp. 228–229.

46. *Minutes of the Military Members of the Army Council*, TNA, WO 163/44, 9 September 1914.

47. Gudmundsson, *British Expeditionary Force*, p. 10.

48. Becke, *Order of Battle of Divisions, Part I: The Regular Army Divisions*, pp. 100 and108.

49. Gudmundsson, *British Expeditionary Force*, p. 10.

50. A. F. Becke, *Order of Battle of Divisions, Part 3A: New Army Divisions (9-26)* (London: HMSO, 1938), pp. 16, 24, 32, 42, 51, 59, 68, 76, 84, 92, and 100.

51. Becke, *Order of Battle of Divisions, Part I: The Regular Army Divisions*, p. 120.

52. Ibid., pp. 28, 36, and 34.

53. A. F. Becke, *Order of Battle of Divisions, Part 2A: The Territorial Force Mounted Divisions and the First-Line Territorial Force Infantry Divisions (42-56)* (London: HMSO, 1936), pp. 64, 72, 80, 88, 96, and 104.

54. Bruce Gudmundsson, *The British Army on the Western Front, 1916* (Oxford: Osprey, 2007), pp. 42–43.

55. Mitchinson, *Defending Albion*, pp. 98–120.

56. For a short discussion of transfers between the Territorial Force and the Regular Army, see *Army Council, Minutes and Precis* entry for 16 January 1915, TNA, WO 163/21.

57. *Hansard*, House of Commons, 8 March 1916, Vol. 80, column 516.

58. *Hansard*, House of Commons, 11 May 1916, Vol. 82, columns 985–999.

59. Gudmundsson, *The British Army on the Western Front*, pp. 43–45.

60. To get a sense of the change in the nomenclature of Territorial Force units, see the various organizational charts in Becke, *Order of Battle of Divisions, Part 2A.*

61. For a brief overview of this system, see James, *British Regiments*, p. 130.

62. On 1 August 1914, 268,777 officers and men were serving with units of the Territorial Force and 2,082 were members of the Territorial Force Reserve. War Office, *Statistics,* pp. 30. The estimate of three-quarters of a million men recruited into (or appointed to commissions in) the Territorial Force between August 1914 and May 1916 is in keeping with the official figure of 725,842 men enlisted into that body between August 1914 and December 1915. War Office, *Statistics*, p. 366.

63. Between August 1914 and December 1915, some 725,842 men enlisted into the Territorial Force. This figure does not include officers. Neither does it include the substantial number of men who seem to have joined between December 1915 and May 1916.

64. At the start of December 1915, all but 101,359 of the 913,108 officers and men serving in the Territorial Force had volunteered for service overseas. War Office, *Statistics*, p. 139.

65. In May 1916, a total of 2,965,776 officers and men were serving in the British Army. In March 1918, the figure was 3,889,990. These figures include both the Territorial Force and the Regular Army, but exclude the Indian Army, the contingents of the self-governing Dominions, and small colonial corps of various kinds. War Office, *Statistics*, pp. 229–231.

66. The total figure for cavalry regiments includes the three Special Reserve regiments and the composite regiments of Household Cavalry, but no second-line Yeomanry regiments. The figure for infantry regiments only includes units intended for service with armies in the field and thus excludes garrison and training units. James, *British Regiments*, pp. 15, 33, 24, and 126.

Chapter 4: World War I Aviation

1. On the French Air Service before World War I see Charles Christienne and Pierre Lissarague, *A History of French Military Aviation* (Washington: Smithsonian Institution Press, 1986), pp. 46–51.

2. On the German General Staff thinking on aviation before World War I see James Corum and Richard Muller, *The Luftwaffe's Way of War: German Air Force Doctrine 1911–1945* (Baltimore: Nautical and Aviation Press, 1998), pp. 20–36.

3. For the full text of Germany's 1913 air manual see Corum and Muller, pp. 37–45.

4. John Morrow, *The Great War in the Air* (Washington: Smithsonian Institution Press, 1993) pp. 22, 44–45.

5. Ibid., pp.84–85.

6. Peter Supf, *Die Geschichte des deutschen Flugwesens*, vol. II (Berlin: Verlagsanstalt Hermann Klemm, 1935), p. 262.

7. Christienne and Lissarague, pp. 78–80.

8. Morrow, *The Great War in the Air*, pp. 110–111.

9. Peter Kilduff, *Germany's First Air Force 1914–1918* (Osceola WI: Motorbooks International, 1991), p. 67.

10. The Friedrichshafen G III (designed by Zeppelin and Dornier) carried 3,000lb of

bombs and had a five-hour endurance. The Gotha G IV bombers, which the Germans used to bomb England and on the Western Front in 1917, were powered by two 260hp engines and carried a 1,100lb bomb load. Brian Philpott, *Encyclopedia of German Military Aircraft* (London: Bison Books, 1981), pp. 48–49.

11. On the development of fighter planes and tactics in World War I see Richard Hallion, *Rise of the Fighter Aircraft 1914–1918* (Baltimore: Nautical and Aviation Publishing, 1984).

12. Christienne and Lissarague, pp. 140–142.

13. On the *Luftstreitkräfte* organization in World War I see Major a. D. Freiherr von Bülow, *Geschichte der Luftwaffe* (Frankfurt: Verlag Moritz Diesterweg, 1934), pp. 88–135.

14. On aircraft production during the war see Christienne and Lissarague, pp. 157–158.

15. Ibid., p. 157

16. For the most complete account of the German aircraft industry in World War I see John Morrow, *German Air Power in World War I* (Lincoln: University of Nebraska Press, 1982). See especially pp. 95–96, 119. See also Christienne and Lissarague, pp. 157–158. For an overview of the German aviation industry see Terry Treadwell and Alan Wood, *German Fighter Aces of World War I* (Gloucestershire: Tempus, 2003), pp. 185–316.

17. Georg Neumann, *Die deutschen Luststreitkräfte im Weltkriege* (Berlin: E.S. Mittler, 1920), pp. 268–269.

18. Dennis Winter, *The First of the Few: Fighter Pilots of the First World War* (Athens: University of Georgia Press, 1983), p. 36.

19. In April 1917, during the Arras offensive the RFC threw pilots into the battle with only 15 hours' total flight training, which explains the high British losses in that campaign. See Hallion, pp. 72–73, 160–161.

20. In the summer of 1917 the RFC took its top fighter pilots such as James McCudden from the front and sent them to teach fighter tactics in the operational squadrons. On British training losses see John Morrow, *The Great War in the Air*, p. 318.

21. Hallion, pp. 28–32; see also Christienne and Lissarague, pp. 94–98.

22. Christienne and Lissarague, pp. 95–98.

23. Ibid., pp. 110–112.

24. Morrow, *German Air Power in World War I*, p. 91.

25. Leon Wolff, *In Flanders Fields: The 1917 Campaign* (New York: Time Books, 1963), pp. 162–179.

26. Ibid., pp. 141–142.

27. H. A. Jones, *The War in the Air Vol. VI* (Oxford: Clarendon Press, 1934), pp. 118–119.

28. As the Flanders campaign began the Germans deployed seven flak groups with 252 guns and 28 searchlights to that sector – a considerable force by World War I standards. See Kriegswissenschaftlichen Abteilung der Luftwaffe, *Entwicklung und Einsatz der deutschen Flakwaffe und des Luftschutzes im Weltkrieg* (Berlin: E. S. Mittler, 1938), p. 97.

29. In 1917 German flak guns shot down 467 Allied planes and went on to down more than 700 in 1918. See Edward Westermann, *Flak: German Anti-Aircraft Defenses, 1914–1945* (Lawrence: University Press of Kansas, 2001), p. 24. Georg Neumann, *Die deutschen Luststreitkräfte im Weltkriege* (Berlin: E.S. Mittler, 1920), p. 590.

30. Peter Gray and Owen Thetford, *German Aircraft of the First World War* (London: Putnam, 1962), pp. 136–139, 150–153.

31. Morrow, *The Great War in the Air*, p. 216.

32. George Questor, *Deterrence Before Hiroshima* (New Brunswick: Transaction Books, 1986), pp. 18–29.

33. Raymond Fredette, *The Sky on Fire*, (New York: Holt, Reinhart and Winston, 1966), p. 262.

34. For a thorough account of the whole campaign see George K. Williams, *Biplanes and Bombsights: British Bombing in World War I* (Maxwell AFB, AL: Air University Press, 1999).

35. David Divine, *The Broken Wing: A Study in the British Exercise of Airpower* (London: Hutchinson, 1966), pp. 142–143.

36. On the many technical developments associated with the World War I strategic bombers see William Fischer, *The Development of Military Night Aviation to 1919* (Maxwell AFB, AL: Air University Press, 1919).

37. Westermann, pp. 21–27; Georg Neumann, *Die Deutschen Luftstreitkräfte im Weltkrieg* (Berlin: E.S. Mittler, 1921), pp. 275–286.

38. See John Ferris, 'Fighter Defence Before Fighter Command: The Rise of Strategic Air Defence in Great Britain', *Journal of Military History* 63, 1999, 845–884.

39. On the German interdiction and strategic campaigns see James Corum, 'Starting from Scratch: The Luftstreitkräfte Builds a Bomber Doctrine, 1914–1918', *RAF Air Power Review*, Vol. 6, spring 2003, pp. 60–77. On the French 1917 bombing campaigns see Christienne and Lissarague, pp. 114–118.

40. Stephen Budiansky, *Air Power* (New York: Viking Press, 2003), p. 112.

41. On the US Army Air Service organization and employment in the battles of late 1918 see James Cooke, *Billy Mitchell* (Boulder: Lynne Rienner, 2002).

42. Morrow, *German Air Power in World War I*, pp. 95–96, 119.

43. In 1918 reforms in the training programme ensured that the British pilots were better prepared for combat. The British brought their fatal accident rate in training down from 0.37 fatalities per 1,000 flying hours in 1916 to 0.25 in 1918. See Lee Kennett, *The First Air War 1914–1918* (New York: The Free Press, 1991), p. 128.

44. Ibid., pp. 120–124.

45. Morrow, *The Great War in the Air*, p. 297.

46. On the German 1918 offensives see Rod Paschall, *The Defeat of Imperial Germany 1917–1918* (Chapel Hill NC: Algonquin Books, 1989) and Randal Gray, *Kaiserschlacht 1918* (Oxford: Osprey, 1991).

47. Morrow, *The Great War in the Air*, p. 310.

48. *Revue De L'Aeronautique Militaire*, July/August 1925.

49. The Fokker D 7 with the BMW engine could climb to 5,000 metres in 16 minutes, an astounding climb rate for the time. See Morrow, *The Great War in the Air*, p. 301. See also Kenneth Munson, *Aircraft of World War I* (Garden City: Arco, 1977), pp. 93–94; and Hallion, p. 306.

50. Treadwell and Wood, p. 137. The difference that the Fokker D 7 made in the air war is

notable. Lieutenant Wolfram von Richthofen, Manfred's cousin, flew an obsolescent Fokker Triplane in the intense air battles of April and May 1918 but failed to shoot down a single Allied aircraft. When issued a Fokker D 7 in June 1918 he went on to shoot down eight Allied aeroplanes by November. See James Corum, *Wolfram von Richthofen: Master of the German Air War* (Lawrence: University Press of Kansas, 2008), pp. 68–70.

51. Morrow, *German Air Power in World War I*, p. 138.

52. Budiansky, p. 114.

53. Christienne and Lissarague, p. 130.

Chapter 5: The Global War at Sea, 1914–18

1. For details see Volker R. Berghahn, *Der Tirpitz Plan: Genesis und Verfall einer innenpolitischen Krisenstrategie unter Wilhelm II* (Düsseldorf: Droste, 1971), pp. 173–201; Holger H. Herwig, *'Luxury' Fleet: The Imperial German Navy 1888–1918* (London: George Allen & Unwin, 1980); Michael Epkenhans, 'Imperial Germany and the Importance of Sea Power', in Nicholas A. M. Rodger (ed.), *Naval Power in the Twentieth Century* (London: Macmillan, 1996), pp. 27–40.

2. Szögyeny to Goluchowski, 5 February 1900, cited in Paul M. Kennedy, *The Rise of the Anglo-German Antagonism, 1860–1914* (London, 1980), p. 241.

3. Christopher Clark, *The Sleepwalkers: How Europe Went to War in 1914* (London: Allen Lane, 2012), pp. 147–149, has rightly pointed out this aspect. However, he underestimates the fact that Germany's naval planners had more far-reaching aims in mind.

4. The best account of Churchill's naval policy is Christopher M. Bell, *Churchill & Seapower* (Oxford: OUP, 2013), pp. 15–48.

5. Undated memo by Tirpitz, probably May 1914, cited in Epkenhans, *Die wilhelminische Flottenrüstung 1908 –1914: Weltmachtstreben, industrieller Fortschritt, soziale Integration* (Munich: Oldenbourg, 1991), p. 391.

6. For German war-planning see Ivo N. Lambi, *The Navy and German Power Politics, 1862–1914* (London: Allen & Unwin, 1984), pp. 390–415; Frank Nägler, 'Operative und strategische Vorstellungen der Kaiserlichen Marine vor dem Ersten Weltkrieg', in Michael Epkenhans, Jörg Hillmann, and Frank Nägler (eds.), *Skagerrakschlacht: Vorgeschichte – Ereignis – Verarbeitung* (Munich: Oldenbourg, 2009), pp. 51–54.

7. Bell, *Churchill*, pp. 42–48. For the quote see p. 53. Also James Goldrick, 'The Battleship Fleet: The Test of War, 1895–1919', in J. R. Hill (ed.), *The Oxford Illustrated History of the Royal Navy* (London: University Press, 1995), pp. 223–296.

8. Kurt Assmann, *Deutsche Seestrategie in zwei Weltkriegen* (Heidelberg, 1957), p. 30.

9. Bell, *Churchill*, pp. 19–26.

10. Lambi, *The Navy*, p. 408.

11. See table on page 78.

12. Bell, *Churchill*, pp. 51–52; Nicholas Lambert, *Planning Armageddon: British Economic Warfare and the First World War* (Cambridge, MA: Harvard University Press, 2012).

13. Werner Rahn, 'Die Kaiserliche Marine und der Erste Weltkrieg' in Stephan Huck (ed.), *Ringelnatz als Mariner im Krieg 1914–1918* (Bochum: Winkler Verlag, 2003), pp. 39–89; Michael Epkenhans, *Mein lieber Schatz! Briefe von Admiral Reinhard Scheer an seine Ehefrau August – November 1918* (Bochum: Winkler Verlag, 2006), pp. 20–26.

14. Eric W. Osborne, *The Battle of Heligoland Bight* (Bloomington: Indiana University Press, 2006), especially pp. 27–46, 100–120.

15. Paul G. Halpern, *A Naval History of World War I* (London, 1994), pp. 21–50.

16. Andrew Lambert, 'The German North Sea Islands, the Kiel Canal and the Danish Narrows in Royal Navy Thinking and Planning, 1905–1918', in Epkenhans and Gerhard P. Groß (eds.), *The Danish Straits and German Naval Power 1905–1918* (Potsdam: Militärgeschichtliches Forschungsamt, 2010), pp. 35–62.

17. Werner Rahn, 'Die Seeschlacht vor dem Skagerrak: Verlauf und Analyse aus deutscher Perspektive', in Epkenhans et al. (eds.), *Skagerrakschlacht* (Munich: Oldenbourg), pp. 139–196; Andrew Gordon, *The Rules of the Game: Jutland and British Naval Command* (Annapolis: Naval Institute Press, 1997).

18. See the Emperor's speech in Wilhelmshaven on 5 June 1916, cited in Gerhard Granier (ed.), *Die deutsche Seekriegsleitung im Ersten Weltkrieg, vol. 2* (Koblenz: Bundesarchiv, 2000) pp. 97–99.

19. German losses in men (killed, wounded, or taken prisoner) amounted to 3,058; British losses to 6945. The difference in tonnage was 61,180:115,025 tons. Figures according to Rahn, 'Die Seeschlacht vor dem Skagerrak', in Epkenhans et al. (eds.), *Skagerrak*, p. 188.

20. See Scheer's report to the Emperor, 4 July 1916, in *Seekriegsleitung*, vol. 2, pp. 106–109.

21. Halpern, *Naval History*, pp. 183–222; Werner Rahn, 'The Naval War in the Baltic, 1914–1918: A German Perspective', in Michael Epkenhans et al. (eds.), *The Danish Straits*, pp. 75–77.

22. Quote from a Secret Service Memorandum of the German Navy (1934), cited in Rahn, 'The Naval War in the Baltic', in Epkenhans et al. (eds.), *The Danish Straits*, p. 81.

23. Goldrick, 'The Battleship Fleet', pp. 299–300.

24. Andrew Gordon, *The Rules of the Game*.

25. On the Austro-Hungarian Navy see Lawrence Sondhaus, *The Naval Policy of Austria-Hungary 1867–1918* (West Lafayette: Purdue University Press, 1994), pp. 257–378; Halpern, *Naval History*, pp. 51–70, 139–178, 381–402.

26. Paul G. Halpern, *The Battle of the Otranto Straits: Controlling the Gateway to the Adriatic in WWI* (Bloomington: Indiana University Press, 2004), especially pp. 35–99.

27. Sondhaus, *The Naval Policy of Austria-Hungary*, pp. 307–308.

28. On the Turkish Navy see Halpern, *Naval History*, pp. 223–261.

29. Ibid., pp. 109–124.

30. Memo by Admiral Capelle with Tirpitz's remarks, 17 May 1914, cited in Epkenhans, *Flottenrüstung*, p. 399.

31. Lambi, *The Navy*, p. 410.

32. Halpern, *Naval History*, p. XX.

33. Richard Guilatt and Peter Hohnen, *The Wolf: How one German Raider Terrorized the Southern Seas during the First World War* (London: Bantam Press, 2009).

34. Nicholas Lambert, *Sir John Fisher's Naval Revolution* (Columbia: University of South Carolina Press, 1999).

35. Admiral Sir John Fisher in 1904 and 1914, cited in Geoffrey Till, *Sea Power: A Guide for the Twenty-First Century* (London: Frank Cass, 2004), p. 63. For a good survey of submarine development in Britain see Nicholas Lambert (ed.), *The Submarine Service, 1900–1918* (London: Ashgate, 2001), pp. IX–XXIX (introduction) and for the German Navy see Bodo Herzog, *Deutsche U-Boote 1906–1966* (Herrsching: Pawlak, 2001), pp. 36–37.

36. Lambert, *The Submarine Service*, pp. XXXVI–XXXVIII.

37. Sondhaus, *The Naval Policy of Austria-Hungary*, pp. 264–266, 286–289.

38. Halpern, *Naval History*, pp. 42–44, 311–312, 441–444.

39. Sondhaus, *The Naval Policy of Austria-Hungary*, pp. 291–292, 337–338.

Chapter 6: The French Army Between Tradition and Modernity

1. See François Cochet, *Survivre au front, 1914–1918, les soldats entre contrainte et consentement* (Saint-Cloud: Soteca/14-18 Editions, 2005).

2. The section that is responsible for the preparation of operations.

3. Quoted by Lieutenant-Colonel Rémy Porte, 'Deployment and manoeuvring instructions for future warriors in the Great War as seen by the Military Journal of Foreign Armed Forces (1911–1914)', in François Cochet (ed.), *Former les soldats au feu, premier volume de la collection l'Expérience combattante, 19e–21e siècles* (Paris: Rive Neuve editions, 2011), p, 97.

4. John Keegan, *The First World War*, French translation (Paris: Perrin, 2003), pp. 31–32.

5. See Marie-Thérèse Bitsch, *Belgium between France and Germany* (Presses de la Sorbonne, 1994).

6. Plan XVII is in fact thanks to the generals Castelnau and Berthelot.

7. Stephane Tison, 'The savagery of the fighting on the Western Front in 1914', in François Cochet (ed.), *The Battles of the Marne. Ourcq of Verdun (1914 and 1918)* (Saint-Cloud: Soteca/14-18 Editions, 2004), p. 52.

8. Figures given by Colonel Frederic Guelton in *The French Army in 1918* (Saint-Cloud: Soteca/14-18 Editions, 2008), pp. 90 and 94.

9. See Captain R. Bourchon, *Course in Trench Artillery* (Bourges, 1917).

10. Quoted by Henri Ortholan, 'The technique of mine warfare' in *The Great War, 14–18*, No. 19, April–May 2004, p. 9.

11. On all aspects of gas warfare, see Olivier Lepick, *The Great Chemical War* (PUF, 1998).

12. See Williamson Murray, *Air Wars, 1914–1945* (Paris: Otherwise, 1999), foreword by Patrick Facon.

13. Ibid., p. 51.

14. Quoted by Henri Ortholan, *Tank Wars, 1916–1918* (Bernard Giovanangeli Publisher, 2007), p. 24.

15. See Lieutenant-Colonel Rémy Porte, *La Direction des Services Automobiles des armées et la motorisation des armées françaises (1914-1918), vues à travers l'action du commandant Doumenc* (Lavauzelle, 2004), and also *La mobilisation industrielle, 'premier front' de la Grande Guerre?* (Saint-Cloud, 14/18 Éditions, 2006).

16. Quoted by Colonel Frederic Guelton, *The French Army*, p. 26.

17. First section: numbers; second section: information; third section: operations.

18. See General André Bach, *Executed as an Example, 1914–1915* (Paris: Tallandier, 2003).

19. General Robert A. Doughty, *Pyrrhic Victory: French Strategy and Operations in the Great War* (The Belknap Press, 2005).

Chapter 7: German Tactical Doctrine and the Defensive Battle on the Western Front

1. Erich von Falkenhayn, *General Headquarters 1914–1916 and its Critical Decisions* (London: Hutchinson, 1919) p. 35.

2. Quoted in Holger Afflerbach, 'Planning Total War? Falkenhayn and the Battle of Verdun, 1916', in Roger Chickering and Stig Förster, eds., *Great War, Total War. Combat and Mobilization on the Western Front, 1914–1918* (Cambridge: Cambridge University Press, 2000), p. 118.

3. Wilhelm Solger, *Studien betr. Die Umstellung im Westheere vom Bewegungs–zum Stellungskriege*, no. 1, p. 4, in Bundesarchiv-Militärarchiv (hereafter BA-MA) W 10/51151.

4. Ibid.

5. Ibid.

6. Carl Groos and Werner von Rudolff, eds., *Infanterie-Regiment Herwarth von Bittenfeld (1.Westfälisches) Nr. 13 im Weltkriege 1914–1918. Nach den amtlichen Kriegsakten und privaten Aufzeichnungen* (Oldenburg, Berlin: Stalling, 1927), p. 117.

7. *Exerzier-Reglement für die Infanterie vom 29. Mai 1906* (Berlin, 1906).

8. Chef des Generalstabes, ed., *Gesichtspunkte für den Stellungskrieg* (Berlin, 1915).

9. Falkenhayn, p. 249. Allegedly, Falkenhayn mentioned these ideas in a 'Christmas memorandum' to the Kaiser on Christmas 1915; see Falkenhayn, p. 239. The text of this memorandum only appears in Falkenhayn's memoirs and it has therefore been argued that the memorandum too was written in 1919 to justify in retrospect why Verdun was never captured.

10. *Experience of the German 1st Army in the Somme Battle 24th June –26 November 1916, issued on 30 January 1917, translated into English 3 May 1917* (British Library, general reference section, 9086.C.9), p. 10.

11. Erich Ludendorff, *My War Memories 1914–1918*, 2 vols. (London: Hutchinson, without year), vol. 1, p. 266.

12. *Chef d. Gen.St. des Feldheeres. M.J. 10000 Betr.: Kriegführung und Generalstab, 22.11.1916*, in, BA-MA PH 3/3.

13. *Vorschriften für den Stellungskrieg für alle Waffen. Teil 8. Grundsätze für die Führung in der Abwehrschlacht im Stellungskriege* (Berlin, 1916).

14. Edward L. Spears, *Prelude to Victory* (London: Cape, 1939), p. 490.

15. Kronprinz Wilhelm, *My War Experiences* (London: Hurst and Blackett, 1923), p. 269.

16. John M. Bourne, 'Flandern', in Gerhard Hirschfeld, Gerd Krumeich, and Irina Renz, eds., *Enzyklopädie Erster Weltkrieg* (Paderborn: Schöningh, 2004), pp. 489–494, here p. 492.

17. Ernst Jünger, *In Stahlgewittern* (Berlin: Mittler, 1942), p. 217.

18. Ludendorff, vol. 2, p. 480.

19. Kronprinz Wilhelm, p. 267.

20. Ernst Jünger, *Das Wäldchen 125. Eine Chronik aus den Grabenkämpfen 1918* (Berlin: Mittler, 1941, first edition 1925), pp. 7–8.

21. Jünger, pp. 33–34.

22. Wilhelm Deist, 'The Military Collapse of the German Empire: The Reality Behind the Stab-in-the-Back Myth', in *War in History*, vol. 3, number 2 (1996), pp. 186–207.

23. These figures have been obtained from Deist, pp. 203–204.

24. Klaus-Jürgen Müller, *General Ludwig Beck. Studien und Dokumente zur politisch-militärischen Vorstellungswelt und Tätigkeit des Generalstabschefs des deutschen Heeres 1933–1938* (Boppard: Harald Boldt, 1980), p. 326.

25. See Ludendorff's order from 6 July 1918 in BA-MA PH 5/I/37, pp. 5–6.

26. *Chef des Generalstabes, II Nr. 10162 op., 4 September 1918*, BA-MA PH 3/3, p. 63.

Chapter 8: The Rollercoaster of Austria-Hungary's World War I Experience

1. Jozsef Galantai, *Die österreichisch-ungarische Monarchie und der Weltkrieg* (Budapest: Corvina 1979); Samuel R. Williamson Jr., *Austria-Hungary and the Origins of the First World War* (New York: Palgrave Macmillan, 1991); Günther Kronenbitter, *'Krieg im Frieden': Die Führung der k.u.k. Armee und die Großmachtpolitik Österreich-Ungarns 1906–1914* (Munich: Oldenbourg, 2003); Manfried Rauchensteiner, *Der Tod des Doppeladlers: Österreich-Ungarn und der Erste Weltkrieg* (Graz: Styria, 1993).

2. Norman Stone, 'Die Mobilmachung der österreichisch-ungarischen Armee', in *Militärgeschichtliche Mitteilungen* 2 (1974), pp. 67–95; Graydon Tunstall, *Planning for War against Russia and Serbia: Austro-Hungarian and German Strategies, 1871–1914* (New York: Columbia University Press, 1993).

3. Sir Basil Liddell Hart, *History of the First World War* (London, 1930; reprinted Pan Book, 1972), p. 107.

4. Lothar Höbelt, '"So wie wir haben nicht einmal die Japaner angegriffen": Österreich-Ungarns Nordfront 1914/15', in Gerhard P. Groß (Hg.), *Die vergessene Front: Der Osten 1914/15* (Paderborn: Schöningh, 2006), pp. 87–119.

5. Rudolf Jerabek, *Potiorek: General im Schatten von Sarajevo* (Graz: Styria, 1991), pp. 108–201.

6. William A. Renzi, *In the Shadow of the Sword: Italy's Neutrality and Entrance into the Great War, 1914–1915* (New York: Peter Lang, 1987); Gian Enrico Rusconi, *L'azzardo del 1915: Come l'Italia decide la sua guerra* (Bologna: Il Mulino, 2005).

7. Graydon A. Tunstall, *Blood on the Snow: The Carpathian Winter War of 1915* (Lawrence: Kansas University Press, 2010).

8. Franco Cabrio, *Uomini e mitragliatrici nella grande guerra*, 2 vols. (Novale: Rossate, 2008/09).

9. Richard C. Hall, *Bulgaria's Road to the First World War* (Boulder: Indiana University

Press, 1996); Wolfgang-Uwe Friedrich, *Bulgarien und die Mächte 1913–1915* (Stuttgart: Steiner, 1985).

10. Christos Theodoulou, *Greece and the Entente August 1, 1914 – September 25, 1916* (Salonika: Zeno, 1971); David Dutton, *The Politics of Diplomacy: Britain and France in the Balkans in the First World War* (London: Tauris, 1998).

11. Lothar Höbelt, 'Montenegro and the Central Powers 1915–16', in *Festschrift for Jean-Paul Bled* (forthcoming).

12. Timothy C. Dowling, *The Brusilov Offensive* (Bloomington: Indiana University Press, 2008); Rudolf Jerabek, *Die Brussilowoffensive 1916: Ein Wendepunkt der Koalitionskriegführung der Mittelmächte* (Vienna, 1982) is an unpublished Ph.D. thesis that contains a wealth of material on military planning in 1915–16.

13. The foremost expert, Glenn Torrey, has now collected his articles in a monograph: *Romania and World War I* (Jasi/Oxford: Center for Romanian Studies, 1998).

14. The best survey of the problem still is Gary Shanafelt, *The Secret Enemy: Austria-Hungary and the German Alliance 1914–1918*, East European Monographs 187 (New York: Columbia University Press, 1985).

15. For their achievements as a force see Paul Halpern, *The Naval War in the Mediterranean 1914–1918* (London: Naval Institute Press, 1987); Paul Halpern, *The Battle of the Otranto Straits: Controlling the Gateway to the Adriatic in World War I* (Bloomington: Indiana University Press, 2004); Wladimir Aichelburg, *Die Unterseeboote Österreich-Ungarns*, 2 vols. (Graz: Akademische Druck- U. Verlagsanstalt, 1981).

16. John Milton Cooper Jr., 'The Command of Gold Reversed: American Loans to Britain, 1915–1917', in *Pacific Historical Review* 45 (1976), pp. 209–230; here p. 228; Justus D. Doenecke, *Nothing Less than War: A New History of America's Entry into World War I* (Louisville: The University Press of Kentucky, 2011); Vaclav Horcicka, 'Austria-Hungary, Unrestricted Submarine Warfare, and the United States' Entrance into the First World War', in *International History Review* 34 (2012), pp. 245–269.

17. D. Stevenson, *French War Aims against Germany* (Oxford: OUP, 1982), p. 74; Wolfgang Steglich, *Die Friedenspolitik der Mittelmächte* (Wiesbaden: F. Steiner, 1964).

18. Wolfgang Steglich (ed.), *Die Friedensversuche der kriegführenden Mächte im Sommer und Herbst 1917* (Stuttgart: F. Steiner, 1984), p. 19.

19. HHStA, PA I 504, fol. 842 (1 August 1917).

20. See the official history: *Österreich-Ungarns letzter Krieg*, vol. 7 (Vienna, 1937), pp. 57, 70; Hans Linnenkohl, *Vom Einzelschuß zur Feuerwalze: Der Wettlauf zwischen Technik und Taktik im Ersten Weltkrieg* (Bonn: Bernard und Graefe, 1996), p. 187.

21. Mark Thompson, *The White War: Life and Death on the Italian Front 1915–1919* (London: Faber and Faber, 2008), pp. 242–245, 279–282; Lord Hankey, *The Supreme Command 1914–1918* (London: Allen and Unwin, 1961), pp. 607–608, 671–672, 693–697.

22. Cyril Falls, *Caporetto* (London: Weidenfeld & Nicolson, 1966).

23. See Austria's equivalent of Hansard: *Stenographische Protokolle des Abgeordnetenhauses des österreichischen Reichsrates*, XXII. Session, pp. 2812, 2895.

24. Ottokar Czernin, *Im Weltkriege* (Berlin: Mittler, 1919), p. 356.

25. Peter Fiala, *Die letzte Offensive Altösterreichs* (Boppard: Harald Boldt, 1967).

26. Details in Maximilian Polatschek, *Österreichisch-ungarische Truppen an der Westfront 1914–1918* (Ph.D. Vienna, 1974).

27. Wilfried Fest, *Peace or Partition: The Habsburg Monarchy and British Policy 1914–1918* (London: St. Martins, 1978).

28. Betty Miller Unterberger, *The US, Revolutionary Russia and the Rise of Czechoslovakia* (Chapel Hill: University of North Carolina Press, 1989).

29. Josef Kalvoda, *The Genesis of Czechoslavakia* (Boulder: East European Monographs, 1986), p. 393.

30. For Hungarian politics see Jozsef Galantai, *Hungary in the First World War* (Budapest: Corvina, 1989); Gabor Vermes, *Istvan Tisza: The Liberal Vision and Conservative Statecraft of a Magyar Nationalist* (New York: East European Monographs, 1985); in German: Geza A. v. Geyr, *Sandor Wekerle 1848–1921* (Munich: Oldenbourg, 1993).

31. Lothar Höbelt, 'Late Imperial Paradoxes: Old Austria's Last Parliament 1917–18', in *Parliaments, Estates & Representation* 16 (1996), pp. 207–216; Lothar Höbelt, 'Karl I. der "Teufelspuk" und die Deutschböhmen', in Andreas Gottsmann (ed.), *Karl I. (IV.): der Erste Weltkrieg und das Ende der Donaumonarchie* (Vienna: Austrian Academy of Sciences 2007), pp. 47–58; *Sbornik Dokumentu k vnitrnimu vyvoji v Ceskych zemich za 1.Svetove Valky 1914–1918*, Vol. 4: Rok 1917 (Prague: Státní ústrední archiv, 1996).

32. On Czech politics, see Victor Mamatey, 'The Union of Czech Political Parties in the Reichsrat 1916–18', in Robert A. Kann (ed.), *The Habsburg Empire in World War I* (Boulder: 1977 East European Quarterly, 1977), pp. 3–28; H. Louis Rees, *The Czechs during World War I* (New York: Columbia University Press, 1992).

33. Richard Lein, *Pflichterfüllung oder Hochverrat? Die tschechischen Soldaten Österreich-Ungarns im Ersten Weltkrieg* (Vienna: Litt Verlag, 2011); Christian Reiter, 'Die Causa Infanterieregiment 36: Zur Problematik der Tschechen in der k.u.k. Armee im Ersten Weltkrieg', in Heeresgeschichtliches Museum (Hg.), *Der Erste Weltkrieg und der Vielvölkerstaat* (Vienna, 2012), pp. 179–241.

34. John Leslie, *Austria-Hungary's Eastern Policy in the First World War, August 1914 – August 1915* (Ph.D. Cantab., 1975); Richard W. Kapp, 'Bethmann-Hollweg, Austria-Hungary and Mitteleuropa, 1914–1915', in *Austro-Hungarian History Yearbook* 19/20 (1983/84), pp. 215–236; Achim Müller, *Zwischen Annäherung und Abgrenzung: Österreich-Ungarn und die Diskussion um Mitteleuropa im Ersten Weltkrieg* (Marburg: Tectum, 2001).

35. Jan Zupanic, *Rakousko-uhersko a Polska otazka za prvni svetove valky* (Prague, 2006); Damian Szymczak, *Miedzy Habsburgami a Hohenzollernami. Rywalizacja niemicko-austro-wegierska w okresie I wojny swiatowej a odbudowa panstwa polskiego* (Krakow: Avalon, 2009).

36. Lothar Höbelt, 'Die austro-polnische Lösung – eine unendliche Geschichte', in Heeresgeschichtliches Museum (Ed.), *Der Erste Weltkrieg und der Vielvölkerstaat* (Vienna, 2012), pp. 35–54.

37. Joseph Rothschild, *Pilsudski's Coup d'Etat* (New York: Columbia University Press, 1966), pp. 25–34.

38. Hew Strachan, *The First World War*, vol. 1 (Oxford: OUP, 2001), pp. 1043–1046.

39. M. Christian Ortner, *Die österreichisch-ungarische Artillerie von 1867 bis 1918* (Vienna , 2007), pp. 551, 577ff.

40. *Österreich-Ungarns letzter Krieg VII*, table 10; *Reichsarchivwerk XIV*, p. 33.

41. J. Robert Wegs, 'Transportation: The Achilles Heel of the Habsburg War Effort', in Robert A. Kann (ed.), *The Habsburg Empire in World War I* (Boulder, East European Quarterly, 1977), p. 121; Emil Homann-Herimberg, *Die Kohlenversorgung in Österreich während des Krieges* (Vienna/New Haven: Holder-Pichler-Tempsky, 1925), pp. 99, 105.

42. Quotes from the correspondence between Tisza and Stürgkh printed in Gustav Gratz and Richard Schüller, *Der wirtschaftliche Zusammenbruch Österreich-Ungarns: Die Tragödie der Erschöpfung* (Vienna/New Haven: Holder-Pichler-Tempsky, 1930), pp. 246, 266.

43. General Landwehr, *Hunger: Die Erschöpfungsjahre der Mittelmächte 1917/18* (Zurich: Amalthea 1931), pp. 211, 220, and 252.

44. Stephan Horak, *The First Treaty of World War I: Ukraine's Treaty with the Central Powers of February 9, 1918* (Boulder: Columbia University Press, 1988); Clifford F. Wargelin, 'A Huge Price of Bread: the First Treaty of Brest-Litovsk and the Break-Up of Austria-Hungary, 1917–1918', in *International History Review* 19 (1997), pp. 757–788; in German: Wolfram Dornik & Peter Lieb (eds.), *Die Ukraine zwischen Selbstbestimmung und Fremdherrschaft 1917–1922* (Graz, Leykam, 2011).

45. Maureen Healy, *Vienna and the Fall of the Habsburg Empire: Total War and Everyday Life in World War I* (Cambridge: CUP, 2004), p. XXX; Hans Loewenfeld-Russ, *Die Regelung der Volksernährung im Kriege* (Vienna/New Haven: Holder-Pichler-Tempsky, 1926), pp. 156, 173.

Chapter 9: The Imperial Russian Army and the Eastern Front in World War I, 1914–17

1. Allan K. Wildman , *The End of the Russian Imperial Army*, Vol. 1 (New Jersey: Princeton University Press, 1980), p. 65.

2. Richard W. Harrison, *The Russian Way of War: Operational Art, 1904–1940* (Lawrence: University Press of Kansas, 2001), p. 40.

3. Norman Stone, *The Eastern Front, 1914–1917* (Penguin, 1998), p. 37.

4. Harrison, *The Russian Way*, p. 47 disagrees and regards Gumbinnen as a German victory.

5. Geoffrey Jukes, *The First World War: The Eastern Front 1914–1918* (Oxford: Osprey, 2002), p. 20.

6. Harrison, *The Russian Way*, p. 48.

7. Ibid., pp. 46–47.

8. Jukes, *The Eastern Front*, p. 23.

9. Ibid., p. 22.

10. Harrison, *The Russian Way*, p. 58.

11. Ibid., p. 58.

12. Jukes, *The Eastern Front*, p. 28.

13. Robert B. Asprey, *The German High Command at War* (New York: Warner, 1991), p. 183.

14. C. R. M. F. Cruttwell, *A History of the Great War 1914–1918* (Oxford: Clarendon Press, 1936), p. 173.

15. N. Stone, *The Eastern Front*, p. 129.

16. A. A. Brusilov, *A Soldier's Notebook* (London: Macmillan, 1930), p. 140.

17. Jukes, *The Eastern Front*, p. 35.

18. N. Stone, *The Eastern Front*, p. 139.

19. Jukes, *The Eastern Front*, p. 36.

20. N. Stone, *The Eastern Front*, pp. 175–176.

21. Asprey, *The German High Command*, pp. 186–187.

22. Wildman, *The End of the Russian Imperial Army*, p. 92.

23. Brusilov, *A Soldier's Notebook*, p. 171.

24. David R. Stone, *A Military History of Russia* (Santa Barbara, CA: Praeger, 2006), p. 162.

25. Wildman, *The End of the Russian Imperial Army*, p. 89.

26. N. Stone, *The Eastern Front*, p. 227.

27. Ward Rutherford, *The Tsar's War* (Cambridge: Ian Faulkner Publishing, 1992), p. 205.

28. N. Stone, *The Eastern Front*, p. 231.

29. Ibid., pp. 235–237.

30. N. Stone, *The Eastern Front*, p. 251.

31. Harrison, *The Russian Way of War*, p. 63.

32. Ibid., p. 65.

33. Brusilov, *A Soldier's Notebook*, p. 243.

34. David R. Jones, 'Imperial Russia's Forces at War', in Millet and Murray (eds.), *Military Effectiveness, Vol. 1, The First World War* (London: Allen & Unwin, 1988), p. 307.

35. Eric Lohr, 'War and Revolution', in D. Lieven (ed.), *The Cambridge History of Russia, Vol. II, Imperial Russia 1689–1917* (Cambridge: Cambridge University Press, 2006), p. 663. See also Wildman, *The End of the Russian Imperial Army*, p. 120.

36. Jukes, *The Eastern Front*, p. 68.

Chapter 10: ANZACs and the Rocky Road to Tactical Effectiveness, 1916–17

1. Andrew Macdonald, *On My Way to the Somme: New Zealanders and the Bloody Offensive of 1916*, (Auckland: HarperCollins, 2005), pp. 71–72, p. 138.

2. Peter Simkins, 'Co-Stars or Supporting Cast? British Divisions in the "Hundred Days", 1918' in Paddy Griffith (ed.), *British Fighting Methods in the Great War* (London: Frank Cass Publishers, 1996), pp. 54–55; Dale Blair, *Dinkum Diggers: An Australian Battalion at War* (Carlton South: Melbourne University Press, 2001), p. 130; Glyn Harper, *Dark Journey: Three Key New Zealand Battles of the Western Front* (Auckland: HarperCollins, 2007), pp. 206–208; Tim Cook, *Shock Troops: Canadians Fighting the Great War 1917–1918* (Toronto: Penguin Group, 2008), p. 380.

3. N. M. Ingram, *Anzac Diary: A Nonentity in Khaki* (Christchurch, Treharne Publishers: 1987) p93

4. Vincent Jervis, diary, 17 April 1918, ATL, MS-Papers-2241.

5. *New Zealand Herald*, 1 April 1918, National Library of New Zealand (NLNZ).

6. John Lee, 'Command and Control in Battle: British Divisions on the Menin Road Ridge, 20 September 1917', in Sheffield and Todman (eds.) *Command and Control* (Chalford: Spellmount Ltd, 2007), pp. 120–122.

7. Paddy Griffith, *Battle Tactics of the Western Front: The British Army's Art of Attack 1916–18* (London: Yale University Press, 1994), p. 194.

8. Andrew Russell, 'A Fine Address', in *Chronicles of the NZEF, 1916–1918* (newspaper), 17 October 1917, NLNZ, National Newspaper Collection (NNC), p. 104.

9. Ibid.

10. Ibid.

11. Ibid.

12. Ibid.

13. *Training Notes*, 1st New Zealand Infantry Brigade, ANZ, WA70/3/3/9a, this folder includes, for instance: *Further Notes on Operations, 20th and 26th September 1917* (Second Army), *The Enemy's Tactical Methods East of Ypres* (Second Army), *Notes on Dealing with Hostile Machine Guns in an Advance* (Second Army).

14. Bill Rawling, *Surviving Trench Warfare: Technology and the Canadian Corps, 1914–1918* (Toronto: University of Toronto Press, 1997), pp.136–137.

15. *Syllabus of Training for Week Ending 11th August, 1917*, 2 August 1917, 1st Australian Infantry Brigade, War Diary, AWM, 23/1/25; 1st Australian Infantry Brigade, War Diary, July 1917, AWM, 23/1/24.

16. 1/7th Battalion, The Royal Warwickshire Regiment, War Diary, September 1917, NAUK, WO/95/2756; 1/8th Battalion, The Royal Warwickshire Regiment, War≈Diary, September 1917, NAUK, WO/95/2756; 1/5th Battalion, Gloucester Regiment, War Diary, September 1917, NAUK, WO/95/2763; 9th Scottish Rifles, War Diary, June–September 1917, NAUK, WO/95/1772; 11th Royal Scots, War Diary, September 1917, NAUK, WO/95/1772; 12th Royal Scots, War Diary, September 1917, NAUK, WO/95/1773; 6th King's Own Scottish Borderers, War Diary, September 1917, NAUK, WO/95/1772.

17. Charles Carrington, *Soldier from the Wars Returning* (London: Hutchinson & Co, 1965), pp. 174–177.

18. Andy Simpson, *Directing Operations: British Corps Command on the Western Front 1914–18* (Stroud: Spellmount Ltd, 2006), p. 224; Gary Sheffield, *Forgotten Victory – The First World War: Myths and Realities* (London: Headline Book Publishing, 2002), p. 220.

19. Communication delays undermined the ability of formation commanders to make timely decisions.

20. Ian Malcolm Brown, *British Logistics on the Western Front, 1914–1919* (Westport: Praeger Publishers, 1998), p. 9; Sheffield, 'Foreword', in Simpson, *Directing Operations*, p. xv.

21. Geoffrey Hayes, Andrew Iarocci, and Mike Bechthold, *Vimy Ridge: A Canadian Reassessment* (Waterloo: Wilfrid Laurier University Press, 2007), 'Afterthoughts', p. 313.

22. Simpson, p. 226; Peter Simkins, '"Building Blocks": Aspects of Command and Control at Brigade Level in the British Army's Offensive Operations, 1916–1918', in Sheffield and Todman (eds.) *Command and Control*, p. 151.

23. Simpson, *Directing Operations*, pp. 223–224.

24. Simkins, 'Building Blocks', p. 151.

25. Ibid.

26. Sheffield, *Forgotten Victory*, p. 196.

27. Ian Passingham, *Pillars of Fire: The Battle of Messines Ridge, June 1917* (Stroud: Sutton Publishing, 2004), p. 178.

28. Griffith, *Battle Tactics*, p. 150.

29. Carrington, *Soldier*, p. 194.

30. Charles Bean, *Official Histories – First World War: Volume IV – The Australian Imperial Force in France, 1917* (Sydney: Angus and Robertson Ltd, 1941), p. 849, pp. 854–856, pp. 864–865.

31. 49th Division had relieved the New Zealand Division in II Anzac's sector.

32. A. M. J. Hyatt, *General Sir Arthur Currie: A Military Biography* (Toronto: University of Toronto Press in association with Canadian War Museum, 1987), p. 81.

33. Rawling, *Trench Warfare*, pp. 151–166.

34. Ibid., pp. 155 and 165.

35. Dean Oliver, 'The Canadians at Passchendaele', in Liddle (ed.) *Passchendaele in Perspective* (London: Leo Cooper, 1997), p. 262.

36. Mark Humphries, *The Selected Papers of Sir Arthur Currie: Diaries, Letters and Report to the Ministry, 1917–1933* (Waterloo, Canada: LCMSDS Press of Wilfrid Laurier University, 2008), pp. 51–59.

37. Andrew Macdonald, *Passchendaele: The Anatomy of a Tragedy* (Auckland: HarperCollins, 2013), p. 223

38. Griffith, *Battle Tactics*, p. 193.

39. Rawling, *Trench Warfare*, pp. 217–223.

40. Ibid., p. 223.

41. Ibid., pp. 217–223.

42. Peter Simkins, 'The War Experience of a Typical Kitchener Division: The 18th Division, 1914–1918', in Hugh Cecil and Peter Liddle (eds.), *Facing Armageddon: The First World War Experience* (Barnsley: Pen & Sword, 1996), pp. 297–313; Humphries, p. 80.

43. Ewing, p. 228.

44. Humphries, *Selected Papers*, p. 80.

45. Christopher Pugsley, *The Anzac Experience: New Zealand, Australia and Empire in the First World War* (Auckland: Reed Publishing, 2004), p. 176; Carrington, *Soldier*, pp. 174–177.

46. Simkins, *18th Division*, p. 300.

47. *Command and Control*, p. 139.

48. Ibid., pp. 127–132

49. Simkins, 'Co-Stars or Supporting Cast?', p. 53.

50. Ibid., p. 56.

51. Ibid.

52. Simpson, *Directing Operations*, p. 217.

53. Ibid., p. 175.

54. Pugsley, *The Anzac Experience*, p. 166.

Chapter 11: A Sideshow of a Sideshow?

1. Lawrence first used this term 'sideshow of a sideshow' in an article entitled 'The evolution of a revolt', which was published in *The Army Quarterly and Defence Journal* of October 1920. He later re-used it in *Seven Pillars of Wisdom* (Penguin edition, 1988), Book 4, Chapter XLVIII, p. 281.

2. For those interested in Lawrence, the authorized biography by Jeremy Wilson is an excellent starting point. See Jeremy Wilson, *Lawrence of Arabia: The Authorized Biography* (London: Heinemann, 1989). See also John E. Mack, *The Prince of Our Disorder* (Little, Brown & Co, 1978).

3. See James Barr, *Setting the Desert on Fire: T. E. Lawrence and Britain's Secret War in Arabia* (London: Bloomsbury, 2006). For information on the Great Arab Revolt Project, visit the project website at <http://www.jordan1914-18archaeology.org>.

4. Eugene Rogan, *The Arabs: A History* (Penguin 2nd edition, 2012). See also David Murphy, *The Arab Revolt, 1916–18: Lawrence Sets Arabia Ablaze* (Oxford: Osprey, 2008), pp. 5–8.

5. Murphy, *The Arab Revolt*.

6. Apart from the British forces of the EEF, there were also French troops in theatre. The French would send their own mission to the Hejaz and some of their officers and troops would cooperate with the Arab Northern Army in 1917 and 1918. See James Barr's *A Line in the Sand: Britain, France and the Struggle That Shaped the Middle East* (W. W. Norton & Co, 2012). See also Christophe Leclerc, *Avec T.E. Lawrence en Arabie: la mission militaire française au Hejaz, 1916–1920* (Harmattan, 1998).

7. Leclerc, *Avec T. E. Lawrence en Arabie*.

8. Murphy, *The Arab Revolt*, p. 26.

9. William Facey and Najdat Fathi Safwat (eds.), *A Soldier's Story from Ottoman Rule to Independent Iraq: The Memoirs of Jafar Pasha al-Askari* (London: Arabian Publishing, 2003).

10. Lawrence, *Pillars*, p. 200.

11. See Barr, *Setting the Desert on Fire*. See also Michael Asher's *Lawrence: The Uncrowned King of Arabia* (London: Viking, 1998). This latter is an excellent biography with a strong emphasis on military aspects.

12. T. E. Lawrence Papers, Bodleian Library, Oxford. Ms.Eng.c.6738, folio 139.

13. Lieutenant-General Sir Aylmer Haldane, *The Insurrection in Mesopotamia, 1920* (1922). See also David Murphy, 'T. E. Lawrence and the Iraq rebellion of 1920' in *Journal of the T. E. Lawrence Society* (forthcoming, 2013–14).

14. See Lawrence, *Pillars*. See also Michael Asher on Lawrence and desert travel in his *Lawrence: The Uncrowned King of Arabia*.

15. Ibid. See also Murphy, *The Arab Revolt*.

16. Joyce Papers, Liddell-Hart Centre for Military Archives, King's College, London. I/AC, 1 April 1917.

17. Ibid. See also Lawrence, *Pillars*.

18. See Murphy, *The Arab Revolt*.

19. James P. Hynes, *Lawrence of Arabia's Secret Airforce* (Barnsley: Pen and Sword, 2010). See also L.W. Sutherland's excellent wartime memoir, *Aces and Kings* (Naval & Military Press New edition, 2009).

20. Joyce Papers.

21. Ibid.

22. Joyce Papers, Joyce to Clayton, 17 September 1917.

23. Joyce Papers.

24. Ibid.

25. Hynes, *Lawrence of Arabia's Secret Airforce*.

26. Lawrence, *Pillars*, pp. 192–202.

27. See Mesut Uyar and Edward J. Erickson, *A Military History of the Ottomans from Osman to Atatürk* (Westport: Praeger, 2009). This is an excellent study of the subject and it also provides a useful guide to the wider literature.

28. Murphy, *The Arab Revolt*, pp. 24–27.

29. For reports of recent excavations and also useful bibliographies, see the website of the Great Arab Revolt Project, <http://www.jordan1914-18archaeology.org>.

30. Murphy, *The Arab Revolt*, pp. 80–82.

31. T. E. Lawrence Papers, Bodleian Library, Oxford. Ms.c.6742, folio 105.

32. Murphy, *Lawrence of Arabia*, pp. 40–41, 42–43. See also Murphy, *The Arab Revolt*, pp. 62–63, 64–65, 68.

33. Barr, *Setting the Desert on Fire*, p. 256.

34. See Murphy, *The Arab Revolt*, pp. 76–79. See also Cyril Falls, *Military Operations, Egypt and Palestine* (2 vols., London: HMSO, 1930).

35. Russell McGuirk, *The Sanusi's Little War: The Amazing Story of a Forgotten Conflict in the Western Desert, 1915–1917* (Arabian Publishing, 2007).

36. Saul Kelly, *The Hunt for Zerzura: The Lost Oasis and the Desert War* (Westview Press, 2002). See also Ralph Bagnold's own account of desert travel, in particular, *Libyan Sands: Travel in a Dead World* (London: Travel Book Club, 1935).

Chapter 12: The Reluctant Pupil

1. Byron Farwell, *Over There: The United States in the Great War, 1917–1918* (New York: W. W. Norton & Company, 1999), p. 238. Many elements of this chapter appeared in an earlier form as 'Preferring to Learn from Experience: The American Expeditionary Force in 1917', in Peter Dennis and Jeffrey Grey, eds., *1917: Tactics, Training, and Technology* (Canberra: Australian History Military Publications, 2007).

2. Mark Grotelueschen, *The AEF Way of War: The American Army and Combat in World War I* (Cambridge: Cambridge University Press, 2007), p. 10.

3. Robert Bruce, *A Fraternity of Arms: America and France in the Great War* (Lawrence: University Press of Kansas, 2003), p. 122; Adrian Lewis, *The American Culture of War: The History of U.S. Military Force from World War II to Operation Iraqi Freedom* (New York: Routledge, 2007), p. 25.

4. Minutes of a Meeting between Pershing and Robertson, 10 January 1918, WO 106/466. War Office Papers, The National Archives, London.

5. David Trask, *The AEF and Coalition Warmaking, 1917–1918* (Lawrence: University Press of Kansas, 1993), p. 61.

6. James Rainey, 'The Questionable Training of the AEF in World War I', in *Parameters*, Vol. 22 (Winter 1992–1993), p. 89.

7. Grotelueschen, *The AEF Way of War*, p. 12.

8. Timothy Nenninger, 'Tactical Dysfunction in the AEF, 1917–1918', in *Military Affairs*, Vol. 51, No. 4 (October, 1987), p. 179.

9. E. T. Dawnay, Report on Command in the AEF, 28 May 1918, WO 106/513. War Office Papers, The National Archives, London.

10. Chief of the Imperial General Staff Report on American Training, WO 106/474. War Office Papers, The National Archives, London.

11. Timothy Nenninger, *The Leavenworth Schools and the Old Army: Education, Professionalism, and the Officer Corps of the United States Army, 1881–1918* (Westport, Connecticut: Greenwood Press, 1978), pp. 36–39.

12. 'Effect of the New Tactics on the Operations of Infantry', in *Infantry Journal* 11 (September–October 1914), pp. 242–246; quoted in Grotelueschen, *The AEF Way of War*, p. 17.

13. Grotelueschen, *The AEF Way of War*, p. 20.

14. James Rainey, 'Ambivalent Warfare: The Tactical Doctrine of the AEF in World War I', in *Parameters*, Vol. 13 (September 1983), pp. 35–37.

15. John Pershing, *My Experiences in the World War*, Military Classics Series edition (Blue Ridge Summit, Pennsylvania: TAB Books, 1989), Vol. 1, p. 153.

16. Grotelueschen, *The AEF Way of War*, p. 31.

17. Ibid., pp. 36–39.

18. Ibid., p. 40. Additionally, as the war progressed, several American units served in battle alongside and under the command of the French Army or the BEF. Although American units, especially those brigaded within the French or British military structures, doubtless absorbed some aspects of Allied military doctrine, Pershing and his staff did their best to guard pristine American units from the baleful influence of 'European-ness'.

19. Memorandum for [AEF] Chief of Staff from Colonel Harold B. Fiske, 4 July 1918. Quoted in Bruce, *Fraternity of Arms*, p. 120.

20. Nenninger, 'Tactical Dysfunction', p. 178.

21. The preceding two quotes are from Farwell, *Over There*, pp. 100–101.

22. General Robert Alexander to Adjutant General, US Army, 13 December 1919, quoted in, Grotelueschen, *The AEF Way of War*, p. 31.

23. General W. Kirke to the C.I.G.S., 28 June 1918, WO 106/513. War Office Papers, The National Archives, London.

24. Pershing, *My Experiences*, Vol. 1, pp. 364–365.

25. Quoted in Trask, *The AEF and Coalition Warmaking*, p. 113; and Farwell, *Over There*, p. 216.

26. Farwell, *Over There*, p. 217.

27. Lieutenant-General J. P. Du Cane, 'Notes on American Offensive Operations', November 1918. WO 106/528. War Office Papers, The National Archives, London.

28. As an army commander Pershing had French forces under his command, just as Haig and the British often did, and even the French sometimes had British forces under their command.

29. Robert Blake, ed., *The Private Papers of Douglas Haig, 1914–1919* (London: Eyre & Spottiswoode, 1952), p. 329.

30. Farwell, *Over There,* p. 236.

31. Trask, *The AEF and Coalition Warmaking*, 128.

32. Du Cane, 'Notes on American Offensive Operations', November 1918. WO 106/528. War Office Papers, The National Archives, London

33. Ibid.

34. Rainey, 'Ambivalent Warfare', p. 41.

35. Notes on the American Army, WO 106/513. The National Archives, London War Office Papers.

36. Pershing, *My Experiences*, Vol. 1, p. 153.

37. Grotelueschen, *The AEF Way of War*, pp. 53–55.

Chapter 13: The German Occupation of the Ukraine, 1918

1. Hauptstaatsarchiv Stuttgart (HStA Stuttgart), M46/15. Fernspruch Heeresgruppe Linsingen Ia 13204 v. 16 February 1918.

2. Fritz Fischer, *Germany's Aims in the First World War* (London: Chatto & Lindus, 1967). This once ground-breaking book first published in German in 1961 initiated the so-called 'Fischer debate' in the 1960s. Today it must be considered outdated, as a number of later studies have proven that there was no German war aims master plan. For the Ukraine see particularly Winfried Baumgart, *Deutsche Ostpolitik 1918: Von Brest-Litowsk bis zum Ende des Ersten Weltkrieg* (Vienna and Munich: Oldenbourg, 1966); Oleh S. Fedyshyn, *Germany's Drive to the East and the Ukrainian Revolution 1917–1918* (New Jersey: Rutgers University Press, 1971).

3. HStA Stuttgart, M 46/16.Korps Knoerzer. Abt. Ia Nr. 214 v. 6 March 1918. An Generalkommando I. A.K.

4. Winfried Baumgart (ed.), *Von Brest-Litovsk zur deutschen Novemberrevolution: Aus den Tagebüchern, Briefen und Aufzeichnungen von Alfons Paquet, Wilhelm Groener und Albert Hopman, März bis November 1918* (Göttingen: Vandenhoek und Ruprecht, 1971), p. 317.

5. Bundesarchiv Berlin (BArch), R 3101/1314. Bericht über Eindrücke in der Ukraine von Oblt.d.Res. Colin Ross.

6. BArch, N 754/10. Kosch's letter to his wife from 26 March 1918.

7. HStA Stuttgart, M 46/15.Fernspruch Heeresgruppe Linsingen Ia 13204. 16 February 1918.

8. Bayerisches Hauptstaatsarchiv – Kriegsarchiv (BayHStA-KA), Bay.Landsturm Regt. 1, Armee Abt. Gronau. Ia Nr. 09570 geheim 17 February 1918. Verhalten dem Feinde gegenüber beim Vorgehen aus unseren Linien.

9. BayHStA-KA, Kav.Div., Bd. 20. Bezirk Wolhynien. Generalkommando XXII. R.K. Ia Nr. 222 op. 29 March 1918. BayHStA-KA, Kav.Div, Bd. 18. Generalkommando (z.b.V.) Nr. 52. Ia Nr. 4774. 7 April 1918. Korpsbefehl. BArch, R 3101/1168. Reichswirtschaftsstelle bei der Deutschen Ukraine Delegation an den Staatssekretär des Reichswirtschaftsamts. 17 August 1918.

10. BayHStA-KA, 15. Res.Inf.Brig., Bd. 7. Korps Knoerzer Abt. Ib Nr. 528. 24 March 1918. Besondere Verordnungen (Zusammenfassung der bisher erlassenen wichtigsten Bestimmungen).

11. HStA Stuttgart, M 46/21.215. Infanterie-Division. Abt. Ia Nr. 6111/18 op. 24 May 1918. See also BA-MA, N 46/171. In these daily reports of Heeresgruppe Eichhorn-Kiew the word 'prisoners' is hardly mentioned in April/May 1918. In contrast, no obvious evidence can be drawn from the records of 15. Res.Inf.Brig. about the shooting of prisoners.

12. HStA Stuttgart, M 46/9. War Diary of Korps Knoerzer, entry from 14 June 1918. HStA Stuttgart, M 411/394. War Diary of III./Landwehr Infanterie Regiment 121, entry of 14 June 1918. However, the war diary of 52. Landwehr Brigade remains silent on this execution.

13. HStA Stuttgart, M 46/20.Bericht über das Gefecht bei Taganrog im Besonderen und über die nach dem Gefecht erfolgte Erschießung der gefangenen Bolschewiki. 11 August 1918. Indeed, it seems the Bolsheviks did not take any German prisoners, either, since the start of the battle. BayHStA-KA, 4. Chevauleger Regiment, Bd. 1. Report Chev. Regt 4. to 7 Brigade from 12 June 1918, 3.30hrs.

14. BArch, RH 61/2315. Verteilung der deutschen und k.u.k. Divisionen am 26 October 1918.

15. Baumgart, *Brest-Litovsk*, p. 348.

16. BArch, R 3101/1341. Handelsvereinigung für Getreide, Futtermittel und Saaten. Ukraine-Bericht Nr. 149. 23 December 1918.

17. BayHStA-KA, Kav.Div., Bd. 21. Heeresgruppe Eichhorn. Ia Nr. 1094/18. 23 May 1918.

18. BArch, N 776/45. Generalleutnant v. Watzdorf. Personal Diary Entry from 7 April 1918.

19. BayHStA-KA, Kav.Div., Bd. 22. Heeresgruppe Eichhorn Ia Nr. 507/18. 3 May 1918.

20. BayHStA-KA, 15. Res.Inf.Brig., Bd. 7. Heeresgruppe Eichhorn-Kiew. Ia Nr. 1595/18. 9 June 1918. An Generalkommando XXVII. Res.Korps

21. BayHStA-KA, 15. Res.Inf.Brig., Bd. 7. Bayr. 15. Res.Inf.Brigade Nr. 3236 Adj. 11 June 1918.

22. Baumgart, *Brest-Litovsk*, p. 442.

23. Ewan Mawdsley, *The Russian Civil War* (Edinburgh: Birlinn Ltd, 2008), p. 49.

24. BayHStA-KA, Kav.Div., Bd. 21. Heeresgruppe Eichhorn-Kiew. Ia Nr. 1094/18. 23

May 1918. See also BayHStA-KA, 15. Res.Inf.Brig., Bd. 7. Heeresgruppe Eichhorn-Kiew. Ia Nr. 946/18. 17 May 1918.

25. BayHStA-KA, Kav.Div., Bd. 20. Heeresgruppe Eichhorn. Abt. Ia Nr. 2825/18. 18 July 1918.

26. HStA Stuttgart, M46/16. Heeresgruppe Eichhorn. Abt. Ia Nr. 3086/18. 26 July 1918.

27. The dominantly positive evolution pictured in the report of 15th BRIB is mirrored by a similar report from 4. Bayer. Kavallerie Brigade. BayHStA-KA, 4. Kav.Brig., Bd. 4. Bayer. 4. Kavallerie Brigade. Nr. 107/I. 21 September 1918. An das K.B. Kriegsministerium München. Verwendung der 4. Kav.Brig. in der Zeit v. 16 August–21 September 1918.

28. BayHStA-KA, 15. Res.Inf.Brig., Bd. 7. K.Bayr.15.Res.Inf.Brigade. Nr. 4460. 15 July 1918. Merkblatt für Unterweisung von Führern und Mannschaften für ihr Verhalten im besetzten Gebiet und bei Unternehmungen. See also: BayHStA-KA, 4. Kav.Brig., Bd. 4. Gruppe Tannstein. Nr. 3020/I. Gerichtliche Verfahren gegen Landeseinwohner. 11 September 1918.

29. The Bavarian Cavalry Division in Wolhynia gave an even more damning assessment on the militia: 'corrupt, ill-disciplined, coward and on the other hand brutal'. BayHStA-KA, Kav.Div., Bd. 21. Bezirk Wolhynien West. Bay.Kav.Division. Ia Nr. 3276 W. v. 19 September 1918. Betr.: Stimmung im Lande

30. Orest Subtelny, *Ukraine. A History* (Toronto: University of Toronto Press, 2009), p. 355.

BIBLIOGRAPHY

Chapter 1: Commanding Through Armageddon

Cassar, George, *Kitchener's War: British Strategy from 1914 to 1916* (Washington: Brassey's, 2004)

Doughty, Robert, *Pyrrhic Victory: French Strategy and Operations in the Great War* (Cambridge, MA: The Belknap Press of Harvard University Press, 2005)

Foley, Robert, *German Strategy and the Path to Verdun: Erich von Falkenhayn and the Development of Attrition, 1870–1916* (Cambridge: Cambridge University Press, 2005)

French, David, *British Strategy and War Aims, 1914–1916* (London: Allen and Unwin, 1986)

Gooch, John, *The Plans of War: The General Staff and British Military Strategy, 1900–1916* (New York: John Wiley, 1974)

Greenhalgh, Elizabeth, *Victory Through Coalition: Britain and France during the First World War* (Cambridge: Cambridge University Press, 2005)

Herwig, Holger, *The First World War: Germany and Austria-Hungary, 1914–1918* (London: Arnold, 1997)

Jeffrey, Keith, *Field Marshal Sir Henry Wilson: A Political Soldier* (Oxford: Oxford University Press, 2006)

McMeekin, Sean, *The Russian Origins of the First World War* (Cambridge, MA: The Belknap Press of Harvard University Press, 2011)

Mombauer, Annika, *Helmuth von Moltke and the Origins of the First World War* (Cambridge: Cambridge University Press, 2001)

Neiberg, Michael, *Foch: Supreme Allied Commander in the Great War* (Washington: Brassey's, 2003)

Philpott, William, *Anglo-French Relations and Strategy on the Western Front, 1914–1918* (London: Macmillan, 1996)

Prete, Roy, *Strategy and Command: The Anglo-French Coalition on the Western Front* (Montreal: McGill-Queen's University Press, 2009)

Prior, Robin and Wilson, Trevor, *Command on the Western Front: The Military Career of Sir Henry Rawlinson* (Barnsley: Pen and Sword, 2004)

Sheffield, Gary, *The Chief: Douglas Haig and the British Army* (London: Aurum Press, 2012)

Stone, Norman, *The Eastern Front, 1914–1917* (New York: Penguin, 1975)

Strachan, Hew, *The First World War, To Arms* (Oxford: Oxford University Press, 2003)

Chapter 2: German Operational Thinking in World War I

Citino, Robert M., *The German Way of War: From the Thirty Years' War to the Third Reich* (Lawrence: University Press of Kansas, 2005)

Ehlert, Hans, Epkenhans, Michael and Groß, Gerhard P. (eds.), *Der Schlieffenplan: Analysen und Dokumente* (Paderborn: Ferdinand Schöningh, 2006)

Foley, Robert, *German Strategy and the Path to Verdun: Erich von Falkenhayn and the Development of Attrition, 1870–1916* (Cambridge: Cambridge University Press, 2005)

Förster, Stig and Nagler, Jörg (eds.), *On the Road to Total War: The American War and the German Wars of Unification 1861–1871* (Cambridge: Cambridge University Press, 1997)

Groß, Gerhard P., 'Development of Operational Thinking in the German Army in the World War Era', in *Journal of Military and Strategic Studies*, vol. 13, no. 4 (2011)

Groß, Gerhard P. (ed.), *Die vergessene Front: Der Osten 1914/15. Ereignis, Wirkung, Nachwirkung* (Paderborn: Ferdinand Schöningh, 2006)

Naveh, Shimon, *In Pursuit of Military Excellence: The Evolution of Operational Theory* (London: Routledge, 1997)

Showalter, Dennis E., 'German Grand Strategy: A Contradiction in Terms?', in *Militägeschichtliche Mitteilungen*, vol. 48 (1990)

Strachan, Hew, 'The War Experienced: Command, Strategy, and Tactics, 1914–18', in John Horne (ed.), *A Companion to World War I* (Oxford: Blackwell Publishing, 2012)

Wallach, Jehuda L., *The Dogma of the Battle of Annihilation: The Theories of Clausewitz and Schlieffen and Their Impact on the German Conduct of Two World Wars* (Westport: Greenwood Press, 1986)

Chapter 3: The Expansion of the British Army During World War I

Atkinson, Christopher T., *The Seventh Division, 1914–1918* (London: John Murray, 1927)

Becke, A. F., *Order of Battle of Divisions, Part I: The Regular Army Divisions* (London: HMSO, 1935)

——, *Order of Battle of Divisions, Part 2A: The Territorial Force Mounted Divisions and the Frist-Line Territorial Force Infantry Divisions (42–56)* (London: HMSO, 1936)

——, *Order of Battle of Divisions, Part 3A: New Army Divisions (9–26)* (London: HMSO, 1938)

Brown, W. Baker et al., *History of the Corps of Royal Engineers, Volume V* (Chatham: The Institution of Royal Engineers, 1952)

Edmonds, J. E., *Military Operations, France and Belgium, 1914* (London: Macmillan, 1922)

Gudmundsson, Bruce, *The British Expeditionary Force, 1914–1915* (Oxford: Osprey, 2005)

——, *The British Army on the Western Front, 1916* (Oxford: Osprey, 2007)

Haldane, R. B., *Before the War* (London: Cassell, 1920)

——, *Richard Burdon Haldane: An Autobiography* (London: Hodder and Stoughton, 1929)

Headlam, John, *The History of the Royal Artillery, Volume II* (Woolwich: Royal Artillery Association, 1937)

James, E. A., *British Regiments, 1914–1918* (Dallington: Naval and Military Press, 1998)

Maurice-Jones, K. W., *The History of Coast Defence Artillery in the British Army* (Woolwich: Royal Artillery Institution, 1959)

Mitchinson, K. W., *Defending Albion: Britain's Home Army, 1908–1919* (Basingstoke: Palgrave Macmillan, 2005)

——, *England's Last Hope, the Territorial Force, 1908–1914* (Basingstoke: Palgrave Macmillan, 2008)

Smithers, A. J., *The Fighting Nation, Lord Kitchener and His Armies* (London: Leo Cooper, 1994)

Spiers, Edward M., *Haldane: An Army Reformer* (Edinburgh: University Press, 1980)

United Kingdom War Office, *Statistics of the Military Effort of the British Empire During the Great War* (London: HMSO, 1922)

Watson, Charles M., *History of the Corps of Royal Engineers, Volume III* (Chatham: The Royal Engineers Institute, 1915)

Chapter 4: World War I Aviation

Budiansky, Stephen, *Air Power* (New York: Viking Press, 2003)

Christienne, Charles and Lissarague, Pierre, *A History of French Military Aviation* (Washington: Smithsonian Institution Press, 1986)

Cooke, James, *The U.S. Air Service in the Great War, 1912–1919* (Westport: Praeger, 1996)

Corum, James and Muller, Richard, *The Luftwaffe's Way of War: German Air Doctrine 1911–1945* (Baltimore: Nautical and Aviation Press, 1998)

Franks, Norman, Guest, Russell and Frank Bailey, *Bloody April ... Black September* (London: Grub Street, 1995)

Grattan, R. F., *The Origins of Air War: Development of Military Air Strategy in World War I* (London: Taurus, 2009)

Kennett, Lee, *The First Air War 1914–1918* (New York: The Free Press, 1991)

Hudson, James J., *Hostile Skies: A Combat History of the American Air Service in World War I* (Syracuse: Syracuse University Press, 1997)

Johnson, Herbert Allen, *Wingless Eagle: U.S. Army Aviation Through World War I* (Chapel Hill: University of North Carolina Press, 2001)

Kilduff, Peter, *Germany's First Air Force 1914–1918* (Osceola, WI: Motorbooks International, 1991)

Morrow, John, *German Air Power in World War I* (Lincoln: University of Nebraska Press, 1982)

——, *The Great War in the Air: Military Aviation from 1909 to 1921* (Washington: Smithsonian Institution Press, 1993)

Shores, Christopher, Franks, Norman and Guest, Russell, *Above the Trenches* (London: Grub Street, 1990)

Winter, Dennis, *The First of the Few: Fighter Pilots of the First World War* (Athens: University of Georgia Press, 1983)

Chapter 5: The Global War at Sea, 1914–18

Berghahn, Volker R., *Germany and the Approach of War in 1914* (New York: St. Martin's Press, 1973)

Corbett, Julian S. and Newbolt, Henry, *History of the Great War*, vol. 5 of 9 (London: Longmans, Green 1920–31)

Epkenhans, Michael, *Grand Admiral Alfred von Tirpitz: Architect of the German High Seas Fleet* (Washington D.C.: Potomac Books, 2008)

Goldrick, James, *The King's Ships Were at Sea: The War in the North Sea August 1914–February 1915* (Annapolis: Naval Institute Press, 1984)

Halpern, Paul A., *Naval History of World War I* (London: UCL Press, 1994)

Herwig, Holger H., *'Luxury' Fleet: The Imperial German Navy 1888–1918* (London: Allen & Unwin, 1980)

Horn, Daniel, *The German Naval Mutinies of World War I* (New Brunswick, NJ: Rutgers University Press, 1969)

Kennedy, Paul M., *The Rise and Fall of British Naval Mastery* (New York: Scribner's, 1976)

——, *The Rise of the Anglo-German Antagonism 1860–1914* (London: Allen & Unwin, 1982)

Lambi, Ivo N., *The Navy and German Power Politics, 1862–1914* (London: Allen & Unwin, 1984)

Marder, Arthur J., *From the Dreadnought to Scapa Flow*, 5 vols (London: Oxford University Press, 1961–70)

Sondhaus, Lawrence, *The Naval Policy of Austria-Hungary, 1867–1918: Navalism, Industrial Development, and the Politics of Dualism* (West Lafayette, Indiana: Purdue University Press, 1994)

Watts, Anthony J., *The Imperial Rus3sian Navy* (London: Arms & Armour, 1990)

Chapter 6: The French Army Between Tradition and Modernity

Cochet, François (ed.), *Les batailles de la Marne. De l'Ourcq à Verdun (1914 et 1918)* (Saint-Cloud: Soteca/14-18 Editions, 2004)

——, *Survivre au front, 1914–1918. Les poilus entre contrainte et consentement* (Saint-Cloud: Soteca/14-18 Editions, 2005)

Doughty, Robert A., *Pyrrhic Victory: French Strategy and Operations in the Great War* (Cambridge, MA: The Belknap Press, 2005)

Herwig, Holger, *The Marne, 1914: The Opening of World War I and the Battle That Changed the World* (New York: Random House, 2011)

Les Armées Françaises dans la Grande Guerre, 106 vols. (Paris: Imprimerie Nationale, 1922–37)

Ousby, Ian, *The Road to Verdun: World War I's Most Momentous Battle and the Folly of Nationalism* (New York: Random House, 2003)

Pedroncini, Guy, *Les mutineries de 1917* (Paris: Publications de la Sorbonne, Presse Universitaires de France, 1983)

Rolland, Denis, *La grève des tranchées. Les mutineries de 1917* (Paris: Imago, 2005)

Van Evera, Stephen, 'The Cult of the Offensive and the Origins of the First World War', *International Security*, vol. 9, no. 1 (Summer 1984)

Chapter 7: German Tactical Doctrine and the Defensive Battle on the Western Front

Boff, Jonathan, *Winning and Losing on the Western Front: The British Third Army and the Defeat of Germany in 1918* (Cambridge: Cambridge University Press, 2012)

Förster, Jürgen, 'Evolution and Development of German Doctrine 1914 and 1945', in Gooch, John (ed.), *The Origins of Contemporary Doctrine* (London, 1997)

Gudmundsson, Bruce, *Stormtroop Tactics: Innovation in the German Army, 1914–1918* (Westport: Praeger, 1989)

Howard, Michael, 'Men Against Fire: Expectations of War in 1914', in Steven E. Miller, Sean M. Lynn-Jones , and Stephen van Evera (eds.), *Military Strategy and the Origins of the First World War* (Princeton: Princeton University Press rev. ed., 1991)

Jünger, Ernst, *In Stahlgewittern* (1st ed., 1920)

Linnenkohl, Hans, *Vom Einzelschuß zur Feuerwalze: Der Wettlauf zwischen Technik und Taktik im Ersten Weltkrieg* (Koblenz: Bernard & Graefe, 1990)

Lupfer, Timothy T., *The Dynamics of Doctrine: The Changes in German Tactical Doctrine During the First World War* (Fort Leavenworth: Combat Studies Institute, 1981)

Stachelbeck, Christian, *Militärische Effektivität im ersten Weltkrieg. Die 11. Bayerische Infanteriedivision 1915 bis 1918* (Paderborn: Ferdiand Schöningh, 2010)

Storz, Dieter, '"Aber was hätte anders geschehen sollen?" Die deutschen Offensiven an der Westfront 1918', in Jörg Duppler, and Gerhard Groß (eds.), *Kriegsende 1918. Ereignis, Wirkung, Nachwirkung* (Munich: Oldenbourg, 1999)

Strohn, Matthias, *The German Army and the Defence of the Reich: Military Doctrine and the Conduct of the Defensive Battle 1918–1939* (Cambridge: Cambridge University Press, 2010)

Watson, Alexander, *Enduring the Great War: Combat, Morale and Collapse in the German and British Armies, 1914–1918* (Cambridge: Cambridge University Press, 2008)

Chapter 8: The Rollercoaster of Austria-Hungary's World War I Experience

Fest, Wilfried, *Peace or Partition: The Habsburg Monarchy and British Policy 1914–1918* (London, New York: St Martin's Press, 1978)

Galantai, Jozsef, *Die österreichisch-ungarische Monarchie und der Weltkrieg* (Budapest: Corvina, 1979)

Healy, Maureen, *Vienna and the Fall of the Habsburg Empire:Total War and Everyday Life in World War I* (Cambridge: Cambridge University Press, 2004)

Höbelt, Lothar '"So wie wir haben nicht einmal die Japaner angegriffen". Österreich-Ungarns Nordfront 1914/15', in Gerhard P. Groß (ed.), *Die vergessene Front. Der Osten 1914/15* (Paderborn: Ferdinand Schöningh, 2006), pp. 87–119

Rauchensteiner, Manfried, *Der Tod des Doppeladlers. Österreich-Ungarn und der Erste Weltkrieg* (Graz: Verlag Styria, 1993)

Renzi, William A., *In the Shadow of the Sword: Italy's Neutrality and Entrance Into the Great War, 1914–1915* (Bern, New York: Peter Lang, 1987)

Shanafelt, Gary, *The Secret Enemy. Austria-Hungary and the German Alliance 1914–1918*, East European Monographs 187 (New York: Columbia University Press, 1985)

Stone, Norman, 'Die Mobilmachung der österreichisch-ungarischen Armee', in *Militärgeschichtliche Mitteilungen* 2 (1974), pp. 67–95

Tunstall, Graydon, *Planning for War against Russia and Serbia: Austro-Hungarian and German Strategies, 1871–1914* (New York: Columbia University Press, 1993)

——, *Blood on the Snow: The Carpathian Winter War of 1915* (Lawrence: University Press of Kansas, 2010)

Williamson, Samuel R. Jr., *Austria-Hungary and the Origins of the First World War* (New York: Macmillan, 1991)

Chapter 9: The Imperial Russian Army and the Eastern Front in World War I, 1914–17

Brusilov, A. A., *A Soldier's Notebook* (London: Macmillan, 1930)

Davidian, Irina, 'The Russian Soldier's Morale from the Evidence of the Tsarist Military Censorship', in Hugh Cecil and Peter H. Liddle (eds.), *Facing Armageddon: The First World War Experienced* (London: Leo Cooper, 1996)

Groß, Gerhard, ed., *Die vergessene Front. Der Osten 1914/15. Ereignis, Wirkung, Nachwirkung* (Paderborn: Ferdinand Schöningh, 2006)

Harrison, Richard W., *The Russian Way of War, Operational Art, 1904–1940* (Lawrence: University Press of Kansas, 2001)

Jones, David R., 'Imperial Russia's Forces at War', in Millet and Murray (eds.), *Military Effectiveness, Vol.1, The First World War* (London: Allen & Unwin, 1988)

Jukes, G., *The First World War, The Eastern Front 1914–1918* (Oxford: Osprey, 2002)

Stone, Norman, *The Eastern Front, 1914–1917* (London: Penguin, 1998)

Strachan, Hew, *The First World War, Vol. 1: To Arms* (Oxford: Oxford University Press, 2001)

Wildman, A., *The End of the Russian Imperial Army*, Vol. 1 (New Jersey: Princeton University Press, 1980)

Chapter 10: Anzacs and The Rocky Road to Tactical Effectiveness, 1916–17

Bean, Charles, *Official Histories, First World War: Volume III: The Australian Imperial Force in France, 1916* (Sydney: Angus and Robertson Ltd, 1941)

——, *Official Histories, First World War: Volume IV: The Australian Imperial Force in France, 1917* (Sydney: Angus and Robertson Ltd, 1941)

Blair, Dale, *Dinkum Diggers: An Australian Battalion at War* (Carlton South: Melbourne University Press, 2001)

Harper, Glyn, *Dark Journey: Three Key New Zealand Battles of the Western Front* (Auckland: HarperCollins, 2007)

Carrington, Charles, *Soldier from the Wars Returning* (London: Hutchinson & Co Ltd, 1965)

Cecil, Hugh, and Liddle, Peter, eds., *Facing Armageddon: The First World War Experience* (Barnsley: Pen & Sword, 1996)

Cook, Tim, *Shock Troops: Canadians Fighting the Great War 1917–1918* (Toronto: Penguin Canada, 2009)

Griffith, Paddy, ed., *British Fighting Methods in the Great War* (London: Frank Cass Publishers, 1996)

Hayes, Geoffrey, Iarocci, Andrew, and Bechthold, Mike, eds., *Vimy Ridge: A Canadian Reassessment* (Waterloo: Wilfred Laurier University Press, 2007)

Humphries, Mark, *The Selected Papers of Sir Arthur Currie: Diaries, Letters and Report to the Ministry, 1917–1933* (Waterloo, Canada: LCMSDS Press of Wilfrid Laurier University, 2008)

Hyatt, A. M. J., *General Sir Arthur Currie: A Military Biography* (Toronto: University of Toronto Press in association with Canadian War Museum, 1987)

Ingram, N. M., *Anzac Diary: A Nonentity in Khaki* (Christchurch: Treharne Publishers, 1987)

Liddle, Peter, ed., *Passchendaele in Perspective: The Third Battle of Ypres* (London: Leo Cooper, 1997)

Macdonald, Andrew, *On My Way to the Somme: New Zealanders and the Bloody Offensive of 1916* (Auckland: HarperCollins, 2005)

——, *Passchendaele: The Anatomy of a Tragedy* (Auckland: HarperCollins, 2013)

Millett, Allan and Murray, Williamson, eds., *Military Effectiveness, Volume 1: The First World War* (Cambridge: Cambridge University Press, 2010)

Passingham, Ian, *Pillars of Fire: The Battle of Messines Ridge, June 1917* (Stroud: Sutton Publishing, 2004)

Prior, Robin and Wilson, Trevor, *Passchendaele: the Untold Story* (New Haven: Yale University Press, 2002)

Pugsley, Christopher, *The Anzac Experience: New Zealand, Australia and Empire in the First World War* (Auckland: Reed Publishing, 2004)

Rawling, Bill, *Surviving Trench Warfare: Technology and the Canadian Corps, 1914–1918* (Toronto: University of Toronto Press, 1997)

Robbins, Simon, *British Generalship on the Western Front 1914–18: Defeat into Victory* (Abingdon: Frank Cass, 2005)

Sheffield, Gary, *Forgotten Victory – The First World War: Myths and Realities* (London: Headline, 2002)

Sheffield, Gary, and Todman, Dan, eds., *Command and Control on the Western Front*, (Stroud: The History Press, 2007)

Simpson, Andy, *Directing Operations: British Corps Command on the Western Front 1914–18* (Stroud: Spellmount Ltd, 2006)

Stewart, Col. H., *The New Zealand Division 1916–1919: A Popular History Based on Official Records* (Auckland: Whitcombe & Tombs, 1921)

Chapter 11: A Sideshow of a Sideshow?

Asher, Michael, *Lawrence: The Uncrowned King of Arabia* (London: Penguin, 1998)

Barr, James, *Setting the Desert on Fire: T. E. Lawrence and Britain's Secret War in Arabia* (London: Bloomsbury, 2006)

Brown, Malcolm, ed., *The Letters of T. E. Lawrence* (London: Dent, 1988)

——, *T. E. Lawrence: The Selected Letters* (New York: Norton, 1989)

——, *Lawrence of Arabia: The Life, the Legend* (London: Thames & Hudson, 2005)

——, *Lawrence of Arabia: The Selected Letters* (London: Max, an imprint of Little Books, 2007)

Garnett, Edward, *The Letters of T. E. Lawrence* (London: Doubleday, Doran & Company, 1938)

Graves, Robert, *Lawrence and the Arabs* (London: Jonathan Cape, 1927)

James, Lawrence, *The Golden Warrior: The Life and Legend of Lawrence of Arabia* (London: Abacus, 1990)

The Journal of the T. E. Lawrence Society

Korda, Michael, *Hero: The Lfe and Legend of Lawrence of Arabia* (London: Harper Perennial, 2011)

Lawrence, T. E., *Seven Pillars of Wisdom* (privately printed in 1922 and 1926; first public edition, London: Jonathan Cape, 1935)

——, *The Revolt in the Desert* (first edition, London, Jonathan Cape: 1927)

Leclerc, Christophe, *Avec Lawrence en Arabie: la mission militaire française au Hezaz, 1916–20* (Paris: Harmattan, 1998)

Liddell Hart, Basil, *T. E. Lawrence: In Arabia and After* (London: Jonathan Cape, 1934)

Mack, John E., *The Prince of Our Disorder* (London: Little, Brown & Company, 1978)

Mohs, Polly A., *Military Intelligence and the Arab Revolt: The First Modern Intelligence War* (London: Routledge, 2008)

Mousa, Suleiman, *T. E. Lawrence: An Arab View* (Oxford: Oxford University Press, 1966)

Murphy, David, *The Arab Revolt 1916–18: Lawrence sets Arabia ablaze* (Oxford: Osprey Publishing, 2008)

——, *Thomas E. Lawrence* (Oxford: Osprey Publishing, 2011)

Nicolle, David, *Lawrence and the Arab Revolts* (Oxford: Osprey Publishing, 1989)

Uyar, Mesut and Erickson, Edward J., *A Military History of the Ottomans: From Osman to Atatürk* (Santa Barbara, CA: Praeger Security International, 2009)

Wilson, Jeremy, *Lawrence of Arabia: The Authorized Biography* (London: Heinemann, 1989)

Chapter 12: The Reluctant Pupil

Blake, Robert, ed., *The Private Papers of Douglas Haig, 1914–1919* (London: Eyre & Spottiswoode, 1952)

Bruce, Robert, *A Fraternity of Arms: America and France in the Great War* (Lawrence: University Press of Kansas, 2003)

Dennis, Peter and Grey, Jeffrey, eds., *1917: Tactics, Training, and Technology* (Canberra: Australian History Military Publications, 2007)

Farwell, Byron, *Over There: The United States in the Great War, 1917–1918* (New York: W. W. Norton & Company, 1999)

Grotelueschen, Mark, *The AEF Way of War: The American Army and Combat in World War I* (Cambridge: Cambridge University Press, 2007)

Kennedy, David, *Over Here: The First World War and American Society* (New York: Oxford University Press, 1980)

Lewis, Adrian, *The American Culture of War: The History of US Military Force from World War II to Operation Iraqi Freedom* (New York: Routledge, 2007)

Neiberg, Michael, *The Second Battle of the Marne* (Bloomington: Indiana University Press, 2008)

Nenninger, Timothy, *The Leavenworth Schools and the Old Army: Education, Professionalism, and the Officer Corps of the United States Army, 1881–1918* (Westport, Connecticut: Greenwood Press, 1978)

——, 'Tactical Dysfunction in the AEF, 1917–1918', *Military Affairs*, vol. 51, no.4 (October 1987)

Pershing, John, *My Experiences in the World War*, Military Classics Series edition (Blue Ridge Summit, Pennsylvania: TAB Books, 1989)

Rainey, James, 'Ambivalent Warfare: The Tactical Doctrine of the AEF in World War I', *Parameters*, vol. 13 (September 1983)

——, 'The Questionable Training of the AEF in World War I', *Parameters*, vol. 22 (Winter 1992–93)

Sheffield, Gary, *Forgotten Victory –The First World War: Myths and Realities* (London: Headline, 2001)

Trask, David, *The AEF and Coalition Warmaking, 1917–1918* (Lawrence: University Press of Kansas, 1993)

Travers, Tim, *The Killing Ground: The British Army, the Western Front, and the Emergence of Modern War, 1900–1918* (London: Allen and Unwin, 1987)

Chapter 13: The German Occupation of the Ukraine, 1918

Baumgart, W. (ed.), *Von Brest-Litovsk zur deutschen Novemberrevolution. Aus den Tagebüchern, Briefen und Aufzeichnungen von Alfons Paquet, Wilhelm Groener und Albert Hopman. März bis November 1918* (Göttingen: Vandenhoek und Ruprecht, 1971)

Baumgart, W., *Deutsche Ostpolitik 1918. Von Brest-Litowsk bis zum Ende des Ersten Weltkrieg* (Vienna and Munich: Oldenbourg, 1966)

Dornik, W., Lieb, P. et al., *Die Ukraine zwischen Selbstbestimmung und Fremdherrschaft 1917–1922* (Graz: Lit-Verlag, 2011)

Fedyshyn, O., *Germany's Drive to the East and the Ukrainian Revolution 1917–1918* (New Jersey: Rutgers University Press, 1971)

Golczewski, F., *Deutsche und Ukrainer 1914–1939* (Paderborn: Ferdinand Schöningh, 2010).

Groß, G. (ed.), *Die vergessene Front. Der Osten 1914/15* (Paderborn: Ferdinand Schöningh, 2006)

Holquist, P., *Making War, Forging Revolution: Russia's Continuum of Crisis, 1914–1921* (Cambridge: Cambridge University Press, 2002)

Lincoln, B., *Red Victory: A History of the Russian Civil War* (London: Simon & Schuster, 1989)

Liulevicius, V., *War Land on the Eastern Front: Culture, National Identity and German Occupation in World War I* (Cambridge: Cambridge University Press, 2000).

Mawdsley, E. *The Russian Civil War* (Edinburgh: Birlinn, 2008)

Steinberg, O., *Spiridonova: Revolutionary Terrorist* (London: Methuen & Co, 1935)

Subtelny, O., *Ukraine: A History* (Toronto: University of Toronto Press, 2009)

INDEX

References for maps and tables are in **bold**

G

H